The
Right Side
of Normal

Understanding and Honoring
the Natural Learning Path for
Right-Brained Children

Cindy Gaddis

Excitement for the release of *The Right Side of Normal:*

Please notify me when your book is finished! I was one of these kiddos and I was schooled in a left-brained environment. It has taken me great efforts to gain confidence in my natural learning style as an adult.
—Lynn

I can't wait for your book to be finished! We've been following your Yahoo groups for years and you've given us confidence in our right-brained son's method of learning. We've recommended you to many, many people with similar kids.
—Julie

I am waiting on pins and needles for the book.
—Cassidy

Hi Cindy, I live in the UK and am a member of your Yahoo group. The group has made life for me and my son so much easier. I would love to buy a copy of your book when it is finished.
—Jackie

I am extremely excited your book is done. Your words of encouragement and the advice you have so generously shared with so many has changed my view of the world and the way I can now (confidently) raise my children. I can allow them to be who they are and revel in their uniqueness. I have also been able to heal the damaged right-brained child I was so I can be a better mom for them. I can't wait to get my copy, and more to share, as I did your CDs, to open more minds about the wonders of the right-brained world. Thank you so much.
—Lauralee

When will the book be ready? I need it ASAP.
—Mary

Thank you for all of your "out-of-the-box," thoughtful, kind, practical, and beyond all else, inspiring words...can't wait for the book!
—Julia

Acknowledgments

Understanding and honoring the natural learning path for right-brained children encapsulates my life's work and I have developed a passion around the topic that has spanned more than 20 years now. There have been many individuals and groups of people who have inspired and encouraged me to complete this book in order to help others.

I would like to acknowledge and thank my first on-line friend I met in person, Rebecca Jaxon, for believing in me enough to invite me to speak at my first conference on the topic of right-brained learners. It was the enthusiastic responses of participants I received after those first presentations that made me realize this information was so needed. Since then, I'm humbled by the hundreds of people who have approached me during and after my conference presentations to share how my information was life-changing for their families after their often painful and damaging prior experiences with learning. It's these heartfelt stories of creative, inquisitive, yet misunderstood children that motivated me to put a voice to this valid learning path.

Through my e-mail group forum, *Homeschooling Creatively,* I'm honored to learn along with the thousands who have joined the group. Each gave me the opportunity to more succinctly verbalize what the natural learning path for right-brained children looks like in all its diversity.

I would like to particularly acknowledge my right-hand gal, Stephanie Elms, who fully embraced my shift in perspective about right-brained learning and shares her compassionate and empathetic voice to others on the path. She also offered her services in co-moderating *Homeschooling Creatively* while I focused on writing my book. Without her efforts, families wouldn't have received the continued support needed to understand a new educational model of learning.

About 18 months ago, several women stepped forward from *Homeschooling Creatively* to be a strong catalyst in my push to commit the time needed to finish my book. I would like to acknowledge and thank April Rose Undy, whose big picture views helped me define the focus of my book in the early weeks and months, and whose humor lightened my days. I would like to acknowledge and thank Sandra Reimer for freely offering her expertise and invaluable insights into the book publishing process. I'm grateful for her editing direction in the early weeks and months and for forwarding certain elements to her husband, Wes Reimer, for his input and advice. Julie Antolick Winters provided consistent feedback and editing assistance in the early weeks and months to get me moving in the right direction, as did Lisa Campbell Blocker, Karen Mack Davis, Benjiman and Abigale Miles, Kirsten Ruark Sonner, Mary Bennett, Kim Starlene Graham, Sofie Couch, Angela McGinn, and Jennifer when time permitted.

I'm also honored to have many photographer friends who allowed me to use their photos of their children in my book. Thanks to Robin Jenkins Duralia, Stephanie Elms, Lori R. Godaire, Marianne PS Stern, and Teresa Loos.

A special thank you to two unschooling pioneers who offered valuable support: Linda Dobson and Pat Farenga. I was fortunate to find Linda to edit my book with me. We were a perfect example of well-matched interaction styles and her input was invaluable in polishing my book while staying true to its purpose. I'm grateful to Pat Farenga for believing in me and my information early on and giving me confidence and professional support to complete my book.

My most profound thanks and acknowledgment goes to my children, who taught me everything I know as I observed and translated what they showed me worked for them. I'm especially grateful to my firstborn son, whose spirited temperament forced me to understand and honor another way to live and learn; to my daughter, who "gets me" the most and is always my sounding board and my traveling/speaking companion; and to my husband, Weston, for his confidence in my abilities to write this book, and for all the extra duties he took on so I could have enough time to write.

Introduction

Strengths-Based Learning

Just as there are always two sides to every story, science and research show us there are two working sides to the brain that impact learning: the left brain specialties and the right brain specialties. Schools use a scope and sequence[1] that favors the strengths and gifts of a left-brained dominant person,[2] which works well for these learners. Here's a small sample:

- ❖ Schools instruct in a sequential manner, such as learning addition and multiplication in the younger years. This then prepares students to learn algebra and geometry when they're older (see Chapter Seven).

❖ Schools are product-driven. This is why they have children create physical work (products) that they can sort and classify based on right and wrong answers, completed tasks, and definable measurements. The focus is on *what* is learned (see Chapter Nine).

❖ Schools are word- and symbol-focused. This is why they pursue early reading acquisition, math fact drilling, and handwriting practice (see Chapter Seven).

Right-brained dominant people[2] learn in a completely opposite manner. Here's a small sample:

❖ Right-brained people learn best in a global, big picture manner, allowing them to experiment with the bigger ideas, such as algebra and geometry, in the younger years. This then motivates them to learn the detailed tasks, such as math facts, when they're older (see Chapter Seven).

❖ Right-brained people are process-driven. This is why they enjoy projects that utilize experimentation, creativity, and/or exploration. It's the act of discovery, innovation, and knowing *why* something works that drives learning (see Chapter Nine).

❖ Right-brained people are picture-focused. They learn best with visual, pictorial, mental work that encourages mental visualization, such as read-alouds, mental math activities, and/or an oral history documentary (see Chapter Seven).

The school environment doesn't work well for these learners. It's time to tell the other side of the learning story and introduce a scope and sequence that honors the right-brained process and the people who use it.

Right-brained children learn in a completely different manner than their left-brained peers.

Because most of us were schooled in a left-brained manner, we learned to value left-brained traits, too. If we have right-brained children, though, we'll soon notice they do things differently. For instance:

➢ Do you hear your child say "this is stupid," or constantly question why they are asked to do something?

➢ Do math facts not come easily to your child, or is your child a "late reader?"

➢ Does your child provide answers on his homework, but can't explain how he got them, or does your child have trouble "showing his work?"

➢ Does your child occupy himself with something like building with LEGO®, drawing, or playing while you read aloud to him?

➢ Does your child watch TV or listen to music while doing his homework, or does your child doodle on his homework?

➢ Does your child have trouble completing tasks or keeping track of homework, or do people say your child daydreams instead of concentrating?

➢ Does your child struggle with spelling, have difficulty putting together a legible sentence, resist handwriting or have difficulty with it?

Listening to music helps a right-brained child better concentrate.

Or, alternatively:

> ➤ Does your child have a knack for current technology?

> ➤ Does your child go on and on telling stories, or does your child enjoy dressing up in interesting costumes or creating complicated play scenarios?

➤ Does your child spend hours doing one of the following: computers/video games, cooking/gardening, music/dance, building/electronics, art/photography, fashion/sewing, puzzles/mazes, math/numbers, or theater/showmanship?

➤ Does your child craft, draw, or build something in intricate detail?

➤ Does your child ask profound questions or know interesting facts that leave you wondering where he learned them?

➤ Does your child show compassion for the cares of the world and want to make a difference, or does your child act as an emotional gauge in the home?

➤ Did your child have an interest in ancient history, mythology (such as dragons or unicorns), other cultures, the sciences (including dinosaurs), or nature and animals at a young age?

> ➢ Does your child remember directions to places she's only been to once, or have a keen visual memory for stories or movies he heard or saw only once?

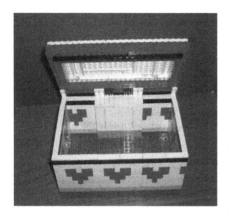

Right-brained children can build with detailed precision and creativity.

If you recognize your child possesses many of these attributes, you may have a right-brained learner. These are intelligent, creative, and inquisitive children who often seem to flounder in school. The reality is *creative children love to learn, but hate to be taught.* They resist or perform poorly because we are not teaching in the way they learn. We use left-brained teaching methods on a right-brained child. The good news and hope within this book is that there exists a valid and strengths-based educational approach best suited for right-brained learners and, with it, they flourish and thrive.

Consciously or subconsciously, our society believes that the scope and sequence created for our schools that favors left-brained thinkers is "the norm." It's held up as the measure of intelligence. For example, a current benchmark declares that reading can and should be accomplished through phonics by the age of 6 to 7 years. Around this, parents hold their breath, waiting to discover where their children will be classified. If a child reads before the benchmark, she's "smart as a whip" or "gifted." If he reads at the expected time, he's "average." Look out if she reads after that time frame! At best, she's either "lazy," "not living up to potential," or "stupid." At worst, the child is disordered. Broken. Learning disabled. The truth is that it's *normal* for right-brained children to learn to read at a later age. Left-brained benchmarks shouldn't be the only "normal" that children are held to in a scope and sequence.

The solution is to allow right-brained children to learn on a different time frame that honors their gifts and strengths. This doesn't mean we should follow the current left-brained scope and sequence, and then just wait a little longer. It means right-brained learners' success requires a totally different scope *and* sequence.

✓ The right-brained child needs different resources for learning than those currently found in school.
✓ The right-brained child needs a different skill development focus than found in school.
✓ The right-brained child needs a different time frame for learning than the one expected in school.

If *all* of these differences are honored, right-brained children will learn various subjects as joyfully and painlessly as their left-brained counterparts.

Right-brained children learn subjects at different times with different resources.

What's our current solution? We attempt to "fix" right-brained learners. We remediate when they don't meet left-brained expectations (i.e., dyslexia programs). We medicate their behaviors (i.e., Ritalin). We even "jump-start" natural biological occurrences through exercises (i.e., vision tracking). There are consequences to these common "solutions." Some children decide they are "stupid" and take that notion into adulthood. Some children develop anxiety, depression, or grow angry as they are made to feel worthless. Some children decide they "just don't care" and "do the minimal," as if oppositional, because they want to feel some control over the fact that they can't live up to the left-brained expectation. Some children self-medicate through alcohol or drugs in their teen years to ease the pain of not feeling "good enough." And some children get a learning disability label and live *down* to that expectation believing they are deficient in some way.

Right-brained learners are the most labeled children in our schools. There are so many labels they often overlap[3] as professionals scramble to justify the discrepancy between the obvious intelligence and creativity displayed by these children and their inability to perform to the expectations of the school setting. Why is it that behind practically every learning disability label (ADD/ADHD, dyslexia, learning disabled, dysgraphia, twice exceptional, dyscalculia, etc.) is a right-brained learner? Where are the left-brained learning disabled children? They're difficult to find because left-brained children are flourishing in the left-brained learning environment! The good news is that when right-brained children are placed in a right-brained learning environment, they will also flourish and learning disability labels will all but disappear.

Maria Montessori said, "Free the child's potential, and you will transform him into the world." One important way to do this is by **understanding and honoring the natural learning path for right-brained children** that inherently develops their strengths and gifts. This book exhorts *shifting perspective* about learning disabilities by showcasing the *natural learning path* of the right-brained learner. This book further shares how we as parents, educators, and mentors can help facilitate *strengths-based learning* that celebrates **the right side of normal** allowing the right-brained learner to thrive.

References and Notes

[1] A scope and sequence is a term used in school to delineate a list of skills to be taught (scope), and the order in which the skills are taught (sequence).

---

[2] See Chapter One for an explanation of the left-brained and right-brained labels.

[3] Linda Kreger Silverman, Ph.D., was the first who helped me recognize the overlapping of criteria in learning disabilities in her book: Silverman, Linda Kreger. *Upside-Down Brilliance: The Visual-Spatial Learner.* Denver: DeLeon Publishing, Inc., 2002. See Chapter Three in this book for more details.

Table of Contents

Section Three:
Common Subject Differences 185

Section Four: Common Labels 325

Preface

The Story of How It All Began

- ❖ Your child is not living up to his potential.
- ❖ My child is so resistant.
- ❖ Your child is an underachiever.
- ❖ I have a struggling learner.
- ❖ My child is behind.
- ❖ He's just a late bloomer.
- ❖ I think your child has a learning disability.
- ❖ My child is so smart, but I don't understand why he can't do (fill in the subject).
- ❖ She's lazy.
- ❖ My child thinks he's stupid.

In 1998, I finally joined the technological world around me by hooking up to the Internet. I was excited to discover e-mail group lists. Finally, I had easy access to connect with others who chose a path similar to mine in teaching my own children.

I don't know what I was expecting, but I was confused and surprised to hear story after story of struggles, labels, years of remediation, and statements like those at the start of this chapter about children who reminded me a lot of my own, especially my oldest. Where were the positive stories describing life with this creative and inventive, albeit high-maintenance, personality? Though I recognized a strong spirit in my son, his childhood had overall been a delight. I was determined to figure out what was going on.

Life with my creative, albeit high-maintenance, personality son had overall been a delight.

I remember the moment I first chose a different learning path for my children. Like many parents of 5 year olds, I pre-registered my oldest son in the local kindergarten. It was the pre-screening day, and I showed up excitedly with my son in hand. Excitement turned to disappointment when I learned my son would go off into a room with the "screening experts" while I filled out registration paperwork. Disappointment turned into annoyance when I felt I was being told I would interfere with my son's performance if I observed.

I thought, "Boy, they don't understand that I enjoy watching my son try new things and being excited about his adventures. I don't worry and fret and question; I cheerlead and enjoy and share his surprise with him." At that moment, standing before the screeners as my child in hand looked up at me, I fought a short-lived inner battle: Do I take a stand, or do I relent?

I relented. An invisible force took me in the direction they wanted me to go as I waved encouragingly to my son following the screeners.

I sat down in my little area where I received a folder stuffed with papers to be filled out. I'm going to be here all day, I thought. I took a deep breath and pulled out the first sheet. It started off requesting basic information, but before long I grew uncomfortable with some of the questions. *Tell us your child's birth story.* What? Why do they need that? I wrote N/A. *Names and ages of siblings.* Now I'm thinking, Okay, you're taking my oldest child from me, making me feel like the bad guy; why should I give you information about my other children when it's not legally required? Wow, am I getting paranoid now? I wrote N/A. Why did I suddenly feel like all the responsibility for making decisions as my son's mother was at risk? That invisible force pushed me to fill out another paper or two, and then enough was enough. Somehow I reclaimed my mother's instinct; I shoved the papers into the folder and walked out without completing them.

I found my smiling oldest son where we had separated. The screeners informed me he passed with flying colors. I smiled, nodded, took my son's hand, and we walked out of the school. I felt robotic at that moment, like I was going through the motions because that's what everyone does. Trouble was nothing made sense as to why I was doing it. I let the feeling envelop me. I didn't shake it off or chase it away. I just let it sit to see where it might lead me.

A few days later, the word "homeschool" popped into my head. Where did that come from? My husband and I were both successful, straight-A public school students. We both excelled in athletics of all types. Socially, we were at the top of the game. Heck, we were even high school sweethearts! As high school seniors, we often dreamt together about what our future family would be like. It inevitably involved sporting events to watch our sure-to-be-athletic children. We envisioned ourselves as popular parents among their friends. And now I was considering homeschooling—on a gut instinct.

Although I don't homeschool for religious reasons, my beliefs align beautifully with doing so.

I asked around at church to see if anyone homeschooled. I was given a name and eagerly contacted her. Eventually, I realized I had met my perfect mentor. She began by asking me questions for self-discovery. *So, what style of homeschooling do you think you would like to do?* Huh? There are styles? My mentor gave me a summary of the various homeschooling styles. She assured me that I'd know the style I wanted when I read it. Well, sure enough, there it was—what we'd been doing all along since birth—the style called unschooling.[1] *How fortunate! That's the style of homeschooling I do so I have a lot of resources for you.* She gave me a huge stack of books and publications. I devoured the information.

After a few months of dedicated research on homeschooling, and more particularly, unschooling, it was time to make a decision about school. I initiated nightly pillow talks with my husband about the idea of unschooling. Initially, he rejected the idea, mainly for the same reason I balked at the beginning. We shared a subconscious thought that our children would follow in our footsteps and be those school success stories. We discussed the fact our son pursued interests in subjects that were not offered at his age in school. We realized homeschooling could provide a unique opportunity for our son to continue to learn in areas that excited him. As discussions progressed, we were both on board in the commitment to undertake this new style of learning environment.

Even with all my research, support from my amazing mentor, and observations my husband and I began to make about our oldest son and his learning, I had much to *unlearn*. My oldest son had to show me how to fully embrace this way of learning when the expected "formal learning process" was supposed to begin. It's funny how naturally and easily it existed in our home, interactions, and learning environment before the magical age of 5 arrived. Somehow, crossing that "official school age" threshold made me momentarily lose my mind. I wanted to revert right back to how I was taught, which made the most sense to me.

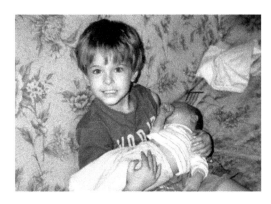

The birth of my fourth child saved the education of my first.

My fourth child was due that Labor Day before my son was supposed to start school, so I only half-joke that the birth of my fourth child saved the education of my first. With four children 5 years old and under, my hands were full. I certainly didn't have time to control and direct my oldest son's learning life. But, as I stood still and took care of the needs of a newborn, I had lots of opportunity to observe and read and reflect on what I was noticing about my children's learning. I had lots of opportunity to *shift my perspective* and understand that children can continue to be curious, engaged, and inquisitive because they are compelled from within to know things. Receiving these early lessons from my children allowed a home environment that encouraged each child to go about learning in the way that made the most sense to him or her.

Please understand that as a previously successful left-brained [2] student, I felt drawn to left-brained teaching practices. But like you, I am a devoted parent (and/or motivated teacher) who wants to provide the best possible learning opportunities for my children. As the adult in the equation, I can shift and change and be flexible. I can open myself up to once again be taught. Though my children were but little people, I understood their worth was as great as anyone's, and they deserve respect and admiration. And so my eyes were opened, little by little, until amazing insights became apparent.

Since that fateful day at the school, each of my seven children has shown me how he or she will live and learn in this world. No two have been alike. Although all seven children favor the right-brained dominant[2] traits, I'll focus on three of them because they taught me the most as I observed learning in those early years. (They're all adults now who have given me permission to share their learning journey in this book.) I'll particularly focus on my first and second sons because they are both *strong* right-brained learners. Betwixt the two of them, they reveal most of the traits of a right-brained learner. For some unique variation, I'll throw in a consistent dose from the rest of my children, who are excited to be featured in this book. Let me introduce them.

My artist son.

My firstborn son will be called my artist son. As a right-brained learner, his preferred creative outlet is drawing. His early interests included history, animals (including dinosaurs), nature, and geography. He spent hours each day expressing himself visually. His secondary creative outlet is video games.

My writer daughter.

My second-born child will be called my writer daughter. She offers both a left-brained perspective in some instances *and* a right-brained viewpoint in others. She's a whole-brained learner with a gravitational pull to the right. As evidence of her left-brained strengths, she was attracted to words at a young age, and often copied books. Using Dr. Seuss™, she taught herself to read at age 5. As evidence of her right-brained strengths, she expressed a rich imagination within her own play world and periodically through short stories. Childhood interests revolved around animals, particularly her large stuffed animal collection, Littlest Pet Shop™ toys and, later, riding horses and training her dogs. In her early teen years she shifted from an animal focus to fantasy writing.

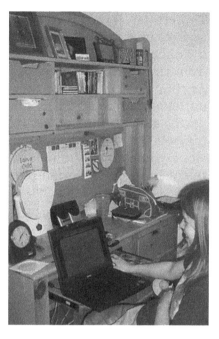

My builder son.

My third-born child will be called my builder son. As a right-brained learner, his preferred creative outlet was building. As a two-year-old he began building tracks for his trains. That evolved into playing with LEGO® at 4 years old, spending hours on various constructions. He built worlds with his hands using

Tinkertoy®, Lincoln Logs®, motorized train track sets, and any other building materials that were available. He also had a knack in his early childhood for mazes and puzzles, going from the children's level to three-dimensional difficulty levels. At that time it became apparent what his secondary creative outlet would be when he showed he had a natural ability with math and numbers as he played around and challenged himself for fun with manipulatives. Other side interests were video games and the mechanics of their creation along with a talent in music through playing the piano.

My electronics son.
Ceiling fans.
Garage door openers.
House design.
Cars.

My forever son.
Books.
Computers.
Videos.
Flipping objects.

My theater son.　　　　*My high energy son.*
Indian lifestyle.　　　　　*Sports.*
Nature.　　　　　　　　*Music.*
Cooking.　　　　　　　*Guns.*
Gardening.　　　　　*Outdoor life.*

The secret to understanding a right-brained child is through his interests during childhood. These introductions share some of my right-brained children's interests. These interests are at the heart of the positive journey my children experienced as they helped me understand this learning style. Don't get me wrong; there were challenges and much that concerned me before I understood the holistic picture of what I was experiencing. For instance, how could my obviously highly intelligent first child not be an early reader, and in actuality, be a late reader? Why was he more interested in ancient Egypt than learning math facts? What about my son who spent hours every day building LEGO®, but wasn't interested in our read-aloud times? Should I be concerned about wordless comic strips, or even worse, the consistently backward written letters? I had all these questions and more, yet trusted my children's path to find answers, as I honed my observation skills.

My observations revealed the path that best serves the right-brained learner. It's different than the one that was right for me as a left-brained learner in school, but it's equally viable.

Sharing this good news about a valid strengths-based learning path for the right-brained child started when a friend invited me to present a workshop at a homeschooling conference in 2000. The following year, I presented more workshops about living and learning joyfully with a right-brained, creative child. I witnessed lives drastically change because of my information, so I've kept sharing. At the same time, I researched material available about this way to process information. During this research I learned there were various "names" given to different attributes of right-brained learners. I didn't know this as I raised my children in a learning environment that simply provided space to *develop one's strengths* in a time frame and pattern that made the most sense to them. It didn't need a name at the time.

Now my passion is to share the good news my children taught me to everyone. I find that sharing the reasons *why* a right-brained child learns in a particular way empowers parents and educators to choose a different path that allows right-brained, creative children to flourish. Developed through my experiential knowledge with the most current research, this book contains that information for your family.

References and Notes

[1] A homeschooling style coined by John Holt to indicate a child-led, interest-based learning environment.

[2] See Chapter One for an explanation of the left-brained and right-brained labels.

Section One

Shifting Perspective

What We Believe.

The way school teaches is the one right way to learning.

Shifting Perspective.

There are as many ways to learn as there are people learning. Schools tend to teach one holistic way, the left-brained way. Another holistic way needs to be added, the right-brained way.

Chapter One describes how the brain works and how that relates to the left- and right-brained information. You'll discover how brain processing preferences impact learning and ultimately our place in the workforce. Strategies on how to apply the left- and right-brained information to ourselves, our children, and our schools will be shared to help your creative child receive a strengths-based education through which he will flourish and thrive.

What We Believe.

Even if I could sort out all the complicated information about learning styles, my child still needs to be able to work within the school system.

Shifting Perspective.

Many professionals have complicated our understanding of learning styles by creating new names to describe old ideas. Going back to the umbrella of left-brained and right-brained learning traits is less complicated and broad enough to encompass how most children process information. Once we recognize these traits, we all need to help spread the good news that there is a valid way for right-brained children to learn joyfully. We should stop accepting methods for helping right-brained children conform to left-brained standards.

Chapter Two highlights some of the top professionals in the field of learning styles and temperaments, especially those related to the right-brained learner. We'll sift through all the different labels and show how each is really describing the right-brained learner. I expose how any good information provided by professionals often gets shifted back into strategies that are developed to help a right-brained child function in the left-brained school. We need to become champions for a right-brained child's right to a strengths-based education that honors his methods and time frames.

What We Believe.
My right-brained child has learning disabilities.

Shifting Perspective.
Labels were created to explain the difference between your child's intelligence and his inability to perform in the classroom. If teachers follow a scope and sequence that favors the natural learning path for right-brained children, learning disabilities would all but disappear.

Common labels for right-brained children are: ADD, ADHD, dyslexia, dysgraphia, dyscalculia, auditory processing disorder, phonological awareness disorder, vision disorders, sensory processing disorder, and other general learning disabilities. Those who are gifted or diagnosed on the autism spectrum are often right-brained learners as well.

Young boys need time to mature, not a label for normal differences.

Chapter Three explores how we value certain academic performances, social styles, and sensory differences found in the left-brained school environment. Using these left-brained

14

standards of measurement, the overspecialization of those in the medical field, and the emphasis on creating test measuring tools, our society pathologizes the legitimate right-brained path to learning.

What We Believe.

The earlier we can start teaching skills, the smarter our children will be.

Shifting Perspective.

Our current culture values fast-paced living, adopts an over-achiever mentality, and functions within jam-packed schedules of activities. No wonder we believe the learning process can be sped up to keep pace with our more-is-better lifestyle. But we can't speed up the brain's readiness for learning. Thousands of studies indicate that formal academics should not be rushed to achieve the best outcome of learning potential.

Imitative learning and mentoring through play is a young child's work.

Chapter Four outlines the research, global, and historical evidences pointing to the ages of 8 to 10 years as the optimal learning time frame for formal studies. The connection between a different learning time frame and academic success for right-brained learners in the early years is introduced.

15

Shift Begins with Me

*At the beginning of each chapter, you'll find a personal experience that helped **shift my perspective**. Without these personal shifts, I wouldn't have been primed to learn the lessons my children had to teach. They opened my eyes to new understandings, discoveries, and realizations about life, learning, and growing up educated. I hope my personal shifts will be a catalyst for your own shifts to learn from your own children. If we don't become right-brained learning advocates, our children will continue to suffer in silence.*

The good news is that the information about how and when right-brained children learn is powerful! With this knowledge, we can dramatically improve the learning lives of right-brained children so that they can thrive and flourish, too.

Chapter One

Reclaiming Our Creative Children

Shift Begins with Me

"You will all write in a journal every day at the beginning of class based on a word I put on the board," explained my psychology instructor at the business college I attended as a young single person. He explained that he wanted us to share our own definition of the word. The words would be big picture ideas with no right or wrong answer. Some of the words were love, fear, faith, and integrity. This class coincided with a time in my life I was feeling particularly confident and competent as I was carving out my new adult identity. When the first word was introduced, I felt a surge of knowledge course through my mind as I was sure my definition would be the highlight of all others. Much to my surprise, as the instructor called on others to share their definitions, I

was humbled by the depth of expression found in these young lives. It took a few more days of the same initial thought pattern and subsequent humbling for me to accept that there are as many meaningful and valid definitions as there are people experiencing the word in question.

It's tricky to try to define something as complex and global as how a brain works. Nobody really knows the real deal, yet it's a topic that has inspired research, studies, and speculation for years. As I have helped support families of right-brained children, common questions crop up as each tries to understand why the right-brained information is relevant to the healthy learning of their children. The answers to these frequently asked questions give us the good news about how right-brained children can flourish in their learning lives with the application of this better information.

How Does the Brain Work?

The brain is divided by a grooved fissure into near-symmetrical halves, the left hemisphere and the right hemisphere. A thick band of nerves called the corpus callosum connects the hemispheres. Roger Sperry, a neurobiologist, conducted split-brain experiments in the 1960s on behalf of epileptic patients in which he completely severed this communication system between the hemispheres.

Corpus
callosum

The corpus callosum provides for communication between the two sides of a normal brain. (Image[1])

He discovered that each side of the brain specializes in high-level cognitive functions equal in complexity. Still, the corpus callosum provides for communication between the two sides of a normal brain at a rate of several billion bits per second. Therefore, there's significant cross-over between hemispheres.

The Right-Brained/Left-Brained Label

We call a person right-brained dominant (or right-brained) if he favors using the specialization traits of the right side of the brain. Likewise, a left-brained dominant (or left-brained) person favors using the specialization traits of the left side of the brain. There are some people (referred to as whole-brained dominant) who use the specialization traits equally between the hemispheres. The first image below represents one of the current lists outlining left-brained specialization traits and right-brained specialization traits. It's depicted in a sequential (left-brained) manner. The second image represents the same in a visual (right-brained) fashion.

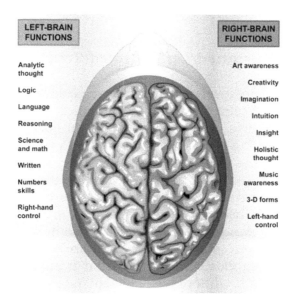

A left-brained version of brain functioning specialties.

A right-brained version of brain functioning specialties.

The Right-Brained/Left-Brained Trait Differences

Although controversy continues regarding the labeling of people as left-brained or right-brained, I have noticed, as have many experts (see Chapter Two), an easily recognizable pattern of learning and temperament traits that frequently go together. For instance, when I describe these traits (see Section Two) at conferences, I see whole audiences nodding in recognition. Inevitably, various individuals approach me and say, "You described my child to a tee" or "Have you been looking in our window?" This can't be coincidence. Whether proven by current studies or not, there's ample anecdotal evidence that supports there are time frame, temperament, and gift/strength differences based on brain processing preferences.

The Right-Brained/Left-Brained Communication

Being left- or right-brained dominant doesn't mean we only use half our brain. Billions of bits of information per second can travel along the nerves that connect the two hemispheres, so naturally there's communication between the hemispheres. I'm simply talking about the brain processing *preferences* that each of us is biologically born to *favor*. With those preferences come the traits that stem from the specialization found in the left or right side of the brain.

Why Does the Brain Dominance Information Matter?

The traits that stem from the specialization found in the left and right sides of the brain impact everything we do. They impact education: how we learn, what we learn, when we learn, and even why we learn. They impact our work: which career we choose, how we work best, and why we work. They impact our relationships: how we interact, how we view others, and how we communicate. In this book, we'll mainly discuss the impact on education, which naturally impacts our future working lives.

Education

Schools teach in a left-brained fashion. They use such formats as sequential scope and sequence resources, short-term memorization, part-to-whole "show me" steps, and verbally based written work (defined in the Introduction). The problem is right-brained people learn best with global interest-based resources, long-term association, whole-to-part conceptual formats, and visual pictorial mental work (defined in the Introduction).

Interest-based, visual, big picture, associative resources work best for right-brained children. (Image[2])

Ever since our population has been schooled, our society tends to value left-brained traits. We've been subconsciously conditioned to believe the left-brained scope and sequence is the norm, but for people who are right-brained dominant, there's a different scope and sequence—a different norm. Thus, in order to expand on what is viewed and accepted as normal, we must first recognize how our system of learning favors left-brained processes. We can then add in and value those processes of the right side of normal.

Education should help an individual discover her passion and purpose in life. Instead, right-brained, creative learners have been misunderstood, overlabeled, unappreciated, and undervalued. This is the result of making these children fit into an environment that is geared toward their weak areas. There's a place for each style of learner in our society, but we can no longer undermine these creative children with outdated schooling practices. Right-brained people have gifts and strengths that should be nurtured as part of a good education.

Work

Education is meant to prepare a person for his life's work. John Taylor Gatto, former New York State Teacher of the Year, in his book *The Underground History of American Education,* espoused that the primary reason for the initial inception of school was to create an obedient workforce similar to what was designed for the German soldiers of the Nazi regime.[3]

However, I believe that we as a nation have matured and deepened our motives since that time. The 21ˢᵗ century needs big picture, creative, innovative thinkers. In an article for *WIRED®* magazine entitled "Revenge of the Right Brain," Daniel Pink encapsulates the changes in our workforce:

> *As the forces of Asia, automation, and abundance strengthen and accelerate, the curtain is rising on a new era, the Conceptual Age. If the Industrial Age was built on people's backs, and the Information Age on people's left hemispheres, the Conceptual Age is being built on people's right hemispheres. We've progressed from a society of farmers to a society of factory workers to a society of knowledge workers. And now we're progressing yet again to a society of creators and empathizers, pattern recognizers, and meaning makers.[4]*

Jeffrey Freed in his book, *Right-Brained Children in a Left-Brained World,* has said, "The software being developed today reflects the right-brained, spatial characteristics of its designers. These are aggressive, forward-thinking individuals who either work for themselves or for innovative companies, and they are living proof that the workforce of the future will require almost none of the skills being focused on in today's classrooms."[5] This book was written over fifteen years ago. The workforce referenced in that quote is that of today, yet our schools continue to languish in old habits.

How Do I Determine Brain Dominance?

Throughout this book you'll find information to help you understand and recognize right-brained learning traits. Just remember, this information is not meant to polarize brain processing preferences. It's meant to be viewed holistically, globally, and intuitively; which, by the way, are all gifts of the right-brained person.

Right-Brained Adult—Right-Brained Child

This information will help those of you who are right-brained embrace and validate your natural process and path to learning. It will definitively prove that you're not broken, and it will showcase valid right-brained strengths and gifts.

As a right-brained adult, you'll need to resist the urge to push right-brained children sooner and harder thinking it will protect them from the hurt you may have experienced as a misunderstood right-brained child. Beware of the "mirror effect" as well. The mirror effect is when we subconsciously dislike something about ourselves and criticize those with

 that same trait, especially our loved ones.

The mirror effect is when we're critical of someone who reminds us of our own traits we dislike.

In this situation, it's important to remember that the strengths and gifts of right-brained children have been historically undervalued and misrepresented. You can provide a well-matched, strengths-based learning environment for your right-brained child that celebrates his particular gifts. You'll receive the opportunity to redefine and heal your own self-image and emotional reaction to these same gifts and strengths. This book shifts the perspective about right-brained traits and specialties that our school-think has promoted as deficient and reveals that these right-brained traits and specialties actually bless the world we live in today with ingenuity, creativity, and innovation.

Left-Brained Adult—Right-Brained Child

We left-brained people will need to resist the temptation to categorize, compartmentalize, or quantify the information about right-brained learning. Because we fit into the left-brained school model so easily, we might believe the fallacy that we are "the smart ones." Yet, logic demands that we acknowledge that our inquisitive, creative right-brained children are smart, too. When we left-brained people discover the information about right-brained, strengths-based learning, we tend to want to forge full steam ahead, applying the "formula" to our right-brained children. In my situation, resisting the temptation to categorize allowed me greater enlightenment about the diversity of learning.

The secret, I discovered, is the timing when I applied the new right-brained information to my child. As I gathered and researched information about how children learn, I filed it away in my efficient left-brained memory system for instant recall as needed. As I observed my children at work or play and I wondered about something, I would search my database of knowledge to see if something I had learned could be used or applied in that instance. This way, what I knew about different learning styles, approaches, or time frames was useful because it emerged from my child's immediate needs. I was not trying to apply it arbitrarily simply from my desire to make something happen based on my limited understanding of a new concept. In other words, as a left-brained person, I needed to release my need to categorize my children and instead connect to my own right side to view them holistically. Since that doesn't come naturally, I had to trust what each child showed he needed in each moment.

How Many Right-Brained Learners Are There?

In an article titled, "Why All Students Need Visual-Spatial Methods," Linda Kreger Silverman, Ph.D., states at her website that, currently, about one-third of the students in our schools are *strong* right-brained learners, and 30% more *moderately* favor the right-brained processing preference. [6] This is the majority of our student population!

I sat down with my artist son and asked him to illustrate some distinctions in our world today compared to yesteryear that might account for this majority. Not only are natural, gene-based creative people entering our world, but our culture-based influences also encourage visual and spatial connections in the brain to be strengthened from a young age.

From oral storytelling—to visual storytelling.

From physical play—to visual play.

From print paper—to visual screen.

From handwriting with print—to keyboarding with visuals.

One is not better than the other; they are simply different ways to process information. Yet we still value print over visual, even when the amount of visual interactions in our culture has exploded. Again, both should be valued versus displacing one narrowly defined value system for another. We are all born with a genetic bent toward a dominant processing preference. Developing a new educational value system begins by understanding what each dominant processing system contributes to our world. It's time to update our educational practices to support both styles of learning in our schools. A right-brained dominant child deserves a scope and sequence that favors her learning path just like the one her left-brained peers enjoy. All learners should have the opportunity to experience joy through well-matched resources and teaching strategies at the same time their different time frames are honored. Our 21st century jobs demand more thinkers who are creative and innovative, the natural strengths of a right-brained dominant person. We need to recognize the traits of right-brained learners in order to give them value in our schools, our society, and our world. We must take a stand to reclaim our creative children and this book shows the way!

References and Notes

[1] Corpus callosum image is taken from: Michael Gazzaniga, Todd Heatherton, Diane Halpern. "Figure 3.28 The Lobes and Hemispheres of the Cerebral Cortex." *Psychological Science, 3rd Edition*. W. W. Norton & Company, 2009.

[2] The resource seen in the image is: Burns, Marilyn. *The I Hate Mathematics! Book*. Little, Brown and Company, 1975.

[3] Gatto, John Taylor. *The Underground History of American Education: A School Teacher's Intimate Investigation into the Problem of Modern Schooling*. Odysseus Group, 2000.

[4] Pink, Daniel. "Revenge of the Right Brain." *WIRED®, February 2005*.

[5] Freed, Jeffrey and Laurie Parsons. *Right-Brained Children in a Left-Brained World: Unlocking the Potential of your ADD Child*. New York: Fireside, 1998.

[6] Silverman, Linda Kreger. "Why All Students Need Visual-Spatial Methods." *Visual Spatial Resource.* n.d. http://www.visual spatial.org/files/allstudnt.pdf (accessed February, 2012).

Chapter Two

When an Apple Is an Apple

Shift Begins with Me

Shortly after our family began homeschooling, I was at a play date with my four children (at the time, ages 1 month, 1 year, 3 years and 5 years old) at the home of my homeschooling mentor with her four children. About an hour later, my friend asked my children if they would like an apple for a snack. They did, so I followed my friend into her kitchen and watched the babies as she started preparing the apples.

As she poised the knife over the apple to begin slicing, I cried, "What are you doing?"

"What?" she asked in surprised confusion.

"Why are you cutting the apple that way? I don't think my children would like it cut differently." I

explained. How could a grown woman not know how to cut an apple correctly, I wondered.

"Well, how do you cut an apple? she queried.

"I cut it down its core, which cuts it in half, and then I cut it in half again down the core, which makes quarters, and then I core it out," I replied gently as I helped her understand what she obviously missed in the home economics department.

She smiled patiently at me. "Well, the reason I cut the apple this way," and she proceeded to slice the apple about a quarter of the way into the apple, against the core, "is because you get an apple star. And my children like the stars."

Sure enough, right before my eyes, was a star! Inside the apple! How did that happen? Why didn't I know there was a star inside of an apple? Do you mean to say there really are different ways to cut an apple of which I was unaware? I'm forever grateful for the "lesson of the apple star." It prepared me to fully open my heart and mind to the unexpected, the undiscovered, the different way, the path that would truly allow each of my children to shine—like a star!

We've got to take a chapter from our creative people and think outside the box, or the apple cutting, as the case may be! If we cut the apple down its center in half and then in perfect quarters and core it, we get a delicious apple treat. The left-brained learning style is valid and good. As a society, we already appreciate the value of this learning style and its optimal scope and sequence. If we cut the apple sideways and enjoy the apple star and eat around it, we get a delicious and fun apple treat. The right-brained learning style is valid and good, too. However, we currently view it as needing to be fixed and to be changed to fit the left-brained scope and sequence.

The good news is there's also an optimal scope and sequence for a right-brained learner. We can't change the apple cut into an apple star into one that is cut down its center any more than we can do the reverse. We need to enjoy the apple star; we need to appreciate and celebrate the right-brained learning style. Both ways are good apples!

Expert Building Blocks

Fortunately, during my research phase of the right-brained learner, I discovered there are professionals leading the way in building our understanding of diverse learning styles and the mismatch of environments prevalent in our classrooms. These professionals gave me a more technical understanding about the right-brained, creative learner that helped me interpret many of the experiences I had with my children.

The secret to making effective changes based on this more useful information is by:

✓ Using consistent and reliable vocabulary
✓ Applying the knowledge to create a better matched learning environment for everyone

As I studied the works of various professionals, the first thing I noticed was the diverse use of vocabulary words. Most of the labels used by professionals describe the *parts* of the right-brained learning style: visual-spatial, dreamer, Edison trait, spatial intelligence, etc. This Heinz 57 approach fragments the information, causing us not to recognize that each is speaking about the same *holistic* person: the learner with a right-brained dominant processing preference. By using different vocabulary to describe different parts of the same learner, it can appear as if we're not speaking of the same thing. It would be like calling an apple a red fruit, fruit that makes juice, or fruit from a tree. Each of these is a descriptive *part* of an apple. To be clear, let's label it by its *holistic* label and call an apple an apple.

Confusing: Red fruit.   *Confusing: Fruit that makes juice.*
Clear: Apple   *Clear: Apple*

The second thing I noticed was how our culture's value system and focus on the left-brained style of learning in school hinder the effective implementation of this more useful right-brained information. In fact, I find that professionals either bend the right-brained information to conform to the left-brained practices, or the conclusions reached are still measured against left-brained standards. Why are we not applying good right-brained information to create well-matched learning environments for right-brained children? If we always do what we've always done, we'll always get what we've always gotten.

Let's start the effective changes by first meeting some of the current contributors to information on learning differences.

Howard Gardner

About 25 years ago in his book called *Frames of Mind*, Howard Gardner identified two types of intelligences that our society values: logical-mathematical and verbal-linguistic. He proposed there are also seven more "types" of intelligences that should be recognized: musical, spatial, kinesthetic, interpersonal, and intrapersonal, with nature and existential being added later. [1] This was my introduction to "learning styles," and I immediately recognized my oldest son as a "spatial learner." However, a couple of other types also fit him, with smidgens of yet a few others. It was the same with me. I couldn't consider myself strongly in one or another of several styles as described by Gardner. This just led to confusion for me, so I simply took away the information that there are different but equally valid ways to learn.

Since that first introduction to these theories, and as I was deciding which pieces of information were most reliable and, more importantly, holistic in their approach, I chose not to identify with Gardner's compartmentalizations. Although I applaud Gardner for expanding our awareness of and appreciation for other ways of thinking, I feel that the intelligences actually fall into the labeling-of-parts category.

For instance, being **musical,** having **spatial** abilities or being attuned to **nature** or spiritual things (**existential**) are *gifts* of the right-brained, creative learner. The **logical-mathematical** and **verbal-linguistic** intelligences are *gifts* of the left-brained learner, though right-brained learners can have a talent in math concepts (especially builder types) or be highly verbal (especially those who are gifted).

Kinesthetic (exploration through one's sense of touch) refers to the way a person gathers information through a sensory channel. It's one of the three most commonly used sensory input media, along with hearing (auditory) and seeing (visual). All three are referred to as *input modalities* (see Chapter Nineteen).

The **interpersonal** and **intrapersonal** intelligences can be compared to the extrovert and introvert information regarding how a person gains and expends energy. It's often considered part of a person's *temperament* or *social style*. Thus, as delineated above, I feel Gardner's intelligences are descriptors pulled from various parts that *impact* learning more than they represent holistic *styles* of learning.

Holistic label: Right-brained. Detailed labels: Kinesthetic, musical, intrapersonal

Gardner's intelligences did encourage the education profession to widen its teaching practices to include diverse methods of learning. If these intelligences are integrated in a classroom, they're often implemented as a choice of *how* a child can express his learning. For example, instead of a written report about the planets, a child can now choose to create a map, sing a song, build a mobile, work with a partner or alone, or delineate the statistics involved with the planets. This is a step in the right direction, but we're still going to study planets, and we're still going to study them in the second semester of third grade, and we're still going to use a textbook resource, and it's still going to come packaged in a neat and presentable product. By honoring only *part* of how children learn, educators fall short in the quest for a deeper *holistic* understanding of how, when, *and* why an individual processes various information.

Thomas Armstrong, Ph.D.

Since Gardner's book describing his philosophy, *Frames of Mind*, is a pretty heavy read, I relied on Thomas Armstrong's interpretations and applications to the classroom setting and children in his book, *In Their Own Way*. In his introduction, Armstrong stated he wrote this book in support of Gardner's theory after quitting his job as a learning disability specialist. Armstrong no longer believed in the labeling going on with most of the children he was being asked to remediate. Instead, he felt the different way these children learn was not understood. [2] Since then, his aggressive stance refuting the attention deficit disorder (ADD) phenomenon with his book, *The Myth of the A.D.D. Child,* has become well known. As mentioned in Chapter Three of this book, ADD is a common label for the right-brained child. The 50 strategies Armstrong delineates for helping a child who appears to have an attention difference are consistent with what works best with a right-brained, creative child.

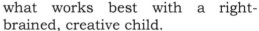

One strategy in Armstrong's book[3] is to promote physical activity.

Armstrong falls into the category of a professional who "gets it" about the right-brained learner (they're not broken but instead are misunderstood and mismatched). Professionals, though, often have to acquiesce to the fact that most right-brained children attend school, so their strategies have to help a child navigate that world.

Jeffrey Freed, M.A.T., and Laurie Parsons

The title of Jeffrey Freed's and Laurie Parsons' book relays this point perfectly: *Right-Brained Children in a Left-Brained World.* As a parent of children who are strong right-brained learners, this was an amazing find. I discovered many *whys* in this goldmine of a book [4] that lead to really *understanding* the right-brained, creative learner. Yet, even with this great information about why right-brained learners do what they do, the authors' focus had to remain on helping these children make it in a mismatched learning environment in order to preserve their self-confidence.

Linda Kreger Silverman, Ph.D.

Linda Kreger Silverman, Ph.D., is another professional who offered a lot of valuable information about right-brained learners in her book, *Upside-Down Brilliance: The Visual-Spatial Learner*. However, she chose to identify these learners with a different (part) vocabulary. Silverman dubbed the phrases "visual-spatial learner" (VSL) to depict the right-brained person, and "auditory-sequential learner" to delineate the left-brained person.[5] The problem with these distinctions is that they imply that the right-brained, creative person will be both visual and spatial in their preferences, and that the left-brained person will be both auditory and sequential in their preferences. However, I have a right-brained artist son who is strong with both the auditory and visual inputs (both are considered input modalities) and is less strong in the spatial arena. My right-brained builder son, on the other hand, skyrockets in the spatial arena and seeks a kinesthetic input, but is weak with auditory and less prone toward visual input. Again, we're talking a lot about input modalities and brain processing *gifts* versus a learning style. Different brain processing systems are more holistic in nature and incorporate not only *how* a person processes information but *why*. More importantly for the early elementary years, different brain processing systems also incorporate *when*.

I also take exception to the title of Silverman's book, *Upside-Down Brilliance*. Although this professional added more depth and knowledge to why the right-brained child learns in a particular manner, she still has the viewpoint that it's "backward" or "upside down" compared to what's "right." Putting the word "brilliance" next to "upside-down" doesn't erase the negative perception implied. These learners are not backward, upside-down, or broken. The right-brained child has a particular preference as to how he approaches material and when he's ready for different skills. There are real and valid reasons for why he learns what he does based on the strengths of the specialized processes of the right side of the brain. The common learning environment in our culture today is steered toward the strengths of the left-brained learner in all aspects (what, why, and when), which happen to be the opposite of what are considered the strengths of the right-brained learner. It's the learning environment that is upside-down for this child because it's set up to emphasize the weaknesses of the right-brained learner.

An upside-down ketchup bottle; now that's brilliant! (Image[6])

Finally, Silverman makes it clear that she's invested in the testing and assessment process within the learning domain because she finds it fascinating and challenging. It certainly makes sense that she would put so much emphasis, therefore, in the right-brained learning domain since these are the children (and adults) most labeled in our schools and society. In fact, there's very little to no labeling for their left-brained peers. Because of her focus on the area of sorting and classifying, Silverman appears to support the existence of a premise for the pathologization of the right-brained learner through labels of disability. At the same time, she does offer strategies to help teachers and students adjust to the left-brained valued classroom.

Dr. Dana Scott Spears and Dr. Ron L. Braund

Dr. Dana Scott Spears and Dr. Ron L. Braund are another set of authors who produced their own categorical naming system. They described the right-brained, creative child as a "dreamer" in their book *Strong-Willed Child or Dreamer?* Spears and Braund created a triadic model that they refer to as cognitive styles.[7] I feel their model coincides strongly with what I call *temperament traits*.

Dreamers are considered creative and sensitive (both strong traits of a right-brained, creative person), which can be combined with the Driver (strong-willed) cognitive style to become Creator types. When a Dreamer is combined with the Diplomat (cautious-compliant) cognitive style, they are considered Relators. Diplomats and Drivers combine to create Doers. In other words, a person can be all of one cognitive style (dreamer, diplomat, or driver) or the cognitive styles can be combined to be classified as relators, creators and doers. Again, I think this model tells us a lot about personality types (and their book has a lot of good information about such things as perfectionism), but it's too complex to steer us in a clear direction as to how, when, and why a right-brained person learns.

Lucy Jo Palladino, Ph.D.

One more example in the renaming department is a book formerly known as *The Edison Trait*, originally linking to the learning traits of Thomas Edison. The author, Lucy Jo Palladino, Ph.D., divides the different styles of learning into *Dreamers, Discoverers, & Dynamos*, which is the current name of the book.[8] From my interpretation, each is actually describing the right-brained, creative learner in various temperaments or creative outlet domains. For example, artist types are usually dreamers, builder types are discoverers, and risky-behavior types who might later be pilots or police officers are dynamos. Therefore, this book can help elaborate on the cross-section of right-brained learners.

My Dreamer.

My Discoverer.

My Dynamo.

Making the Connection

As the various professionals have tried on different names to represent the same style of learner, it all correlates with how people process information. It can appear as if they are trying to come up with alternatives to the obvious—red fruit, fruit that makes juice, fruit from a tree, etc. Why not just call an apple an apple?

It's All in the Name

I prefer to call all of us right-brained and left-brained learners because this encapsulates the holistic nature of processing specialization. I also embrace the term creative learner for right-brained persons because creative expression is at the center of who they are. Without a creative outlet in their lives, they only half live (see Chapter Six). I further embrace the term sequential learner for the left-brained person because order and logic are at the center of how they learn (see Chapter Five).

We need both left-brained learners and right-brained learners (and whole-brained learners) in our world. We complement one another. We often marry the opposite of ourselves. We use the best of each other to make our world go round. It's time that we put our creative people on equal footing with our left-brained people, starting at the earliest ages, in our educational systems. There are few to no labels for left-brained learning practices but a horde of them for the right-brained, creative learner. It's all about what we value. It's about what we've been conditioned to believe is true about what's "normal." There *is* a right side of normal.

Let's Make More Room

Each of these authors and professionals with the different labels and descriptors for the right-brained, creative learner has something positive to offer in his or her theories. However, their offerings are still often siphoned through the school-based learning value system. Thus, the right-brained, creative learner is viewed as someone who is difficult, broken, or needing special arrangements. These professionals find themselves continuing to offer advice to parents and teachers on how to remediate enough with a right-brained child to help him "make it" through the school system. They don't share any information about how this learner can be "normal," without remediation, when the right environment and time frame are honored. Though it's mentioned again and again in each of their books, the reality of the school-based educational value system we often operate under doesn't create a learning environment that supports the natural learning process of the right-brained child. If we are to reclaim this valuable resource, our creative children, we must choose or demand a different way!

Visual, hands-on experimentation is one natural way for right-brained children to learn.

Imagine this. We trust that an optimal reading time frame of between 8 and 10 years old preferred by the right-brained learner is as valid as the 5 to 7 year range preferred by the left-brained populace. We trust there's room for *Dick and Jane®*[9] alongside *Hooked on Phonics®* [10] as a viable pathway to reading acquisition. We trust that it's possible to embrace repetitive written drill of math facts for the sequential learners while offering mental math, manipulative explorations, and visual bibliographies for concept building for the creative learners. We trust learning one's multiplication facts in fifth grade versus third grade still results in mathematical excellence in adulthood. We trust that restoration of the powers of creativity, imagination, and play in the initial elementary years can form the bridge to a stronger representation of reading, writing, and arithmetic later, as indicated in years of studies on brain readiness (see Chapter Four).

The good news I offer through this book that can't be found in any other source is an example of a learning environment for the right-brained child that is completely free of today's schooling practices or psychological testing. I didn't follow a left-brained scope and sequence. I worked hard to decondition my thinking about how education should unfold. I consciously created an environment that encouraged all types of expressions of learning without sharing what I thought that looked like. I widened the window of time in which learning could be attained. I resisted the urge to worry and test when time frames extended beyond those found in school. I squelched the impulse to question and pathologize when I saw different processes emerge. I shifted my lens of acceptable learning practices and saw through eyes without expectations or measurements. Let this book guide your family to a joyful path to learning on the right side of normal for the right-brained, creative learner.

References and Notes

[1] Gardner, Howard. *Frames of Mind: The Theory of Multiple Intelligences.* Basic Books, 1983.

[2] Armstrong, Thomas. *In Their Own Way: Discovering and Encouraging Your Child's Personal Learning Style.* New York: Jeremy P. Tarcher/Putnam, 1987.

[3] Armstrong, Thomas. *The Myth of the A.D.D. Child: 50 Ways to Improve Your Child's Behavior and Attention Span Without Drugs, Labels, or Coercion.* Plume, 1997.

[4] Freed, Jeffrey and Laurie Parsons. *Right-Brained Children in a Left-Brained World: Unlocking the Potential of your ADD Child.* New York: Fireside, 1998.

[5] Silverman, Linda Kreger. *Upside-Down Brilliance: The Visual-Spatial Learner.* Denver: DeLeon Publishing, Inc., 2002.

[6] The *Heinz Tomato Ketchup* upside-down bottle is manufactured by H. J. Heinz Company, headquartered in Pittsburgh, Pennsylvania. Used with permission.

[7] Braund, Ron L. and Dana Scott Spears. *Strong-Willed Child or Dreamer?* Nashville: Thomas Nelson Publishers, 1996.

[8] Palladino, Lucy J. *Dreamers, Discoverers & Dynamos: How to Help the Child Who Is Bright, Bored, and Having Problems in School.* New York: Ballantine Books, 1999.

[9] The *Dick and Jane®* series of graded readers were written by Gray, William S. and Zerna Sharp and published by Scott Foresman and ©Addison-Wesley, Pearson Educational Publishers, Inc. It uses a sight word foundation to teach reading with picture context. I was taught to read with *Dick and Jane®*, the two main characters,

from 1970-1971. I'm a strong left-brained learner, which shows that left-brained learners can benefit from right-brained resources.

[10] Originally released in 1987 by Gateway Educational Products, *Hooked on Phonics®* is a commercial program that uses phonics to teach children to read. Though other phonics programs are mostly used by schools, *Hooked on Phonics®* became known as the stereotype for learning to read by phonics because of their aggressive advertising in the 1990s.

Chapter Three

Unraveling Right-Brained Labels

Shift Begins with Me

As I first began to plot out the wonderful experience I would call homeschooling with my then five-year-old, firstborn son, I envisioned amazing "products" of our efforts to share with any interested friends or family. I remember one project in particular. Logged under social studies, it was an "all about me" book. I would take pictures of him indicating various elements about who he is. He would then write a sentence (you know, for handwriting) sharing information about what the picture shows. Of course this was a good plan because don't all kindergartens across the nation do an "all about me" unit? I would do the same thing, but better (enter stage left: my perfectionism)!

It started falling apart with the first picture. My oldest was having nothing to do with the posed pictures to go in my fabulous book about him (as evidenced by the picture at the start of this chapter). After one picture, I was bribing him already! At about the fourth picture, even bribes didn't work. I found myself resorting to all out threats.

I remember the specific time that my "aha moment" slapped me upside the head. I was stubbornly working on the fancy cover made from wallpaper samples since my oldest was refusing to cooperate with the project. I mused about how lovely and noteworthy the project really was; how could he not see the value in it? And then one of my out-of-body experiences struck: I saw this insanely focused mother hunched over this useless project while simultaneously seeing the joyful intent of my oldest son in the next room pursuing his Venus flytrap interest with passion and purpose. What's wrong with this picture? Then I remembered what I read in an unschooling publication that went something like this: If you think something is so wonderful, do it yourself! That's exactly what I found myself doing, by default. I looked closely at the project, and it was clear. Even I didn't think this project was worth it; I created it strictly as fancy show-me-work.

My oldest son started homeschooling eagerly enough. He figured things would continue as usual, but maybe with some fun things thrown in with my involvement. That was my original intent. I latched onto the unschooling style (see Preface) for our homeschooling endeavor because it duplicated how learning had occurred in our home up until that point, and it was working well for my oldest son. Then my left-brained systematic enjoyment of planning out "the perfect school environment" kicked in. It didn't take long for my son's right-brained learning style to reject my left-brained ideas—no matter how creative! Going forward, I determined I wouldn't usurp the joy of learning by interjecting prideful pursuits, conditioned thinking, or personal preferences into my son's learning life. Instead, I would give value to his process, his time frames, and his interests.

Had I continued forward with the school environment I first created, what labels might have fallen upon my first child? Maybe ADD (attention deficit disorder) for being bored with the adult-created project required of him? Yet he was exploring the intricacies of the live Venus flytrap he learned from as he hand-fed it flies, and was looking up print references regarding his latest interest. How about ODD (oppositional defiant disorder) after he kicked his Sunday school teacher when she told him time was up for coloring his masterpiece? Would he get saddled with dyslexia because he didn't read until 9 years old and wrote certain letters backward until age 10? Or how about gifted-LD since he has a high IQ and yet he didn't share his written abilities until 11 years of age? Does he have dyscalculia if he learned his multiplication facts not in third grade, but in fifth?

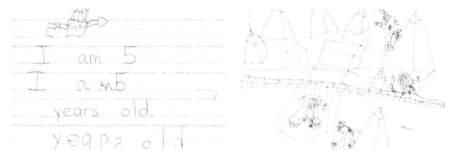

History and drawing captured my 5 year old child's attention more than penmanship. Which one do you think he did on his own initiative?

Our society has become specialized in all its arenas, including the learning domain. At the same time, the overachiever mentality has seeped into our homes and lifestyles and, thus, our expectations of ourselves and our children. We shamelessly and unfairly compare ourselves through our children's performance as we begin to believe that sooner is better, smarter, or more prepared (see Chapter Four). This is evidenced by resources such as Baby Einstein™

products geared toward infants or the recent push for mandatory preschool so children get a "head start." Those who can't live up to the expected performance level at the delineated time frames are paying the price.

Right-brained children are the most labeled learners in our schools. Why is that? Let's examine the attitudes and evidence that show our society is doing a grave disservice to our creative learners, both in how we educate them and how we view them through the lens of labels.

Our Left-Brained Value System

Most of us were mass (public) schooled, and most schools primarily utilize left-brained teaching methods, resources, and time frames. It's human nature to repeat what we experience. In other words, what we know is what we believe to be true. So when we graduate from school, we're inclined to give value to left-brained traits in educational settings. That's why we value the left-brained learning style of early memorization using short-term memory skills, part-to-whole scope and sequence formats of building upon the previous information, and symbolic skill development (see Introduction for definitions). That's why we value it all in a particular age time frame, too, beginning at the ages of 5 to 7. Any child who doesn't function according to this supposed norm may receive academic learning labels.

Academic Labels

I made a list of all the learning disability labels that exist in school for those who don't meet the school norms. There are dyslexia, ADD, attention deficit/hyperactivity disorder (ADHD), dyscalculia, learning disabled (LD), gifted, auditory processing disorder (APD), dysgraphia, and other similar terms. Behind each of these labels is often a right-brained child. These labels are used to quantify the difference between a right-brained child's ability and the school's expected left-brained performance. Instead of attaching labels, the recognition of differences in learning patterns should indicate the need for a different learning environment that utilizes different resources, presentation style, processes, and time frames. Our schools need to accommodate the academic needs of both left- and right-brained children.

Social Labels

I noticed a similar pattern of applying left-brained value systems based on the school environment for the diverse social styles. For instance, what social style is most valued in our society? The extrovert! We notice and give added value to the child who is invited to all the birthday parties and thrives in that environment, the child with many friends who is the life of the party, and the child who is quick to speak eloquently and efficiently.

We give added value to the child who is invited to all the birthday parties.

But what about the other social types? There's the introvert who thinks things through in her mind first and then says a few words with meaning, who has one or two close friends to whom she's loyal and true, or who needs to retreat from time to time to regroup and reenergize. How about the "little professor" who shares his intellectual observations with confidence, who likes to "direct and produce" play scenarios with willing participants, or who flourishes with a small group of like-minded people who

49

discuss the intricacies of a topic? There's also the shy style who warms up slowly in new situations but can assess where she best fits, needs to trust someone before revealing her thoughts to that person, or prefers one-on-one dynamics where her tender heart will be honored. Each of these social styles is valid.

An introvert often has one or two close friends to whom he's loyal and true.

Only one style is placed on the pedestal parents subconsciously aspire to have their children reach: the extrovert with lots of friends who is the first invited to every party. Why? Because this is the social style that can excel best in our schools! We subconsciously value those traits that can flourish in the environment that most of us attended.

Like the remediation procedure in the academic arena, we find ourselves trying to help the shy person "come out of her shell," or get the little professor to tone down his intellect to "fit in," or encourage the introvert to get more friends. We label. We remediate. We negatively connotate. We worry. We forget to value each of these social styles. Each has strengths that add to the variety in the communities in which we live, just like each of the various ways we learn.

Sensory Labels

The way our senses respond to the environment is another category we can add to our growing list of labels. We value those who can process intense levels of input despite such distractions as fluorescent lighting, visually packed walls, odors from carpet glues, and the constant hum naturally emitting from groups of people even on the other side of the wall. Yet, it's common for a right-brained person to have hearing, tactile (touch), olfactory (smell), and/or visual sensitivities that often make it difficult to tolerate the physical classroom environment in a typical school. Should a child wear the latest fad clothing to fit in socially, or do we honor wearing softer, more comfortable clothing against sensitive skin? Do we label these children with sensory processing disorder (SPD) and decide they can't function in the "normal" classroom environment, or do we offer a different style of lighting for sensitive vision and hearing, or different carpet glue for sensitive noses to provide a less stimulating environment? It all comes down to what we value. Each child deserves the freedom to choose an environment that is personally most comfortable. We all need to honor how a child learns, and provide what a child needs to flourish and exercise the strengths of one's individual temperament.

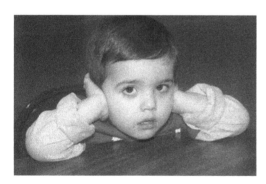

It's common for a right-brained person to have sensory sensitivities.

The good news is there's nothing wrong with the right-brained learning style, the less appreciated social styles, or a sensory sensitive person. As I will repeat again and again, there's also nothing wrong with the left-brained learning style, the extrovert, or the person who can process lots of sensory input easily. To reclaim our creative children though, we need to recognize that we have subconsciously learned to exclusively value traits of left-brained children who excel in the schools. Once we do, we need to learn to understand and equally value traits of right-brained children in our schools. This leads to placing a huge question mark around our labeling system specific to school-related difficulties.

The Myth of Labels

In our trend of specialization, professionals get so bogged down with their particular area of study that they no longer see the forest for the trees. For instance, a right-brained, creative learner can be seen by three different specialists and receive three different diagnoses. The ADD specialist would confirm that label; the dyslexia specialist would confirm that label; and the gifted specialist would confirm a third label. But are they simply describing three different traits of one learning style? We are unique, complex individuals with diverse and intricate parts that work in a complementary pattern to create a whole and beautiful person. Because of overspecialization, dissecting the parts is often used to create pathology through learning disability labels. Instead, the information gleaned regarding the differences in brain processing specialties could be used to promote value in and understanding about the right side of normal.

Overlapping Criteria

Specialized professionals often fail to look for the commonalities in the work of others which results in considerable overlap of criteria. This creates confusion. In her book, *Upside-Down Brilliance: The Visual-Spatial Learner,* Linda Kreger Silverman reveals the following examples[1] to demonstrate what I mean.

❖ Some of the common labels for a right-brained learner are auditory processing disorder (**APD**), sensory processing disorder (**SPD**), **dyslexia**, and **ADHD**. Silverman notes that there are a **lot of commonalities** between each of these labels and the visual-spatial learner (VSL), which translates as a **right-brained learner**. (See Chapters Seventeen, Eighteen, and Nineteen where I clearly explain the connection between these labels and right-brained processing traits.)

❖ Regarding the two labels of **APD** and **ADHD**: There's a **two-thirds overlap in criteria** between these two labels. Silverman goes on to admit that it's difficult to determine the correct diagnosis between certain labels because of the significant overlap in criteria.

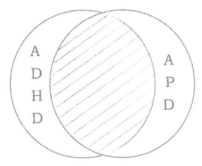

❖ Continuing with the overlap-of-criteria phenomenon, Silverman witnesses a meeting featuring two top professionals in their fields: the expert on **ADHD** and the expert on **overexcitabilities**. [2] A group of diagnosticians trying to determine which diagnosis was applicable to their clients noticed a **significant overlap in criteria**. They wanted these two authority figures to help the group sift through the confusion. The expert response: "They looked at each other, shrugged their shoulders, and both said, 'I don't know. You have to look at each case individually.'"[3]

This might be amusing if lives weren't being destroyed in the labeling process. The overlap of criteria must raise serious questions on its own standing, but when the professionals who profess to specialize in particular areas of expertise can't even differentiate one from another, we must stop the madness and question the foundation upon which we think we stand.

From Disability to Creativity

An important point to remember is that not every right-brained child will have the traits labeled as ADHD, dyslexia, or APD. But most children given these learning labels (and other academic disability labels) are right-brained learners. These labels are the means with which the child is blamed for not fitting into the school environment. They are meant to make us believe that there's something wrong with this child and that the experts can tell exactly what traits are interfering with their learning process. The thing is that most children with these traits have amazing strengths that emerge when placed in an appropriate setting, and can have difficulties when immersed in a mismatched setting.

For instance, take "attention differences" exhibited by a creative, right-brained learner. One of the universal gifts of right-brained learners is an extraordinary imagination (see Chapter Five). The strength of this trait is developed through the enormous amounts of time their brains spend on creative thinking and processing pursuits. This takes attention. If a right-brained learner is engaged in his creative pursuit (see Chapter Six), let's say building with LEGO® blocks, I don't think an attention issue would be found. On the other hand, what happens when he's placed in a school setting with an activity that doesn't facilitate imaginative thinking, such as filling out worksheets? This mind made for creative exercises seeks inspiration out the window or in the recesses of his own mind. Without creative expression, a right-brained learner is half dead. Creativity is sought in any way possible just to feel alive. A right-brained child is simply drawn to his natural bent, like a moth to light.

It's unlikely an attention "problem" exists when a child engages intently in a creative interest, even with distractions!

Silverman concurs:

When VSLs with these [ADHD like] behaviors are placed in challenging, stimulating environments with true peers and loving adults, their symptoms lessen. During times they are engaged in activities that fascinate them, their symptoms often disappear entirely. One-on-one instruction, homeschooling, or computerized instruction may eliminate symptoms that show up in large groups. Annemarie Roeper (psychotherapist and wise woman) advises us to accept each child's individuality, and to adapt our teaching and parenting styles to fit this unique person.[4]

Am I saying that there aren't differences? Nope. There are differences! What I'm saying is that these are *normal* differences inherent in the right-brained processing preference (see Chapter Seventeen). I'm saying there are environments, resources, and appropriate time frames that allow the creative, right-brained learners to flourish and showcase their gifts just as their left-brained counterparts do in the environment, with resources, and time frames that work best for them. That is the good news proclaimed throughout this book.

Creativity Can't Be Measured

Silverman has spent extensive amounts of time and research trying to find a consistent testing result that would help her identify the visual-spatial learner (her name for the right-brained learner). Her conclusion: "While the analysis of subtest patterns tells me a great deal about visual-spatial learners, most of the time I rely on the children's interests. They seem to be more reliable than any particular constellation of subtest scores." [5] That is a noteworthy conclusion! All the individual facets and traits involved in creativity can't be measured.

This criterion of paying attention to the interests of your child is exactly the secret I share with all parents looking to understand their creative children better. What are your child's interests? If they're similar to those shared below, you probably have a right-brained learner.

My list of common creative outlets for right-brained children (see Chapter Six).

One doesn't need a professional degree in order to recognize these amazing learners. Each child will show us if learning is working through active and productive engagement in the learning process. We inadvertently place the blame of poor school performance upon our right-brained children through labels instead of on the faulty belief that there's one correct way to learn. There's more than one right path to learning, to being social, and to interacting with our sensory world. Right now we consider the left-brained characteristics and traits that succeed in the current school as "normal." Educating oneself about right-brained, creative learners will lead to creating a successful learning environment for the right side of normal, too.

References and Notes

[1] Silverman, Linda Kreger. *Upside-Down Brilliance: The Visual-Spatial Learner.* Denver: DeLeon Publishing, Inc., 2002.

[2] Overexcitabilities were coined by Polish psychiatrist and psychologist, Kazimierz Dabrowski, when he noticed that creative/ gifted types have a greater intensity of neural responses. In other words, these children were more easily stimulated and "excited" across a variety of situations. There are five types of overexcitabilities: psychomotor, sensual, imaginational, intellectual and emotional.

[3] Silverman, Linda Kreger. *Upside-Down Brilliance.*

[4] Ibid.

[5] Ibid.

Chapter Four

Earlier Is Not Better

Shift Begins with Me

My oldest son seemed bored and I had morning sickness with my fourth child, so we decided he should try a well-lauded child development center preschool associated with the local university for a half year. Just before his fifth birthday, he began attending two days a week. My son anticipated that the school would feed his interest in meat-eating plants and dinosaurs. As it turned out, the teacher never was able to work it in, and slowly his interest in attending dissipated.

Halfway through the semester, the teacher pulled me aside to ask which preschool my son previously attended. Surprised to discover he'd never attended another preschool, the teacher complimented his social maturity compared to the other children who had been attending various settings for some years. She said that although my son entered mid-year, when connections had already formed among the children, he took a leadership role and established a rapport with the other children. Not only that, she said my son was the most advanced problem-solver, capable of independently working out solutions with his peers.

Just as our family discovered that early formal social programs weren't the prerequisite for social success, this experience helped me also question if the entirety of early learning needed to be looked at more closely.

Comparing "Old Fashioned" Upbringing with Current Trends

I grew up in the era when kindergarten was a half-day filled with cookies and milk, naptime, and playtime. The elementary years included such classics as *Dick and Jane*®, recess three times a day (even in the snow), and a walk home for lunch.

Today, wealthy parents sign up their in utero children at the best preschool. Most children of typical families attend preschool between ages two and three, and kindergarten is the "new first grade." What's more, the unstructured domain of outdoor play, boredom, and free time after school so typical of my day is now replaced with the enrichment activities, after-school programs, and scheduled play dates of this generation's children.

Unstructured free time and boredom prompts creativity and imagination.

Times do change. Both dual-income families and blended families are common today. The world has become more competitive, global, and transient. Our family chose to embrace the potential that came with being "corporate gypsies" for the first nine years of my husband's career (and he switched universities twice prior to that, graduating in six years) which kept us far away from our hometown and family. Though we adopted the new transient lifestyle, we decided to embrace "old fashioned" values for our children, such as lots of unstructured time, space to run around outside, and delayed academics.

Delayed Formal Academics (8 to 10 Years)

I believe that even if all the technologies have encouraged a fast-paced lifestyle, we can't speed up the brain's readiness for formal learning. The idea that someone in some governmental agency somewhere decided that starting school sooner would equate to being better prepared for a global economy doesn't make it true. What we know about how our brain functions doesn't support this supposition.

Research Evidence

In the early stages of deciding to homeschool, and after finding out about the unschooling lifestyle that reflected the early educational years of my oldest child, I sought out material that would support our decision to delay formal academics. I'd heard a lot about Dr. Raymond Moore and his book, *Better Late than Early,* so I picked it up at my local library. What I had anticipated being an easy read about supporting delayed academics in the homeschooling arena was a surprisingly heavily researched book highlighting hundreds of documented brain studies. Over and over again, the overarching conclusions of these studies showed that our brains are not fully developed for the processes necessary for formal academic work with symbolic representations until the ages of 8 to 10 years old. Moore boldly concludes, "... we analyzed over 8000 studies of children's senses, brain, cognition, socialization, etc, and are certain that **no replicable evidence exists for rushing children into formal study *at home or school* before 8 to 10.**" [1] A 2007 Cambridge-based Primary review concurs: "The assumption that an early starting age is beneficial for children's later attainment is not well supported in the research and therefore remains open to question."[2] In other words, hard science supports a different time frame than is currently valued in our country.

Science supports delaying formal academics to between the ages of 8 and 10.

Global Evidence

Global evidence supports the time frame of 8 to 10 years as a turning point in learning. We have more reading difficulties now than ever before. This is a result of too much emphasis on one preferred method of teaching it (phonics-based instruction versus sight word-based), as well as *when* it's taught. Finland, at the top of the educational boards globally, doesn't start schooling until children are age 7. These children also spend the least amount of time in the classroom. In Sweden, formal education also doesn't begin until age 7, reading instruction begins at age 8, and by the time Swedish children are age 10, they are at the top of the literacy charts in Europe.[3]

These global examples of what works should be a starting point in assessing America's poor standing in literacy and academics. Lilian Katz, a professor of education at Illinois University, is an advocate for starting formal academics at 7 years old. She feels teaching children to read between 5 and 6 years seeds a dislike for books later on, especially with boys. "It can be seriously damaging for children who see themselves as inept at reading too early."[4]

Play is more important in the early years, especially for boys.

Historical Evidence

Nations at the top of the academic and literacy charts, as well as brain research, indicate that formal academics are best begun between 8 and 10 years of age. Interestingly, this also coincides with when our Founding Fathers received an education during the Colonial America era. The elite often worked with a tutor between 8 and 10 years of age before entering university level studies in their early teens.[5]

Does this mean there's no learning happening before a child is 8 to 10 years old? Of course not. During colonial times, children learned in their homes. In Sweden, the children are nurtured in a cross-age group with an emphasis on play. Schools can still exist to accommodate the needs of the dual-income family. It's *how* and *when* academic instruction is delivered that should be scrutinized.

How Academic Instruction Is Delivered

As mentioned in Chapter Two, we've made strides in our understanding that different *learning styles* are valid. This has been the main focus of professionals for 25 years and a first step in the right direction. But our schools still fall far short in using different *teaching methods* for different types of learners. Mel Levine wrote a book called *A Mind at a Time* explaining that every mind has value and functions best in its own unique way.[6] Yet Brock Eide, M.D., M.A., and Fernette Eide, M.D., in *The Mislabeled Child,* accuse, "Too often we try to teach children using only a narrow range of options. This narrow approach actually aggravates—and in some cases even causes—many of the learning difficulties children encounter." The Eides conclude that "what they need...is a form of education that is right for children who learn the way they do."[7] We all seem to agree that there are different ways to learn, yet we haven't held our schools accountable by requiring real and legitimate change in the way right-brained children are taught. Instead, we've allowed a labeling epidemic to justify this difference. Our right-brained, creative children pay the price.

When Academic Instruction Is Delivered

Discussion among professionals has occurred for the *how* of learning, even if no one has addressed the significant discrepancy of needs between left- and right-brained learners. But discussion among professionals for the *when* of learning hasn't seemed to have occurred at all. I'm not talking about the discussion that focuses on the start of formal academics, even if those in charge of this decision have obviously ignored all the evidences supporting delayed formal academics to ages 8 to 10. I'm talking about the time frame referred to in the *scope and sequence* schools follow that outlines when children learn certain subjects.

A right-brained scope and sequence would include nature study in the early years.

A professional who hints at the time frame difference best is Stanley I. Greenspan, M.D., in his book, *The Challenging Child*. In a chapter, fittingly, about the right-brained child (or a child identified with one of the labels often associated with the right-brained child, called "The Inattentive Child"), he says:

An interesting point worth remembering is that our schools, in the early years, tend to be biased toward children who are strong auditory-verbal learners [My note: His label for the left-brained person]. *Verbal systems are highly valued as children learn to talk, read, and write. Even if they have trouble picturing math concepts, they can master them in these early years because the simple concepts can easily be memorized. Because the verbal system is so overvalued in those early years, visual-spatial learners* [My note: His label for the right-brained person]*, who can understand math concepts but may not be able to memorize multiplication tables and have more difficulty with reading and writing, are thought to be slower in learning. Verbal children are more apt to be labeled "gifted" in those early years. Later, in high school and beyond, when science and math become more challenging and when even subjects like English and history are more analytical than factual and descriptive, visual-spatial learners (who are very analytical) may begin doing better. Some of the gifted auditory-verbal learners who depended too much on their outstanding memories and never grasped the* *concepts or principles behind what they were learning may begin to struggle.*[8]

What Greenspan described is the time frame differences based on brain processing preferences. The strengths of left-brained children are valued in the early years, so they seem smarter earlier. The strengths of right-brained children are valued in middle school to high school, so they appear to suddenly become smart later. These strengths of the left- and right-brained learners can be linked to doing better, or worse, with certain subjects based on the time frame for learning those subjects. Currently, the scope (what's learned) and sequence (or time frame) used in school for developing different skills and subjects favor the left-brained learners' natural time frame. The good news is there's also a right side of normal.

Currently, formal symbolic academic work begins between 5 and 7 years of age, which works for left-brained learners. Right-brained children learn the various subjects in a completely different order than their left-brained peers (see Chapter Seven). For instance, formal symbolic academic work shouldn't begin until between 8 and 10 years of age for the right-brained learners. Parents and educators initially worry that later isn't a good thing. Let the research, global, and historical evidence in this chapter alleviate those worries to support and value the natural time frame development of the right-brained learner.

My builder son didn't start reading until age 10, but could construct a telephone at age 9.

Stages of Learning

I have identified the time frames of three stages of learning, depicted in the charts below. This chapter introduces the function of each stage while Chapter Seven provides details for the content and subject expression.

Foundation Stage 5 to 7 Years Old		Transition Stage 8 to 10 Years Old		Integration Stage 11 to 13 Years Old	
Left-Brained	Right-Brained	Left-Brained	Right-Brained	Left-Brained	Right-Brained
Symbolic & Word Development	Global & Creative Development	Creative Development	Symbolic Development	Global Development	Word Development
Favor 2-D	Favor 3-D	2-D/start 3-D	3-D/start 2-D	2-D & 3-D	3-D & 2-D
Reading Arithmetic Spelling Writing	Creative Outlets History Science Geography Social Studies	Develop Fluency Of Aged 5-7 LB Subjects Social Studies Geography	Develop Fluency of Aged 5-7 RB Subjects Reading Arithmetic	Develop Fluency of Aged 8-10 LB Subjects History Science	Develop Fluency Of Aged 8-10 RB Subjects Spelling Writing

The first stage of learning is called the Foundation Stage because it focuses on the universal gifts and strengths of each learner (see Chapter Five). Left-brained learners are two-dimensional thinkers who focus on symbolic and word development. Right-brained learners are three-dimensional thinkers who focus on global and creative development. For both left- and right-brained learners, it makes sense that **learning should build upon one's strengths for a firm foundation**.

The second stage of learning is called the Transition Stage because it's the beginning of the integration process of the two hemispheric specializations (see Chapter Seven). This is the time when the right-brained learner *starts* to utilize some of the strengths of the left side of the brain to incorporate two-dimensional thinking. The left-brained learner *begins* to utilize some of the strengths of the right side of the brain to incorporate three-dimensional thinking. The Moores support my theory of a major shift during this stage in their book *Better Late than Early*. They say, "Studies have demonstrated a variety of significant changes in brain maturation between ages 7 and 11. Some of these changes are in the brain's structure, others are in its chemistry and still others in its electrical potential."[9] In 2007, an example of these changes was confirmed in the "largest longitudinal pediatric neuroimaging study reported to date." The study showed that the total gray matter found in the brain peaked for girls at 8.5 years and for boys at 10.5 years.[10] (Gray matter tends to keep learning centered in one area of the brain, which translates to mean that learning is still specialized.[11]) These evidences support my theory that brain specialties *begin* to transition to incorporate other areas of the brain between 8 and 10 years.

The third stage of learning is called the Integration Stage because the established dominant brain preference increasingly integrates the opposite brain specialties so the learner becomes competent in more subjects (see Chapter Seven). Even though each brain processing preference continues to rely heavily on its own specialization (right-brained children are still right-brained dominant and left-brained children are still left-brained dominant), each more fully integrates the less preferred specialty skills. *Better Late than Early* states, "A recent Stanford Research Institute study by Meredith L. Robinson points to the likelihood that the early adolescent years, from 10 to 14, may be the time when most children finally develop the full range of their capacities, or in effect, reach their integrated maturity level."[12] In the 2007 pediatric neuroimaging study mentioned earlier, the white matter of the brain increases significantly at this stage, and the total cerebral volume reaches its highest at 10.5 years for girls and 14.5 years for boys.[13] White brain matter accounts for the best communication throughout the brain[14] as stated in my theory for this developmental stage.

My experiential evidences validate the professional references above that state changes occur in the brain both at the 8 to 10 year time frame and the 11 to 13 year time frame.

I believe more studies and research are warranted in these areas, especially regarding the creative, right-brained learner, to gain more insights as to the best way we can support these learners in our schools.

One of the hardest things I will ask of parents and educators in this book is to wait out the time frame of the creative learner. I didn't come to this conclusion lightly. Though there are thousands of research studies indicating academics shouldn't be rushed, our fast-paced society influences decisions to learn sooner. Moore states a pointed reminder, "We would be aghast at such a performance in medical science. We wouldn't tolerate such ignorance even in the manufacture of our cars."[15] Yet, the research on *when* children optimally learn is ignored. Most experts recognize that the current learning environment in our schools isn't right for everyone, yet they continue to label children when they can't perform in a prescribed manner at a prescribed time. The good news is that there's an optimal learning time frame for right-brained children that showcase their kind of smart in the early years *and* the later years. The next section of this book shares the scope and sequence for the right side of normal.

References and Notes

[1] Moore, Raymond S. and Dorothy N. Moore. *Better Late than Early: A New Approach to your Child's Education.* Reader's Digest Association, 1989.

[2] Coughlan, Sean. "Is five too soon to start school?" *BBC NEWS UK Education.* February 8, 2008. http://news.bbc.co.uk/2/hi/ 7234578.stm (accessed May 23, 2012).

[3] Ibid.

[4] Curtis, Polly. "Under-sevens 'too young to learn to read.'" *The Guardian.* November 22, 2007. http://www.guardian.co.uk/uk/2007/nov/22/earlyyears education.schools (accessed May 23, 2012).

[5] Beliles, Mark A. and Stephen K. McDowell. "Christian Education: The system for any country that wants to be free." *The Mandate.* (April 22, 2008). http://www.forerunner.com/mandate/X0057_ Christian_ Education.html (accessed May 23, 2012).

[6] Levine, Mel. *A Mind at a Time.* New York: Simon & Schuster Paperbacks, 2002.

[7] Eide, Brock and Fernette Eide. *The Mislabeled Child.* New York: Hyperion, 2006.

[8] Greenspan, Stanley I. "The Inattentive Child." *The Challenging Child: Understanding, Raising, and Enjoying the Five "Difficult" Types of Children.* Da Capo Press, 1995.

[9] Moore, Raymond S. and Dorothy N. Moore. *Better Late than Early.*

[10] Lenroot, Rhoshel K., Nitin Gogtay, Deanna K. Greenstein, Elizabeth Molloy Wells, Gregory L. Wallace, Liv S. Clasen, Jonathan D. Blumenthal, Jason Lerch, Alex P. Zijdenbos, Alan C. Evans, Paul M. Thompson, and Jay N. Giedd. *Sexual dimorphism of brain developmental trajectories during childhood and adolescence,* 2007. http:// www.boysadrift.com/2007Giedd.pdf.

[11] Gurian, Michael. *The Purpose of Boys: Helping Our Sons Find Meaning, Significance, and Direction in Their Lives.* Jossey-Bass: 2009.

[12] Moore, Raymond S. and Dorothy N. Moore. *Better Late than Early.*

[13] Lenroot, Rhoshel K. et al. *Sexual dimorphism of brain developmental trajectories during childhood and adolescence.*

[14] Gurian, Michael. *The Purpose of Boys: Helping Our Sons Find Meaning, Significance, and Direction in Their Lives.*

[15] Moore, Raymond S. and Dorothy N. Moore. *Better Late than Early.*

Section Two

The Core Traits

What We Believe.

Children are empty buckets waiting to be filled.

Shifting Perspective.

We all are born pre-wired with unique gifts and inherent weaknesses. We are candles with a small flame. The environment in which we are placed can extinguish that flame—or fan it into a fire.

Chapter Five unveils the core traits of both the right-brained person and the left-brained person. Among these core traits are two universal gifts—traits that are common to all—for each learner. Examples are given that show how each applies the universal gifts in their learning lives.

What We Believe.

The arts are either extra-curricular or a waste of time.

Shifting Perspective.

The arts encourages creative expression. A right-brained person engages in one or more creative outlets throughout his or her life. Learning for a right-brained child revolves around a creative outlet. It's how he makes sense of the world.

Chapter Six describes the creative outlets pursued by right-brained people and reveals how each creative outlet develops particular skills that lead to improved learning ability. Creative outlets are a set of skills in the arts and technology that enhance and promote the use of the universal gifts of the right-brained person. These are computers/video games, art/photography, puzzles/mazes, building/electronics, cooking/gardening, fashion/sewing, theater/showmanship, music/dance, and math/numbers.

What We Believe.

Reading, writing, and arithmetic comes first in learning.

Shifting Perspective.

These are the subjects that use our left hemisphere strengths. For those children born to favor their right hemisphere strengths, other subjects come most easily. The best time to learn each subject is based on the strengths of the favored side of the brain.

Chapter Seven outlines stages of learning for the right-brained child during the time frames of 5 to 7, 8 to 10, and 11 to 13 years of age. It describes and gives examples of how certain core traits are conducive to learning at a particular time and in a particular way.

On the positive side of perfectionism, persistence in the creation process can produce amazing things.

What We Believe.

When a child is disobedient or non-compliant, he's stubborn, oppositional, or strong-willed.

Shifting Perspective.

Resistance is a communication tool used by inexperienced people to indicate something isn't working. The cause of resistance can be a mismatched learning environment, underdeveloped skills, or perfectionism.

Chapter Eight describes and gives examples of the core traits of resistance and perfectionism. Diverse reasons why right-brained children show resistance are showcased, and examples of how to support right-brained children who exhibit the core trait of perfectionism are included.

What We Believe.

Creative people are absent-minded professors with no method to their madness.

Shifting Perspective.

Right-brained people are all about the creative process! To achieve the height of creativity, they need to reach a sense of timelessness.

Chapter Nine describes and gives examples of the core traits of product/process and time/space. This chapter explains how the focus on creativity leads right-brained children to be more interested in the creation *process* instead of an end product. (This is also why a right-brained child exists outside the bounds of time.)

Chapter Five

The Universal Gifts

Shift Begins with Me

Two parents approached me, along with their amazing daughter, after attending my "Understanding the Right-Brained Child" workshop at a conference. They were eager to learn more about how to be facilitators for their creative child who has a passion for learning. I heard how the mother was working with her daughter's love of math by sharing her own passion in the subject, but it was creating disillusionment for both. I saw the sparkle in this incredible daughter's eyes, and I saw the real desire in the parents' eyes to keep that spark alive in their daughter's learning life. Why wasn't it working and what should she do?

The mother figured out through conversations with her daughter that the young lady viewed math like a giant puzzle. This creative daughter found it intriguing to figure out where the missing link in the equation was via algebraic solutions through her gifted visualization skills. Yet, she struggled with simple math facts.

I directed the parents to look at the love of learning exuding from their daughter. I said, "Just feed that! She knows what she loves to do in math. So whatever is emanating from within her, you feed. Having faith that by valuing whatever she loves to pursue, her gifts will be revealed down the road. For today, fan the flame of passion that comes from within her, and that is enough."

This approximately nine-year-old girl didn't take long to show her parents how to fulfill that advice. They came back to me later and said, "Our daughter came out of the play area and said, 'I'm interested in LEGO®. It looks like geometry.'" Since the parents had attended my right-brained learner class, they knew LEGO® was one of the gift areas (see Chapter Six) toward which a creative child could gravitate. We all stood in awe at her cleverness at recognizing the geometric attributes that LEGO® inherently provides. LEGO® it would be, and we smiled at this young person's passion for math and how she wanted to explore her potential in this arena.

Interest-based, child-led learning emanates from within the child outward. As children's learning facilitators, we can be astute observers who translate what we see into additional resources that can feed the flame of passion within the child. Some make it easy, like this young lady. In fact, right-brained learners often are insatiable learners, but they're passionate about areas that aren't highly valued in our society. So these areas of interest—like art, drawing, music, LEGO® building, sewing, gardening, video games, etc.—are often overlooked. To honor the path each type of learner is meant to follow, it's important to value the interests, pursuits, and goals that come from within and through each child. Thus, successful support of learners requires observation of these things.

It's natural that children are drawn to the subjects and activities that engage and expand their foundational strengths and gifts. Unfortunately, it's common to steer right-brained children to the left-brained learning path and strengths. The mother at the conference tried to direct her daughter to arithmetic when she noticed her daughter's interest in math. But closer observation reveals it wasn't math *facts* that intrigued her daughter, but math *concepts*. The young lady was drawn to her natural path as a right-brained learner when she pursued learning concepts before facts. The good news is that there's a natural learning path for this learner. The information in this book will help each of us educating right-brained children create an environment of both resources and time frames well matched to these eager and bright learners.

Core Traits

I presented my first right-brained workshop from a list of traits I created based on my observations of my right-brained children's journeys. After receiving stories of positive change for their families about their right-brained children from attendees to these workshops, I was eager to learn more. I researched others' work regarding the right-brained learner and general knowledge about the brain. I discovered the left and right hemispheres of the brain are mirror images of the other, each specializing in opposing traits. Armed with this understanding, and influenced by lists depicting right hemisphere traits created by professionals in the field, I streamlined my list of attributes to focus on core traits.

Right-brained children are attracted to comic books because this resource supports the picture-based and whole-to-part core traits. (Image[1])

A common characteristic listed for a right-brained learner is "prefers sight words." This isn't what I call a core trait. Why not? A right-brained child typically prefers to learn to read with sight words because of the core traits of the *whole-to-part* preference and the *picture-based* processing. The right-brained child wants to take in the whole word (such as for reading) before understanding its parts (such as for spelling). Since the right-brained child also needs to visualize a picture when learning, these can be created for a whole word but not parts of a word. So, the core traits are *whole-to-part* and *picture based.* These two core traits *impact* how a right-brained child learns to read which *results* in the preference for sight words. These particular core traits also impact spelling, writing, and math strategies as well, to name a few. Understanding how core traits impact learning will affect crucial change for right-brained children when creating a well-matched learning environment.

Below is a list of core traits that showcase the opposing specialties between the brain processing preferences.

Left Hemisphere	Right Hemisphere
reality	*imagination
*word based (symbolic)	*picture based (3-dimensional)
*sequential	global
part	whole
memorization	association
logical (mind)	intuitive (heart)
compliant	resistant
external perfectionism	internal perfectionism
product	process
time	space

*Universal gifts

Universal Gifts

One of the first questions I asked myself was if there are traits common to most right-brained or left-brained people. As noted in Chapter Two, Linda Kreger Silverman delineated these traits as visual-spatial for a right-brained person and auditory-sequential for a left-brained person. And yet, she went on to conclude that the most reliable way to determine if a person is right-brained is if they engage in what I call the creative outlets (see Chapter Six).[2] This shows that the visual, spatial, auditory, and sequential traits Silverman uses to categorize right- and left-brained learners can't be considered universal if these traits aren't good identifiers. My experiential observation after speaking with thousands of right-brained people is that she was on the right track, but the theory needed a little tweaking. I've denoted two particular core traits in the list above to be universally common in each brain processing preference. I call these common traits universal gifts.

Left Hemisphere	Right Hemisphere
reality	***imagination**
*word based (symbolic)	*picture based (3-dimensional)
*sequential	global
part	whole
memorization	association
logical (mind)	intuitive (heart)
compliant	resistant
external perfectionism	internal perfectionism
product	process
time	space

*Universal gifts

Reality vs. Imagination

The first of the two universal gifts of right-brained, creative learners is their extraordinary imaginations. Naturally, childhood is a time of playing pretend and using one's imagination, but with the right-brained child, you'll notice he goes beyond the typical left-brained reality-based elements of expression.

Costume Play

I often use the photo at the beginning of this chapter as a pictorial representation of the difference in imaginations among children. My strong right-brained, creative learner is the child in the king outfit. My youngest child is in the John Deere® tractor costume. They were both excited to receive new Halloween costumes and eager to have their pictures taken in them. My youngest son *loves* John Deere® tractors so was smiling broadly while displaying his find. On the other hand, my creative learner *is* the king in this picture. He's not just showing off his costume; he's portraying his kingliness in expression and actions. There's a difference. It's all about a highly developed imagination.

This creative child displays his imagination through costume play. When he decides he's a police officer, he creatively uses objects and items to depict the various accoutrements. For instance, he dons an older brother's Boy Scout™ shirt as his uniform top, and employs his father's garden belt as his holster. When converting into a soldier, he uses buckled belts crossed over in the front along with a Game Boy® carrying case as a supply kit. From the moment he becomes the police officer or the soldier, he must henceforth be referred to as "police officer" or "soldier." If called by his given name, he becomes visibly upset and corrects your misidentification. My theater son's dress-up and costuming are representations of a creative imagination.

Figure Toy Play

Another of my strong right-brained, creative learners focused his imagination on his toys. He was easy to buy for at Christmas because he was theme-based every season. There was the Power Ranger® season, the Star Wars® season, the Teenage Mutant Ninja Turtle™ season, and a Pokémon® season. This creative child meticulously set up extensive play scenarios and got lost in the drama that unfolded. As a social introvert, my artist son especially enjoyed directing and producing willing peers into his creative process and was fortunate to find other children willing to follow or friends who preferred supporting roles. The gift of the imagination begets amazing fantasy creations.

My theater son also enjoys creating elaborate play scenes.

Stuffed Animal Play

Many of my right-brained children developed special bonds with one or more stuffed animals. When the movie *Toy Story®* first came out, I witnessed the reaction of my two oldest children at the revelation that stuffed toys were alive. They looked at each other and I "heard" the unspoken communication: "I knew it!" My writer daughter carried four to five stuffed cats around all the time for many years. They were ready companions as real to her as any human friend, maybe more. During her early teen, nature hike exploring days, a Pikachu® backpack was as much a required escort as her two pet dogs.

My youngest son is known for his attachment to stuffed animals as his constant buddies as evidenced by the four new additions this past Christmas. He has an uncanny knack for moving them in such a way as to appear life-like. His stuffed "friends" often help me convince my son to do unwanted activities when I engage their help. Even though at 11 years old my youngest son realizes his peers feel stuffed animals are "childish," he openly interacts with his stuffed playmates at home, and secretly in public.

84

My high energy son always has a menagerie of stuffed animal "friends" tagging along.

These life-like attachments mean I could never randomly decide to clean out their collections to donate to others. My children would stare at me in horror at the thought. Certainly Sid from *Toy Story®* didn't help my case any as my children feared a new child wouldn't adore the toy as they had. It wasn't until late teens, just like Andy from *Toy Story 3®*, that enough distance between their rich childhood imagination and grown perspective allowed separation to occur—for some of the toys, anyway. I believe the imaginative quality related to the stuffed animal play strongly identifies them as imaginary friends.

Imaginary Friends

My strong right-brained, creative builder son developed imaginary friends during his childhood. He'd spend hours building with LEGO®, K'NEX®, and such simple devices as paper and tape. When he was asked who his best friends were, his quick and truthful reply was, "My LEGO®." Some felt sorry for him, but I recognized that his passion and happiness were strongly connected to his creative outlet, so I didn't put *my* social perspective on him. Later, this right-brained learner informed me that he had imaginary friends depicted by various LEGO® guys. They were John, Jack, Joe, Jeff, and Jessie (he felt he needed a girl represented). These imaginary friends were around long enough that one served a particular function. John told my son things he didn't know when he needed to know something. He then admitted that

John represented the Holy Ghost (one of our spiritual beliefs). It makes sense that he created a visual image of a non-pictorial belief (see next trait section, "Word Based vs. Picture Based"). Imaginary friends are simply representations of a right-brained, creative learner's extraordinary imagination.

Skewing the Line between Reality and Pretend

With such vivid imaginations, young creative learners easily skew the line between reality and pretend. There are three common instances where a right-brained child may need a different style of support or understanding. The first is the impact TV and other visual media have on this child's highly sensitive nature. The second is the fear a right-brained child often exhibits associated with people dressed up in face make-up or bigger-than-life costumes. The last is the attraction these children have toward the belief in make-believe stories and social customs such as Santa Claus or the Tooth Fairy. All three of these areas stem from the imaginative world that is the foundational trait of a right-brained child.

TV and Visual Media. Visual media are wonderful resources for our visually-based, right-brained children; but they need to be used carefully to protect their highly sensitive natures (see the work of Elaine Aron in *The Highly Sensitive Child*[3]). For instance, because this child needs fairness and has high compassion for humanity, television news programs tend to be a poor choice for these highly sensitive children. Some creative learners will naturally censor themselves, such as my oldest child, who refused to watch a cartoon dinosaur movie for some reason when he was 3 years old. While young, he always asked his father and me if a movie was appropriate for his sensitive nature. On the other hand, those children with impulsivity may find it harder to self-protect so are more willing to request media that negatively impact them, such as those that lead to scary nightmares. I collaborated with my fifth son, who fits this description, by helping him understand he has more time to imaginatively process the visual input if he watches these high-interest, overstimulating media earlier in the day. It's important that a parent be aware of what these highly sensitive people are exposed to on TV and other visual media.

Fear of Clowns and Other Dressed-Up Caricatures. There may be two reasons why the right-brained, creative child experiences a season of fear around clowns and other dressed-up caricatures. The first may be the overwhelming sensory visual impact (see Chapter Nineteen). The second may be that it's too difficult to differentiate between the person and the character. One of my creative children *loved* dinosaurs. He knew all there was to know about more than 50 dinosaurs at age 5 before he was reading. When we learned there would be a dinamatronic display at SeaWorld®, we thought he'd enjoy it. We explained it to him and he was eager to attend. When confronted with the reality of approaching these machines made to look real, he completely melted down and refused to go anywhere *near* the dinosaurs. To get to another park area, we had to pass by the display a time or two. The only way this child would do so was blindfolded! His understanding of dinosaurs was still too greatly married to an immature ability to differentiate between real and pretend.

My artist son's inability to differentiate between reality and pretend during a trip to see a dinamatronic display prompted him to demand he be blindfolded to deal with it.

Social Customs. The creative, right-brained child takes very seriously the social customs we create, such as Santa Claus, the Tooth Fairy, or other make-believe characters. Because of their imaginations, Santa Claus is very real. I discovered I should allow my children to learn about the reality on their own and in their own time frames. This means it usually extends to somewhere around 11 to 12 years before the child is willing to show he understands these customs aren't real. Many right-brained children don't want "the talk" from others verifying that this is so. To soften the transition, we could honestly rally around ideas such as, "We believe in (the spirit of) Santa Claus." These can be very positive, warm memories for our creative children because these bigger-than-life characters draw out their strengths of imagination.

Reality-Based Play

In contrast to the imaginative play of a right-brained child, there's reality play. As a left-brained dominant person, I recall my own childhood summer days with my best friend. One season we made up "shows" that we worked on for days in order to perform them for the neighborhood (which never did happen). In our shows, we never pretended to be another person; we always played "ourselves," sharing our talents. We created commercials in-between acts. Even for these we used real objects, such as our bikes, instead of coming up with imaginary marketing ploys.

I remember my friend and I taking a great interest in "saving the underground spring" in our nearby woods. We spent days and weeks trying to create a path for this underground spring to make its way down to the pond. Both of these childhood endeavors focused on reality-based themes.

Object Manipulation Play

My sister and I enjoyed such indoor activities as putting all of our stuffed animals into a pile in our room and taking turns choosing which we would play with. When this process ended, we couldn't take it much further creatively, so that would end the "play." The same happened with our doll play. I had Crissy and she had Mia[4] and we'd dress our dolls in a clothing set, show it to one another, and repeat. My strength wasn't in imagination but in the manipulation of real objects.

Doll dress-up is an example of a left-brained play activity.

There's a difference between an imagination-based perspective and a reality-based perspective. It's not that the way I played wasn't enjoyable to me, because it was, and it's not that the way I played is "less than" the creative learner and his play process. When we understand how the differences in brain processing preferences impact the learning process, and even the play process, we're better equipped to support all learners by recognizing and creating different environments for different needs.

Left Hemisphere	Right Hemisphere
reality	*imagination
*word based	***picture based**
(symbolic)	(3-dimensional)
*sequential	global
part	whole
memorization	association
logical (mind)	intuitive (heart)
compliant	resistant
external perfectionism	internal perfectionism
product	process
time	space

*Universal gifts

Word Based vs. Picture Based

The second universal gift of right-brained, creative learners is that they think in pictures. I asked one of my right-brained sons what he sees in his brain, and he replied, "It's better than the best three-dimensional computer software available. It's more like the holodeck in *Star Trek®* where you can place yourself in the setting, yet still view it from any angle. It's as if you're really there. It's better than any movie." I've heard thousands of similar explanations of the visual imagery enjoyed by a right-brained person.

Visual Imagery

After careful research on the topic, there's ample empirical evidence supporting the idea that the right-brained learner is amassing a library of pictorial images in his brain's filing system. These are three-dimensional images seen from all angles. Temple Grandin, a person with autism who performs at the top of her field in the area of designing equipment for humanely slaughtering animals, described in her book, *Thinking in Pictures,* how her visual imagery works:

> *I create new images all the time by taking many little parts of images I have in the video library in my imagination and piecing them together. I have video memories of every item I've ever worked with—steel gates, fences, latches, concrete walls, and so forth. To create new designs, I retrieve bits and pieces from my memory and combine them into a new whole. My design ability keeps improving as I add more visual images to my library.[5]*

If a parent or teacher carefully observes, there's evidence of the picture-based three-dimensionality at work in children. I remember observing my builder son when he was heavily into his train interest. He started at 18 months, so young, meticulously linking the die-cast metal Thomas the Tank Engine™ trains together on the kitchen floor. My creative builder would lie down upon the floor, close one eye, and pull the trains toward him, watching one aspect of the train entourage as it passed him. Then, he eagerly moved himself into another angled position and repeated. When he graduated to the wooden train sets at age 3, this three-dimensional visualizing continued as he observed from the top, sides, back and underneath.

My builder son observing three-dimensional angles during train play.

Final evidence emerged when he shifted to LEGO® at 5 years old. This right-brained builder initially assembled the sets as they came packaged. Then, he'd venture off on his own creations as intricate on the inside (where nobody was going to look, right?) as they were on the outside. Further, I was sure he utilized his strong visualization skills in a manner similar to what Temple Grandin described by taking various visual snapshots of his previous LEGO® creation bits and pieces, then combining them in his mind to create a new design. Three-dimensional picture-based thinking is a gift that the right-brained person uses to innovate.

If there's an artist in your midst, you can observe for clues to his picture-based three-dimensional processing nature. The following drawing from my builder son, made when he was around ages 8 to 9, depicts a figure, only half shown, thinking about going to watch a train that will arrive soon. The train is only half shown, as well. The ability to draw some of the parts of a whole image implies the artist has an understanding of the whole but is comfortable sharing only the relevant parts.

Drawing in perspective, using three-dimensional attributes, and creating pictorial imagery can often be seen in drawings of right-brained children at a young age.

If a right-brained person uses visual images to process information, it makes sense that they spend lots of time in their early years building up their mind's library of pictorial images. Thus, the right-brained learner will utilize pictures to develop concepts being pursued.

A Comparative Example

Reading aloud is an activity that easily lets you observe whether the learner is focusing on pictures or words. When I read aloud to my two oldest children individually when they were quite young, I noticed the oldest artist son was always looking at the pictures. My writer daughter, on the other hand, was following the words. In fact, she taught herself to read in this manner.

The early writing process also provides opportunity to discover a picture or word focus. Here's an example during the stage of mirroring a storyline (see Chapter Thirteen). The drawing series below, depicting a scene from *The Lion King*®, comes from my artist son's 8 to 9 year portfolio. It's completely pictorial in nature, yet beautifully captures the story line.

A beautifully depicted (copied) pictorial story. (Image[6])

Next is a sample from my writer daughter's portfolio when she was about the same age, rewriting verbatim, on her own initiative, from the now out-of-print book, *My Cats Nick & Nora* by Isabelle Harper.[7]

Read
Only

Under

Onder
this
line!

It is fun and easy too, here is a book I got from the Lieabry. It is called My Cats Nick And Nora. Every Sunday when my cousin Emmie comes over to my house, the first thing we do is go find Nick and Nora. It isn't always easy. They have lots of places to hide. But no matter where they hide, we always find them. We give them their lessons and because today is their birthday, we make them look especially nice. We invite all their friends and have a birthday party.

A (copied) word-based story.

Although it was a picture book, this is completely word based and provides the same benefits of learning the intricacies of a good story line as did my son's drawings. (See Chapter Fourteen for a discussion of cheating or copying versus modeling or mentoring.)

In our left-brained-based value system, the child who uses words to express her ideas is typically given more credit than the child who uses pictures to express his ideas. The picture-based child would be persuaded to add some words to describe his picture in order to complete the lesson. On the other hand, the word-based child might be encouraged to draw a picture to go with her story as an "added benefit," depending on the age. The words are "required" because that is the goal, while the picture is "extra" because it's not foundational. The good news is that each of these children is simply following his or her preferred path to expressing ideas. Each process is valid.

Right-brained children need different subjects in the elementary years to develop their universal gifts.

The two universal gifts of the left-brained child are thinking in words and sequential processing. These are the traits that should be developed during the early foundational learning years of 5 to 7. School meets this need by introducing reading, spelling and concrete ideas such as community helpers and the human body. The two universal gifts of the right-brained child are thinking in pictures and an

extraordinary imagination. During the foundational years of 5 to 7, these needs are most effectively and naturally met through completely different subjects (see Chapter Sixteen) and the creative outlets (see Chapter Six). Unfortunately, most schools don't address the early subject strengths of right-brained children until later and have cut out of the school budget most creative arts opportunities in the classroom. This means right-brained children begin their school careers without benefit of developing their universal gifts that helps them succeed in learning more easily thereafter. To understand and honor the natural learning path for our right-brained, creative children, changes need to occur in the education establishment to recognize and value the right side of normal.

References and Notes

[1] The resource being used in the image is: Runton, Andy. *Owly:™ The Way Home & The Bittersweet Summer.* Marietta: Top Shelf Productions, 2004.

[2] Silverman, Linda Kreger. *Upside-Down Brilliance: The Visual-Spatial Learner.* Denver: DeLeon Publishing, Inc., 2002.

[3] Aron, Elaine N. *The Highly Sensitive Child.* Three Rivers Press, 2002.

[4] Copyright 1968-1970 Ideal Toy Corporation as noted on the imprint of the dolls.

[5] Grandin, Temple. *Thinking in Pictures and Other Reports from my Life with Autism.* New York: Doubleday, 1995.

[6] The Lion King® is a registered trademark of Walt Disney Pictures registered in the United States Patent and Trademark Office. All images and characters depicted in the movie are copyright © 1994 and 1995 the Walt Disney Company. The drawings found in this body of work based on The Lion King® characters are not intended to challenge any copyright but were the innocent reflection of a young child's enjoyment of a children's movie.

[7] Harper, Isabelle. *My Cats Nick and Nora.* Blue Sky Press, 2002. The copied story found in this body of work is not intended to challenge any copyright but was the innocent learning tool of a young child. Inclusion in this work is strictly being used to demonstrate the value system between written word work and pictorial work.

Chapter Six

Computers Puzzles Art Math Theater Music Building Cooking Fashion

VideoGames Mazes Photography Numbers Showmanship Dance Electronics Gardening Sewing

The Creative Outlets

Shift Begins with Me

My builder son and I arrived at his piano lesson. As usual, my son entered the music room, immediately sat down, and began to play around with music until the instructor was ready to begin. The music mentor sat down, listened to what my builder son was doing, and started imitating him on the other piano in the session room. My son noticed and smiled. The instructor changed rhythms, tempos, etc., and my builder son followed suit without a word between them. They "jammed" like this, learning spatial rhythms and patterns together throughout the half-hour lesson. Suddenly, the mentor realized the time and jumped up, ending the session on behalf of his next student. My builder son and his mentor walked into the lobby and discovered the student wasn't there. The instructor gleamed at my son, exclaiming, "Do you want to go back in and continue?"

Passion. Enthusiasm. Creativity. No formal lesson was given, but a lot of learning occurred. A lot of traditional music *teachers* follow a certain program, focus on theory, and make sure the student has proper form. I instinctively knew that wasn't the type of person my builder son needed to nurture his musical talent. We actually tried one and it ended miserably after a few attempted lessons. My son's enthusiasm for music showed signs of breaking that quickly.

I found it important to find music *mentors*, or practicing musicians, who enjoyed sharing their passion with my son as another musician, albeit a less experienced one. When I found the studio full of practicing musicians, I sensed a shift in perspective. Practicing musicians tend to "share their strategies" versus "teach a particular way." The surge of growth and learning in my son's musical ability within a few sessions proved he was in a well-matched learning environment.

Creative development and expression are at the heart of how a right-brained child learns. It's easy to tell when the right resources or activities are found. The very act of using the resource or doing the activity enhances and develops the strengths and gifts within the person involved. That's what I saw with the right music mentor resource. That's what can be seen in all right-brained children when the activities inherently equipped to enhance and develop their strengths and gifts are the foundation in their lives.

The Role of Creative Outlets in the Early Years

Extraordinary imaginations and visual thinking are the universal gifts of the right-brained learner (see Chapter Five). These universal gifts are noticeable as early as the preschool years. Certainly they're pronounced by the Foundation Stage of learning of ages 5 to 7 (see Chapters Four and Seven). The universal gifts of right-brained children manifest themselves through engagement in one or more of what I term creative outlets. These are computers/video games, art/photography, puzzles/mazes, building/electronics, theater/showmanship, math/numbers, fashion/sewing, cooking/gardening, and music/dance.

For the right-brained learner, deep engagement in one or more of these areas of creative outlet is at the core of development. If these people aren't creatively engaged, they only half live. And yet, our society currently views these pursuits as extracurricular at best, a waste of time at worst. School budget cuts begin with creative outlets even though they should be the center of early years' study for these learners.

Right-brained people are deeply engaged in one or more creative outlets.

I've written about the brain development stage for shifting to formal symbolic work occurring between 8 and 10 years old (called the "age of shifting") for right-brained learners (see Chapter Four). So, what do they do before this shift occurs? The right-brained learner should be pursuing and developing his gifts in the creative outlets. The myriad reasons for this pronouncement should help us understand why the current scope and sequence in our public institutions of learning fall far short of supporting the natural learning process for the creative child.

Inherent Benefits of Creative Outlets

There are inherent benefits as right-brained, creative learners develop one or more of the creative outlets.

> ➢ Creative outlets are naturally formulated to strengthen the universal gifts of the right-brained learner (see Theater/Showmanship section for an example).

> ➢ Creative outlets prepare right-brained learners for later left-brained academic tasks (see Computers/Video Games section for an example).

> ➢ Right-brained learners use their creative outlet to make sense of the world around them (see Building/Electronics section for an example).

> ➢ Right-brained learners process new information by first playing with the ideas through creative outlets (see Math/Numbers section for an example).

> ➢ Creative outlets often lead to a future career path for right-brained learners (see conclusion to this chapter, "Life Work from Creative Outlets," for examples).

That's why it's crucial that creative outlets are recognized, encouraged, and developed throughout a right-brained learner's life, including and especially the early years.

Creative Outlets in Action

When I speak at conferences about the right-brained, creative learner, I specifically use two of my children for two reasons. They both *strongly* identify as right-brained learners and, between the two of them, they pretty much illustrate all the right-brained creative outlets and traits. I will also describe my theater son from time to time for variety. No two creative people are alike. However, as mentioned in Chapter Five, each usually has an extraordinary imagination and thinks in three-dimensional pictorial images. This chapter pronounces that each creative learner also deeply engages in one or more creative outlets as listed at the head of this chapter. We'll see how each creative outlet is represented in these strong right-brained learners in my home.

Computers/Video Games

Visual media have provided opportunities for visual, spatial and imaginative development in many of my right-brained children. It has been used as inspiration on the path to writing, a love of history, and computer programming. Many of us understand the benefits of eye-hand coordination, problem solving, and inference. Computers and video games aren't just the newest technology that every young child accesses; they're an important creative outlet for right-brained learners, just like the very people who created them!

Video games often inspire other subject development.

Inspiration for Writing. Computer and video games have inspired my artist son resulting in a variety of visual-based products. The development of writing is a left-brained favored task often cultivated in right-brained children between 11 and 13 years. Video games inspired my artist son to undertake his writing (see Chapter Thirteen). After discovering someone wrote a novel based on his favorite video game at the time, *The Legend of Zelda®,* he was sorely disappointed in its lack of detail. He decided he could do better, so at age 11 he sat at the computer and began a well-written descriptive narrative of the game he loved. He'd never written in a traditional way before this, yet the writing was outstanding. He made it to about 35 single-spaced typewritten pages before losing interest. However, in his late teens, he again decided to write a novel based on a video game, *Final Fantasy VII®*, and this time he made it to 300+ pages. What these novels had in common was the visual detail he wanted to bring to the story writing process.

Inspiration for History. My artist son's natural love of history grew as he discovered how often video games honored historical accuracy. Therefore, any writings or drawings of even mythical depictions were meticulously historically researched to bring added credibility to his creations. I remember when all the card crazes ignited. My artist son created his own card games using visual images from computer and video games as inspiration while adding carefully researched details.

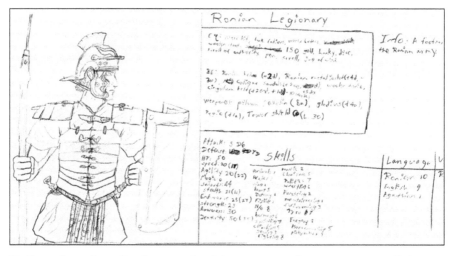

Before drawing the image for his own card game, my artist son researched for historical accuracy.

Inspiration for Computer Programming. Compare the visual inspiration gained by my artist son to the focus of my builder son toward puzzling out the spatial nature behind the creation of computer and video games. My builder son clocked as many hours playing these types of games over the

102

years as his artist brother. But he would initially build LEGO® models of interesting objects depicted in these games, which then progressed to an interest in computer programming beginning around age 13. Instead of looking at the visuals in the games, he contemplated the creation behind the games as he played.

Inspiration for Imagination. My theater son enjoys the inspired fodder found through video games, computers, and other visual media such as movies and television. He usually doesn't get through an entire show before he heads to his dress-up bin. Sometimes he also looks for other resources around the house, with or without permission, to recreate through costuming what he experienced. My theater son needs the whole body experience of any visual media he integrates.

Visual Media Balance. Admittedly, visual media has a captivating quality. I believe in balance for each child within my care. However, balance is different for every person. Further, value gained from the resource needs to be factored in. Video games, the computer, and television are valid creative outlets for a right-brained person. That said, one child may be involved with them for three to four hours a day at a particular age, while another the same age can spend six to seven hours and be in balance. I helped each child understand his unique limits and needs as he matured. This way, by the time they became teens, each was capable of self-governance and balance continued.

When we value visual media, there are diverse positive outcomes, particularly as a creative outlet for a right-brained learner. Pictorial images can be collected for use when translating images into symbolic representations. Inspiration can be garnered for visual detail for other subject areas. Visual media can provide fodder for career options, or it can allow opportunities to try on diverse roles.

Art/Photography

A picture paints a thousand words. This is a common sentiment, yet I don't believe our society believes that a drawn picture can be the precursor to writing for a creative child (see Chapter Thirteen). I'm here to tell you it *can* be for an artist child.

Because a right-brained learner "sees" in pictures, it makes sense that he'll start expressing his ideas as a direct representation from his mind. While he's young, pictures will make sense to him. Therefore, a right-brained child attracted to the art/photography outlet will draw pictures as his first attempt at making sense of and describing his world. As mentioned in Chapter Five, the drawings will start out primarily picture-based, but as time goes by and readiness approaches, words will begin to appear. Because we valued drawing and pictures in our home, beginning explorations of storylines through comics resulted.

Sequential pictures are often an artist's first stories. (Image[1])

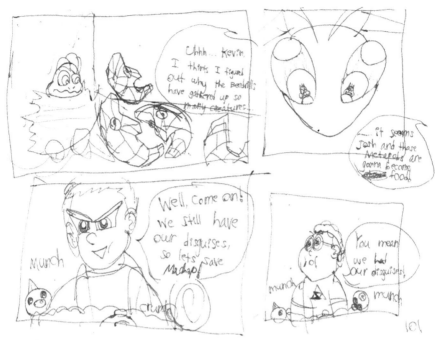

Comics represents a foundational story image with words added for detail. (Image[2])

Because of his propensity for pictorial story-telling, my artist son took a 4-H photography class when he was in the 8 to 10 year time frame. He was particularly drawn to the camera tricks that are part of one type of storytelling.

Visual imagery: Is he really hanging from a wall?

My builder son also had his own way of using the art/photography creative outlet to express himself and develop his gift of spatial awareness. His drawing representations often involved map schematics.

105

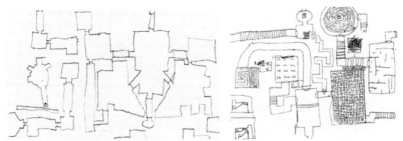

Builder types have their own art form.

For many of my children, drawing was a way for them to express their ideas, whether through visual stories, spatial experimentation, or exploring their interests. Photography was often used as a creative expression of a current interest, whether it was my writer daughter dabbling in nature photography or my theater son capturing his love of animals. Expressing one's ideas is as valid through pictures as it is through words.

Puzzles/Mazes

Parents and teachers often consider puzzles and mazes a preschool precursor to formal academics. However, both of these venues are a laboratory for early spatial development. Builders are especially drawn to these activities, and my builder son was no exception.

Starting as early as 18 months, he put puzzles together right side up, upside down, and backwards. This is because he did it spatially. In his preschool years, my builder son enjoyed visually putting together 100 piece puzzles. By his early elementary years, he advanced to three-dimensional puzzles, quickly working up to the challenging level by mid-elementary. The puzzle building activity is as relevant to spatial development as any you'll find.

Around the age of 4 to 5 years, my builder son became interested in mazes. He drew his own after a while. Below is a sample from his 6-year-old folder. Notice how pictures are involved in the representation. Before the "age of shifting" between 8 and 10 years old, right-brained learners will usually include pictures in everything they do because they still aren't ready to translate into symbols. This is a simple maze, although he did create a two-way solution depicting both persons highlighted in the maze. (As an aside, because of my builder son's intense interest in trains, there always seemed to be a train in every image-based drawing he created.)

A sample maze with images from my builder son.

Because I valued and was amazed by my builder son's interest and skill at creating mazes, I encouraged him. The following sample from his 9-year-old folder shows fantastic spatial development that occurs when we value these creative outlets:

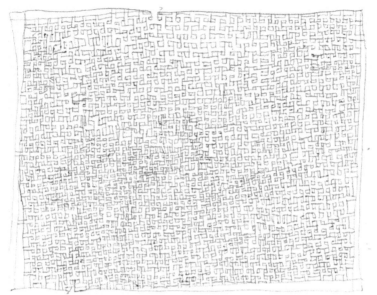

A complex maze showcasing spatial talent.

Notice there's no need for a picture after the "age of shifting" occurs. Young right-brained children often use pictures to help process information because picture-based thinking is a strength. At the same time, I believe my builder son was given enough value for his need to include images as long as he felt he needed (see Chapter Five to see how we often value words over pictures). Once the "age of shifting" occurs between 8 and 10 and integration of the left-brained strengths *begins,* these picture-based strategies will eventually drop because the left-brained tools become available (see Chapters Four and Seven).

Building/Electronics

Along with puzzles and mazes, there are other "normal" childhood activities that promote spatial development through play. At almost 3 years old, my builder son received his first set of wooden train tracks, and he'd construct setups for hours on end. That's spatial awareness. He enhanced his creations by adding other building and construction sets to create whole cities. That's spatial skill. At age 4, LEGO® caught his interest.

When he received a new LEGO® set, my builder son eagerly began sorting the parts meticulously separated in individually wrapped packages. He always built the set as created by the manufacturer first, using the visual directions that came with it. As he became a more competent builder, he explored making his own creations, constructing contraptions before LEGO® assembled kits for that purpose. One time while we visited family in another state, Grandma had a bucket of general piece LEGO®. My builder son, 8 to 9 years old at the time, used every piece available to reconstruct the images on the side of the LEGO® bucket. Here's the photo I took to remember my surprise with his spatial and three-dimensional ability.

Using just the picture on the LEGO® bucket, my builder son created these figures using all the pieces available.

My builder son also processed information with his building outlet to make sense of the world around him. I remember when he learned about the pyramids. First, he drew schematics of the inside design and the outside representation. Then, he constructed a LEGO® creation depicting the same, both inside and out.

Right-brained children use creative outlets to learn about the world.

LEGO® led to TECHNIC™ and my builder son enjoyed incorporating the mechanical and motorized side of things. The final catalyst into his computer programming career path was MINDSTORMS®. My builder son's creative energy was sparked when he programmed the LEGO® robot to perform various maneuvers invented within his mind. It was during this phase that he made the connection between robotic programming and computer game programming.

Math/Numbers

Math is patterns. Patterns are spatial in nature. Math has its own language separate from English or other spoken and written languages. Computers have a language based on mathematical patterns. It makes sense that a builder person would be naturally attracted to math and numbers. Math patterns and concepts are different than memorizing math facts. Chapter Twelve will help differentiate between mathematical patterns and concepts versus arithmetic and facts.

Even though math proficiency often comes with builder types, the stage before the "age of shifting" is still pictorial in nature. Here's a math sample from my builder son's 6-year-old folder. Notice it's picture-based, using a train. He created a visual image to help him process counting by 10s. So, just as train cars "link" together, counting by 10s have a link that connects them.

My builder son uses visual imagery to understand a math concept.

Yet, after the "age of shifting" of 8 to 10 years old, the visuals often disappear from the shown work because right-brained learners more easily translate the workings of their minds into symbols. Here's a sample from my son's 11-year-old folder:

Visual imagery drops once the "age of shifting" occurs.

Since right-brained children often have trouble with arithmetic in the early years, it can be confusing to see math and numbers as a creative outlet for a right-brained learner. As described above, mathematics is about understanding the pattern of numbers, how numbers relate to the world around them, and playing with the deeper concepts of math. This requires completely different tools and methods that ignite the value of math/numbers for the right-brained child (see Chapter Twelve).

Music/Dance

When my builder son had just turned 9 years old, I purchased a piano for myself. I obtained an adult level instruction manual and began to teach myself to play. My builder son noticed and sat down to try. I could tell he was a natural by the way his fingers positioned themselves on the keyboard.

The most interesting part, however, was how my builder son learned to play the notes from my manual. Because I'm a left-brained learner, I process information through a word-based foundation. This means I translate every note symbol into a note name and find each note on the piano, one note at a time. When three notes appear together, if it's an easier pattern, I can use the spatial shortcut. As a right-brained learner, my builder son reads all the notes on the sheet as places in space. He knew that place in space belonged to another place in space on the piano. He didn't know the names of the notes (he wasn't even reading yet), but he could instantly tell where they fell on the piano keyboard. He did this instantly with groups of notes, no matter how difficult the pattern. This, I realized, is how concert pianists exist!

Right-brained learners remember information by association or through visualization, not memorization, as their preferred memory system (see Chapter Seven). This, coupled with amazing spatial skills, is how my builder son played music from memory. When I wanted to play a piece by memory, I had to take a chunk of notes, play each one over and over, and slowly add more pieces of the music until I could remember it all. Frankly, I don't think I could easily memorize a piece of music, particularly without making a mistake.

Right-brained musicians often play spatially or by ear.

My builder son memorizes a piece of music simply by playing it over and over. Also, it seems he has to particularly enjoy the music, whether because he likes the song or enjoys its challenge, in order to put it to memory. So, after playing a piece he enjoys for a week, without knowing it ever happened, he removed the music from the stand "to check if I know it yet." He almost always did. One time, while playing for a music mentor who asked my builder son if he had learned the piece by memory yet, he answered, "I don't know, let me see." He handed the sheet music to the instructor and played it, perfectly. My builder son then giggled, saying, "I can see the music in my head." The

113

visualization skills of a right-brained learner can develop so well as to become like a photographic memory. I believe some body memory was also involved with how my builder son remembered his music pieces.

Theater/Showmanship

Theater is fairly self-explanatory as it pertains to acting and performing on a stage. This includes all the elements that are needed to create movies or theater productions, such as producers, directors, costumers, cameramen, set designers, etc. Showmanship refers to the styles of performing within shows, such as a circus performer, a magician, a comedian, a puppeteer, etc. This is another creative outlet that all three of my right-brained children used in their own way based on their preferred functions of visual, spatial, and imaginative.

Visual Stage. My artist son went through a three-year period when he produced and directed video movies. This is a visual medium of theater/showmanship. My artist son was fortunate enough to have a perfectly matched trio friendship whose roles complemented one another. My artist son was the creative force behind the storyline and how it would appear on screen. One of his friends enjoyed being the star of the show, and the other friend preferred to work behind the camera, adding his wisdom regarding camera angles and tricks. This is a viable visual representation of expressing ideas until the right-brained learner is ready to tackle word print storytelling.

Spatial Stage. My builder son had a one- to two-year season exploring the stop-motion movie-making abilities within LEGO® Studio. This is a complete concentration in the area of spatial ability as each character object has to be meticulously moved inch by inch while synchronizing all the other aspects of the action going on all around it. My builder son spent lots of time creating special effects with the action portions of the objects, which required considerable spatial awareness.

114

Stop-motion movies are a great storytelling expression for builder types. (Image³)

Imagination Stage. My theater son uses a full body experience to process information. Whereas my artist son focuses on the visual aspect of production, and my builder son focuses on the arrangement aspect of production, my theater son has to be an active participant within the framework. He has to feel it and be it and move as part of it. This can be translated as simply pretending and playing, yet the attributes used in play naturally strengthen the area of imagination so important to a right-brained learner.

With no time left or value given for play in our current society's viewpoint, recent research warns of the negative consequences of eliminating play from our children's lives at the same time it showcases the many benefits of play. The act of becoming another person, creating another world, or capturing another lifestyle is expanding knowledge beyond the front door. Dabbling in the theater/showmanship creative outlet has value to the right-brained learner.

Cooking/Gardening

Those who pursue careers of executive chef, English gardener, sous chef, estate gardeners, etc., tend to be right-brained because of the creativity and visualization skills needed. My theater son has taken a high interest in both cooking and gardening as creative outlets from an early age.

This "all boy" son would want a flowering plant from the home improvement store over a toy. He often joined my husband, another right-brained person, as he tended his

115

English garden around our home. My theater son's hands were in the dirt and nurturing the plants as his younger brother focused on the machinery side of yard work. Two different focuses!

English gardening is living art.

My theater son also constantly experiments with food. He doesn't just want to fix himself a sandwich; it has to be some sort of "creation." He likes to mix and match food. My theater son also wasn't afraid to jump right into how to use kitchen tools, even when he had challenges with mixed hand dominance that made proficiency more difficult. It would be easy to not value these things in his life because of his weak areas, which included impulsivity resulting in safety issues. I had to set aside those conditioned responses to give the creative outlet foundation the top priority it deserves in this right-brained learner's early life.

I'm now in the process of finding good cooking mentors for him to nurture his interest. He did take cooking classes for about three months before logistics interfered. We also moved to some acreage to provide gardening space for him to explore. This may include kitchen gardening, raised-bed gardening, berries, fruit trees, and any other gardening experience to which we may be led. Within each of these opportunities lies the ability to create and experiment. The cooking/gardening creative outlet goes beyond the self-help of home economics. It's art!

Fashion/Sewing

I'm a strong left-brained learner. I always had an interest in crafting with needles and taught myself to crochet at a young age. Later, I taught myself to knit, cross-stitch, and embroider. It wasn't until I consciously discovered the differences in brain preference that I noticed what made me different from a right-brained-style crafter.

Left- vs. Right-Brained Crafting. As a left-brained person, I first learned from books with instructions. I also didn't want anyone to teach me because I don't learn from a "watch, then do" focus, but from a part-to-whole dissection of written instructions. Second, I can only make what is printed on a written instruction. I don't know how to improvise and create my own patterns.

With that in mind, I had always found quilting and sewing fascinating, and tried a time or two to figure out how to teach myself. It seemed impossible, and I gave up fairly quickly. With this new information, though, it makes complete sense.

Quilting and sewing take quite a bit of spatial and visual awareness. They're expressions of self-creation. A good quilter sees the patterns she wants to create. A seamstress visualizes how the pattern goes together from a whole-to-part perspective. I often find that my right-brained friends can't read patterns, but they can create unique patterns.

Self-Creation vs. Store-Bought. My artist son wanted to make his own costume for an anime convention he wanted to attend in a month's time. His goal was to recreate a video game character's outfit, but he didn't want to buy it at a store because that wouldn't reflect his own creative expression of it. In other words, he felt that store-bought cheapened the experience. Coincidentally, he made a new friend with a gift for sewing. He asked her to show him how to sew so that he might be able to create the costume he envisioned. My artist son gathered the many materials he needed to complete the costume. He had some Japanese-style outfits that resembled the visual of the costume, so he used those as his pattern. In

no uncertain terms did he sew together this pattern "properly," but he simply "eyed" it from his visual and started to piece it together. The end product was fairly impressive based on zero previous experience.

Fashion design is the translation of a visualized image that must find external expression. (Image[4])

The fashion/sewing creative outlet is a prime example, along with music, of how both left- and right-brained people can enjoy a creative outlet, but how it's processed and, thus, how it's created, and where the gift lies, are in different places. For a right-brained person, it's self-creation that emanates from within outward. It's a translation of a visualized image that must find external expression. This creative outlet provides value to right-brained people.

Life Work from Creative Outlets

After reflecting upon my children's learning journey, I realized that the activities they were significantly engaged in during the ages of 5 to 7 years became the career paths they chose. The foundation for education began with the creative outlets for my right-brained learners. My artist son developed his strong visualization skills from hours and hours, months and months, and years and years of drawing pictures, playing video games, and making card games, comic books, and movies. This led to pursuing his life's work in a Japanese-related field.

118

My builder son developed a strong spatial foundation from his hours and hours, months and months, and years and years of building with LEGO®, arranging train track systems, creating mazes, exploring mathematical concepts with manipulatives, and playing piano without knowing the name of any note. This led him to pursuing his life's work as a video game programmer and mathematician.

I have no doubt that my theater son's hours and hours, months and months, and years and years of pretending, working in the dirt, creating food concoctions, and playing sports is preparing him for his future life's work. Engaging in creative outlets naturally increases the very skills and traits necessary to enhance the gifts of the right-brained learner in ways that bless this world.

By extensively engaging in preferred creative outlets up to the 8 to 10 year time frame, the creative child develops the traits and strengths necessary to navigate the left-brained tasks they'll encounter at the next stage. The strong visualization skills of the right-brained learner developed through creative outlets help them translate the symbols into images that make sense to them. The large library of pictorial images amassed during the time dedicated to creative pursuits enable fast and easy retrieval process to accomplish necessary translations. The extraordinary imagination promotes global thinking and creative solutions for comprehending and answering higher level questions. In essence, the strengths of the creative learner are enhanced and developed to assist them in future academic endeavors. Creative outlets inherently develop the strengths of the right-brained learner so he may joyfully continue academic pursuits in the subsequent learning years.

References and Notes

[1] My artist son's inspiration for this story was: *Jurassic Park*. Directed by Steven Spielberg. 1993.

119

---

[2] My artist son's comic in this example includes images, storylines, and characters created from the Pokémon fad. Pokémon and its many characters are registered trademarks and ©Nintendo. The drawings shown here are not intended to challenge any copyright but are used to demonstrate the positive impact drawing has in the learning life of an artistic, right-brained child.

[3] This image shows my builder son making a stop-motion movie using LEGO® Studio and his various LEGO® building blocks and sets. LEGO® is a registered trademark of The LEGO Group.

[4] This image shows my artist son who made this Auron costume, a character from *Final Fantasy X*, a video game trademarked by and ©2003 Square Enix Co., LTD.

Chapter Seven

The "Right" Time for Learning

Shift Begins with Me

Our class was studying planets in the second grade. Each child presented an oral report on a planet of his or her choice. I chose Venus. It seemed mysteriously accessible. I was fascinated by the whole idea of other planets out there. I wanted to know more! When I presented my report to the class, it simply whetted my appetite for more, so I did something I'd never done before as a shy child. I approached my teacher and asked her if I could do more to learn about the planets. I still remember her shocked expression, her hesitation as she contemplated how to answer a question I could tell she had never been asked before. Haltingly she replied, "I guess you can do another oral report on another planet if you'd like." I don't know what I expected, but I know it wasn't that. I wanted something more real, more concrete, and more hands-on. I tried to create another oral report, but my enthusiasm deflated quickly.

When I had children, I harbored a subconscious memory of this experience that made me ask myself, "How can I create that excitement for learning for my children more often than the one time I experienced it?" The follow-up question became, "And how do I feed that interest when it arises?" The picture at the beginning of this chapter depicts one of many opportunities my children received to benefit from my childhood disappointment, no matter their age. My seventh child was interested in big machinery, and lo and behold, the neighbor started clearing the empty lot next door with a bulldozer. In the evening, under the supervision of his father, my child climbed aboard the resting machine to have an up-close and personal interaction. Since then, he's had other opportunities to ride on and control heavy machinery with an experienced operator.

No matter how much we've been conditioned to consider certain things off-limits to children, I chose to dare say "yes."

More often than not, my children enjoyed subjects and activities I never would have thought to introduce at particular ages. Who knew a 5-year-old would initiate learning ancient history? Not me! That was the exact opposite of me as a learner. I had no interest in history in my elementary years. In fact, I wasn't even introduced to history, in a way that ignited my interest, until I discovered historical fiction with my children! I now know why after researching brain processing preferences.

Stages of Learning Time Frames

Because the left and right hemispheres of the brain are mirror images of each other, each specializing in something different, it makes sense that the educational paths for left- and right-brained learners are opposites of each other. The time frame that schools utilize in teaching various subjects aligns with the left-brained learner stages of learning. I've noticed that right-brained learners acquire subject matter in a different learning pattern than their left-brained counter-parts.

Chapter Four contains an introduction to the time frames of three stages of learning (see chart below).

Foundation Stage 5 to 7 Years Old		Transition Stage 8 to 10 Years Old		Integration Stage 11 to 13 Years Old	
Left-Brained	Right-Brained	Left-Brained	Right-Brained	Left-Brained	Right-Brained
Symbolic & Word Development	Global & Creative Development	Creative Development	Symbolic Development	Global Development	Word Development
Favor 2-D	Favor 3-D	2-D/start 3-D	3-D/start 2-D	2-D & 3-D	3-D & 2-D
Reading Arithmetic Spelling Writing	Creative Outlets History Science Geography Social Studies	Develop Fluency Of Aged 5-7 LB Subjects Social Studies Geography	Develop Fluency of Aged 5-7 RB Subjects Reading Arithmetic	Develop Fluency of Aged 8-10 LB Subjects History Science	Develop Fluency Of Aged 8-10 RB Subjects Spelling Writing

As we continue to learn about and understand the core traits of the right-brained learner in this chapter, these differences in time frame and stages of learning will become clear.

Left Hemisphere	Right Hemisphere
reality	*imagination
*word based	***picture based**
(symbolic)	**(3-dimensional)**
*sequential	global
part	whole
memorization	association
logical (mind)	intuitive (heart)
compliant	resistant
external perfectionism	internal perfectionism
product	process
time	space

*Universal gifts

Symbolic vs. Three-Dimensional

Reading words in a book is both a two-dimensional action and a symbolic one. It's two-dimensional because the page is flat and can only be viewed one way. A picture in a book is two-dimensional because you only see it from one flat angle. Words in a book are also two-dimensional. Three-dimensional viewing, one of the universal gifts of the right-brained learner, is the ability to see an object from every angle as a whole object. A LEGO® block in your hand is three-dimensional; you can see it from every angle, or turn it to see every angle. Your pet dog is three-dimensional. Each of these is concrete. You can touch it; manipulate it; visualize all its components. We created symbols to replace three-dimensional, concrete objects to communicate with one another. Letters are symbols; the letters "d-o-g" combine to represent an actual three-dimensional, concrete object (a dog, in this case). Numbers are symbols; the number 3 actually represents a group of three concrete objects. It might be three dogs, or it might be a cow, a horse, and a sheep. Based on how the different sides of the brain process information, readiness for two-dimensional symbolic work occurs at different times.

Foundation Stage—Developing Universal Gifts

Left-brained learners are ready for this two-dimensional symbolic work in their early years, starting at the age time frame of 5 to 7 years old. This is because of their universal strengths in word-based thinking and sequential ordering. Because of these strengths, the left side of the brain naturally processes the information received from the eyes two-dimensionally. This is why many left-brained learners are more than ready to sequentially figure out the word patterns that entice them to begin reading between the ages of 5 and 7 years old just as reflected in the scope and sequence in most, if not all, of our schools. I remember begging my mother to teach me how to read during the summer between kindergarten and first grade. She simply kept up the mantra of, "Wait until first grade." When I got to first grade, reading enveloped my being and I emerged a reader with no memory of the process whatsoever. As an eager left-brained learner, I was more than ready.

Just like their left-brained counterparts, a right-brained child is also engaging in his universal gifts between the ages of 5 and 7 years: three-dimensional pictorial thinking and imaginative expressions. Because of these strengths, the right side of the brain naturally processes the information received from the eyes three-dimensionally. Thus, the right-brained child continues his focus on the physical, concrete representations of objects to amass a library of pictorial images. A right-brained child collects these images through activities such as play, immersion in one or more of the creative outlets (see Chapter Six), and an attraction to highly visual resources such as television, computer software and the Internet, video games, videos, or highly pictorial books.

Young right-brained children are attracted to highly visual resources.

Skill in using the stored pictures is honed through the use of visualization skills. This happens while being read to, listening to audio books and oral storytelling, interactive play, pretending, and general imaginative creations often developed using the creative outlets. All of these skills are accentuated by studying the subjects of history, science and geography (see Chapter Sixteen), to which a right-brained child is often drawn at the ages of 5 to 7 years. All of these resources create many avenues by which this learner may develop her universal gifts of three-dimensional pictorial thinking and imaginative expression during this time frame.

Transition Stage—Symbolic Development

The right-brained learner is ready for two-dimensional symbolic work starting around the ages of 8 to 10 years old. During this time frame, their primary reliance on the specialization of the right side of the brain shifts to more purposely integrate the specialization of the left side of the brain. This transition allows the learner to begin processing two-dimensional and symbolic work more easily. However, every symbol will still be filtered through the right side of the brain and translated into an image. For example, when a right-brained child learns to read, he'll translate every word into a picture. When puzzling out a math equation, each number is translated into a picture. If the child receives plenty of time to gather a library of pictorial images during the 5 to 7 year range, learning to read and manipulate written numbers during the 8 to 10 year time frame is easier.

126

Conversely, if the right-brained child is asked to view and use symbolic, two-dimensional work before this shift occurs, struggles can result. Because the brain is still processing information from the eyes three-dimensionally, the brain tries to make flat, two-dimensional symbols, such as words, become three-dimensional. This may cause images to float and move, blur, and even appear backward then forward. In other words, when looking at the word c-a-t three-dimensionally, it can be viewed forward as c-a-t or backward as t-a-c because that's how three-dimensionality works. Dr. Raymond Moore states, "If a child is required to develop basic skills in reading, writing, arithmetic, and language arts before the various functions of the brain balance out...he may develop any one of many problems associated with learning failure." [1] Not all right-brained children will develop these issues, but most children with these difficulties will be right-brained.

Left Hemisphere	Right Hemisphere
reality	*imagination
*word based (symbolic)	*picture based (3-dimensional)
*sequential	**global**
part	whole
memorization	association
logical (mind)	intuitive (heart)
compliant	resistant
external perfectionism	internal perfectionism
product	process
time	space

*Universal gifts

Sequential vs. Global

As a young child, I *loved* numbers. I remember sitting on my living room floor deciding that I would write the numbers out sequentially, starting at one and move upward as far as I could write. I envisioned doing this for days on end and got

127

excited about how high a number I could reach. Of course, I tired after a while so it never went very high.

Sequential counting is a left-brained task.

This "fun" activity demonstrates how the mind of a left-brained learner works. Sequentially start at the beginning and progress one step at a time to see how far one can get. A right-brained learner takes a different approach toward a fun math activity. Here's my builder son's "fun" math activity (during church services!) as he takes a number and sees how far he can go while cutting it in half each time.

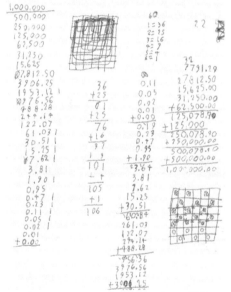

Playing with math ideas is a right-brained task.

My activity represented sequencing, the strength of a left-brained learner; my son's activity represented exploring a global concept, the strength of a right-brained learner. Again, both are valid, and the learning environment inside our mass institutions of learning should offer both avenues of exploration. Changes are particularly needed in the early years to honor the different time frames and processes of acquiring foundational knowledge in preparation for the higher concepts later.

128

Arithmetic to Mathematics—The Left-Brained Way

Let's look at the timing difference with the goal of learning algebra in high school if each learner's early year strengths are utilized. The left-brained learner does well with the current sequential progression of learning numbers, then addition/subtraction, then multiplication/division, and so forth until it's time to apply these concepts to algebra later. At that time, left-brained learners use their foundation with number manipulation (arithmetic) to begin understanding the bigger concepts of negative/positive numbers, variables, math patterns, equality, and so forth (mathematics).

Mathematics to Arithmetic—The Right-Brained Way

For the right-brained child, the learning pattern is opposite but just as viable. In the early years, the right-brained learner needs to explore global concepts that can be visualized, such as negative/positive numbers, variables, math patterns, equality, and so forth (mathematics) so he can build the understanding necessary to be ready to learn algebra later. At that time, right-brained learners use their foundation with math concepts to begin understanding *the reason* to learn math facts, such as addition/subtraction, multiplication/division, and so forth (arithmetic).

As you can see, the goal remains the same—algebra for all in the high school years. But when the strengths of each type of learner are applied, the foundational knowledge needed before algebra begins requires different approaches. The left-brained learner excels at the symbolic sequential manipulation of facts in the early years while the right-brained learner easily visualizes abstract global concepts. It's important to remember that *both* integrate the other ability later, but each works from a foundation based on their respective strengths in math processing.

129

Left Hemisphere	Right Hemisphere
reality	*imagination
*word based (symbolic)	*picture based (3-dimensional)
*sequential	global
part	**whole**
memorization	association
logical (mind)	intuitive (heart)
compliant	resistant
external perfectionism	internal perfectionism
product	process
time	space

*Universal gifts

Part vs. Whole

When I bought our family trampoline, I meticulously took out all the parts, laid them out and accounted for each piece based on the parts page of the assembly instructions. I then proceeded from step one until completion, finding each matching part, reading the instructions to know how it will go together, and puzzling out each step in turn until I understood how it all fit together. This is an example of linear thinking: being able to go from part to whole, one step or part at a time, believing that each will lead to a finished whole product.

After this I visited a friend's house where my children played on their trampoline with her children. I looked at the assembled product and asked my friend who put it together. She replied that her husband did. I asked if he had looked at the instructions or simply at the picture on the front of the box. She sheepishly replied that she'd seen him "eyeing" how it should be assembled from the picture. In typical right-brained fashion, he used the method that made the most sense to him: visualizing from the whole to the parts.

I put my trampoline together starting at step one until completion; a part-to-whole process.

Learning to Read

Left-brained children learn to read in a linear fashion (part-to whole). This is best achieved through phonics instruction. Right-brained children learn to read in a holistic fashion (whole-to-part), best achieved through sight word instruction. Because one of the universal gifts of the left-brained learner is a symbolic, word-driven focus, application of the linear process of learning to read means that the individual sounds and letter identification are part of the reading process. The right-brained learners will also use their foundational strengths to make sense of words through reading. Their three-dimensional pictorial strength is accessed to translate each word into a picture, while their ability to visualize is utilized in order to retain comprehension. This means that knowing the minute parts of words is not necessary at this time.

Foundation and Transition Stages— Writing/Spelling the Left-Brained Way

The part vs. whole traits greatly impact the *development* of the written word: writing stories and spelling words. For the left-brained learner, writing stories and spelling are often learned at the same time as reading acquisition, during the 5 to 7 year time frame. Further development occurs during the 8 to 10 year time frame after reading fluency is attained. This makes sense for left-brained learners because their word-based focus allows them to learn to read primarily from phonics, building words by combining separate sounds. Since writing and spelling utilize part-to-whole word-based sequencing, teaching these subjects at the same time as reading can complement the left-brained learner's understanding of their word-based gift area.

Integration Stage— Writing/Spelling the Right-Brained Way

For the right-brained learner, spelling and writing stories using print are often best delayed until the 11 to 13 year time frame, *after* reading fluency is achieved (usually between 9 and 11 years old). For the right-brained learner, reading is about taking the whole word and creating a picture. This is a translation process, moving from a non-gift area (symbols) to a gift area (pictures). However, spelling uses two double left-brained strengths. In order to spell a word, a right-brained learner sees a picture (right-brained gift), translates the picture to the word (left-brained strength), and then needs to decipher the whole word into its individual sound parts (left-brained strength).

Writing has three left-brained strength requirements. Right-brained learners visualize a whole picture (right-brained strength), translate it into the individual word parts (left-brained strength), break these down into its spelling parts (left-brained strength), and sequence the picture scene in words (yet another left-brained strength). Notice how the skills required to do well with spelling and writing favor the gifts of the left-brained learner: a symbolic, word-driven focus and sequential processes.

Because a right-brained learner uses two entirely different processes, one to learn to read, and another to learn to spell and write, it's not effective for a right-brained learner to learn spelling and writing at the same time he receives reading instruction. Because right-brained learners do best with whole-to-part learning, it's best to master each process independent of the other, establishing the holistic, or whole skill first (reading), followed by the linear, or part skills, last (spelling and writing).

In their book, *The Dyslexic Advantage,* the Eides verify that "the brain systems that help 'translate' nonverbal ideas into words are some of the latest-developing parts of the brain."[2] While awaiting this natural development to occur, there are ways for right-brained children to practice translating scenes into stories. One idea is to look at pictures in story books and make up your own story from the pictures. Along this same idea, a right-brained child could tell a story based on the family photo album. Be creative! Colorforms® can be a good practice tool for right-brained children for developing translation skills for writing stories by assembling the parts of a story through pictures. My artist son was inspired to make his own Colorforms® scenes and figures[3] in order to tell stories.

Each of these tiny homemade Colorforms® figures was meticulously cut out. (Image[4])

A homemade Colorforms® scene.

Although writing using words is not the preferred method to express ideas for the right-brained learner until he reaches the ages of 11 to 13, he expresses ideas in right-brained formats during the 8 to 10 year time frame (see Chapter Thirteen, and above example) in preparation for the transition to writing with words. Further, there are ways to minimize poor spelling habits in the earlier years by understanding the right-brained process to acquiring this skill later (see Chapter Fifteen).

Left Hemisphere	Right Hemisphere
reality	*imagination
*word based (symbolic)	*picture based (3-dimensional)
*sequential	global
part	whole
memorization	**association**
logical (mind)	intuitive (heart)
compliant	resistant
external perfectionism	internal perfectionism
product	process
time	space

*Universal gifts

134

Memorization vs. Association

Right-brained learners have strong long-term memories. This means they like to learn by association. Left-brained learners have strong short-term memories. This means they like to learn by memorization. Never is this more obvious than when our primary-aged children set about to learn math facts.

Math Facts—The Left-Brained Way

As outlined in Chapter Five, the universal gifts of the left-brained learner are symbolic, word-driven focuses, and sequential processes. Therefore, math symbols are included in their natural abilities in the 5 to 7 year time frame when arithmetic is introduced in school. Throw in the preferred teaching method of parts-to-whole sequential building and memorization learning tools, and left-brained learners plug and chug with the best of them. I remember a childhood rush of excitement when given a worksheet full of math equations to solve. I loved applying the memorized sequential formulas I was taught to achieve an answer.

Math Facts—The Right-Brained Way

Right-brained learners prefer to learn math facts based upon whole-to-part associations with global math concepts. In their primary years, my right-brained children explored diverse concepts in math, periodically solving an equation or two in written form to show they understood the translation process. It wasn't until the ages of 11 to 13 years that they achieved immediate recall of multiplication facts (higher arithmetic). Like reading, mathematics is best learned whole-to-part by the right-brained learner. This means providing some arithmetic *exposure* in the primary ages until they build a strong conceptual mathematical foundation and the "age of

135

shifting" (8 to 10 years old) has occurred. Once we began formal academics, my children could apply their gift of holistic imagery by using a visual resource (in their case, a multiplication chart) while performing arithmetic functions until they could effortlessly integrate the knowledge using their visualization strengths.

A visual tool, either bought or homemade, can assist a right-brained child to learn math facts.

Visual Resource Tools

When a right-brained learner uses visual resources as he navigates his way through symbolic work tasks, he's *not cheating.* He's making the most of his strengths.

Visualization Association. My children constantly "looked up" the answers to the problems they were asked to solve on a multiplication chart. After doing this over and over for five to six months, they learned the automatic response because they could instantly visualize the answer on the chart within their minds. A right-brained person often uses the gift of visualization to "memorize" information. An abacus, a number line, or counters are other resources that can achieve the same result.

Mnemonics Association. Yet another resource that taps into the visualization skill of a right-brained learner is mnemonics. These are silly or absurd stories that help the memory process. My builder son discovered a book of mnemonics that teaches the states and capitals.[5] He laughed hysterically over the play on words to pictures. After carrying that book around with him for several weeks, laughing at the absurdities created, he painlessly learned every state and capital. Mnemonics applies the holistic imagery best remembered and stored by the right-brained learner by utilizing the universal gifts of imagination and pictures. However, because mnemonics often use a "play on words" to create the absurdity, right-brained learners will receive the greatest benefit during or after reading acquisition, either in the 8 to 10 year time frame or the 11 to 13 year time frame. In fact, right-brained learners are drawn to silly or absurd reading material as they become fluent readers because of the ease of translation and entertainment benefits. On the other hand, not all visual resources appeal to all right-brained learners. My artist son didn't like mnemonics because "then I would have to learn the word play *and* the correct information."

My son learned all the continents by association through his animal interest.

Interest Association. I saw another example of

learning by association when my oldest son enjoyed a deep interest in animals of all kinds when 5 to 7 years old. With a pictorial animal atlas of the world and other visual resources on particular types of animals (such as sharks, whales, and snakes), my son learned the continents, many countries, all the oceans, and many types of topography in each by knowing where each animal originated. In other words, my son's deep interest in animals served as the "hook" that led him to learn many "parts" associated with the "whole" topic. Interestingly, this strategy is why most successful trivia gamers will be right-brained people because they amass tidbits of information from all manner of sources and store them in long-term memory to be recalled as needed. "Why do you *know* that?" I often exclaim to my husband as he answers trivia, and he inevitably responds, "I don't know. It's just in there."

Left Hemisphere	Right Hemisphere
reality	*imagination
*word based (symbolic)	*picture based (3-dimensional)
*sequential	global
part	whole
memorization	association
logical (mind)	**intuitive (heart)**
compliant	resistant
external perfectionism	internal perfectionism
product	process
time	space

*Universal gifts

Logical (Mind) vs. Intuitive (Heart)

It's been interesting watching my right-brained daughter interact with her left-brained husband. She often makes decisions *"from the heart,"* intuitively. Coming from a home that valued this trait, she wasn't used to someone challenging the validity of her intuitive decision for lack of logical evidence.

Though she's nurturing her logical mind in response, she still primarily wants to be respected and valued for her gift of intuition. I've found that I developed some intuitive thinking by being around so many right-brained people, but I will follow up with logical support from *"within my mind."* We of different traits have much to learn from each other.

Misunderstandings can occur when a right-brained spouse makes decisions intuitively and a left-brained spouse uses logic. (Image[6])

Showing Your Work

A common schooling practice is to "show your work." This is another example of schools mainly adopting left-brained processing practices. Showing your work aligns well with their logical, sequential nature. Take long division, for example. The traditional formula involves many steps to successfully attain an answer. Left-brained learners follow the pattern to its completion and show all the steps along the way. Right-brained learners often get "lost" in all of the part-to-whole, sequential steps on the way to the answer. However, they can apply their own set of tools. A right-brained learner either creates an alternative path to the answer utilizing conceptual understanding, or he engages holistic imagery.

Holistic Imagery—All at Once

I remember teaching an algebra class for my artist son and four of his fellow homeschooling peers. As a left-brained instructor, I shared the sequential formula that led to the correct answers. One time, I observed everyone bent over their notebooks, puzzling out the logical steps to each solution. I noticed my artist son gazing up into the air, so I decided to ask if he needed help. When he saw me out of the corner of his eye, he intercepted my intrusion by quickly raising his finger in a "just a minute" gesture with a, "Sshhh, I've almost got it." Not taking offense since I was used to his processing differences, I waited until he could explain. "It was almost there, and then you made it leave." He'd been anticipating his intuitive revelation to the problem at hand. Let me explain.

Right-brained people think in pictures. All pieces of information are stored in pictures. All information is retrieved in pictures. These pictures can be entire scenes, cinematic movies, or singular images. Therefore, when right-brained learners are puzzling out an answer to something, it appears all at once—as a picture. Often, they have no idea how the answer comes to them. It's intuitive. It's visual or spatial in nature and it comes to them in the finished form. This is why it's frustrating for right-brained learners to be asked how they got an answer, especially in the young years of 5 to 10. Unfortunately, we're conditioned to believe they are either being stubborn or lazy or are cheating.

This same artist son came to me as a young teen and declared, "I'm stupid." That surprised me since it was clear he wasn't. I asked him to clarify his position. He explained, "Whenever I get an answer to a question, it just comes to me all at once. It just appears. I have no idea how it gets there. I'm worried that one day, it won't appear, and then everyone will know that I really don't know anything." That was a very revealing conversation. How unnerving it must be to not understand the process from which you receive your information.

I tried to help him understand that the information has to be inside him, but because of how he receives information, all at once and in its completed form, it makes one think that it's somehow "magic." We need to be patient and value the natural intuitive process of right-brained learners in their young years. Eventually, they'll be able to show their work and explain their process *beginning* in the 11 to 13 year time frame when both hemispheres of the brain reach full integration. It's often fully realized in the 14 to 16 year time frame.

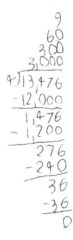

My builder son's self-created long division is now an accepted system. (Image[7])

Right-brained learners take information stored inside their minds and intuitively discover the whole as it forms as an image. Left-brained learners take information stored inside their minds and logically work out the parts to get to the whole. Both are valid processes to information. Only one is valued in our school systems.

Stages of Learning Time Frames Summary

The core traits in this chapter highlight important reasons to provide different learning time frames for the different brain processing preferences.

Foundation Stage (5 to 7 Years)

The ages of 5 to 7 are best focused on the universal gifts of each type of learner. Because the left-brained child enjoys sequential, symbolic, word-based activities, she's ready to tackle reading and beginning arithmetic (addition/subtraction) at the ages of 5 to 7. Because they are part-to-whole word-based learners, left-brained children can learn spelling and writing alongside reading. A right-brained learner is gifted in imaginative, three-dimensional, picture-based activities, so instead enjoys history, science, geography, social studies, (see

Chapter Sixteen) and the creative outlets (see Chapter Six) as his foundation during this time.

Transition Stage (8 to 10 Years)

Around the ages of 8 to 10, the left-brained learner sequentially improves in reading and tackling higher arithmetic (multiplication/division). Left-brained children learn best with part-to-whole sequential processes using memorization as a primary tool. They have the ability to show their work as they go. Creative thinking is integrated through higher level spelling and writing ability, reading comprehension skills, and math story problems. The right-brained learner will shift into the two-dimensional, symbolic realm to begin learning to read and tackle beginning arithmetic. A deeper understanding of the previous subjects occurs during this 8 to 10 year stage for the right-brained child, as well as development of higher skill levels in the creative outlets.

Integration Stage (11 to 13 Years)

As left-brained learners reach the full integration stage and use the weaker hemisphere strengths more reliably, they're ready to develop the global concept strengths of right-brained learners by studying subjects like history and science and taking the other subjects to the highest level. Right-brained learners will more fully integrate the strengths of the left-brained learner: reading (by achieving fluency) and higher arithmetic. This is when the word focus of spelling and writing is tackled as a separate subject from reading because they use completely different techniques to achieve success. Right-brained children learn best with whole-to-part conceptual processes using association as a primary tool. They enjoy various imaginative tools such as mnemonics and the ability to intuitively discover ideas through holistic imagery.

Writing with words often occurs between ages 11 and 13 for right-brained learners.

In Chapter One I mention that the classification of left-brained learners and right-brained learners is not meant to be used to polarize ideas. It's vital that the classification be viewed flexibly. This is also true of these generalized time frame stages. I hope this information shows that there are other valid sequences to learning than just those popularized through the school's scope and sequence favoring left-brained learners. There's also a scope and sequence that honors the right side of normal.

References and Notes

[1] Moore, Raymond S. and Dorothy N. Moore. *Better Late than Early: A New Approach to your Child's Education.* Reader's Digest Association, 1989.

---

[2] Eide, Brock L. and Fernette F. Eide. *The Dyslexic Advantage: Unlocking the Hidden Potential of the Dyslexic Brain.* Hudson Street Press, 2011.

[3] Colorforms® are a flexible vinyl piece that can be placed on a shiny surface and stick, yet are easily moved around. This colorful and artsy toy was first introduced as shapes but has since expanded to themed products. Colorforms® is distributed by University Games Corporation and information can be found at the website http://www.colorforms.com/.

[4] Toy Story® is a registered trademark of Disney Enterprises, Inc. ©Disney/Pixar. My artist son created images inspired from the movie, Toy Story®, and in no way intended to challenge any copyright.

[5] The name of the book my builder son enjoyed is Alvarez, Will Cleveland & Mark. *Yo, Sacramento!* Brookfield: The Millbrook Press, 1994.

[6] This is one of my daughter's engagement pictures. This amazing photo was taken by a talented grown homeschooler and photographer, Jennifer Pinkerton. You can find her website at http://jennimarie.com/.

[7] A similar long division system is called Double Division. A good site is found here: http://www.doubledivision.org/.

Chapter Eight

Loves to Learn;
Hates to Be Taught

Shift Begins with Me

Plan A already failed as I began our first year of homeschooling (see story in Chapter Three) so we were on to Plan B. We slowly tried out some unit study[1] books from time to time over most of the school year. My artist son let me know what he was interested in, I'd find a unit study book on it, and together we'd play around with the ideas in it. Come April, he wanted a unit study on snakes. I couldn't find one, but since we'd done a couple of unit studies, I felt I was up to the task of putting one together myself. The newborn was about seven months old, and with four young ones, it took effort to carve out the time to do so.

We started by going to the library and borrowing a bunch of books about snakes that I could use as fodder. I also gathered what we had at home. By now, we had quite the stack. It took two weeks before I found a weekend to work on it. In the meantime, my artist son went through that stack of books. He was a non-reader, but he asked me a lot of questions about what he saw and asked me to read certain portions.

The weekend came and, boy, did I put together one great unit study, if I do say so myself! It would take five days to complete and my artist son was so excited he could barely contain himself that Sunday night. Monday morning came and he was there with bells on, eager to jump right in. How wonderful to have such an enthusiastic student ready to learn. So, I began with my first lesson. Immediately, my artist son's face fell.

"What's wrong?" I inquired.

"I already know that!" he lamented.

"What do you mean?" I asked incredulously.

"I mean I already know it," he insisted.

"No problem, we'll just skip to the next part," and I continued my lesson plan.

"I already know that, too!" he cried at this point.

Frustrated, I shared with him all that I was going to teach him, and my artist son realized that he knew everything already from going through the resources before I got to them. He was interested in doing a couple of the craft projects, but so ended my fabulous unit study.

Ah, but wait, I noticed that my artist son knew everything you never wanted to know about cobras and pythons and constrictors, but nothing about rattlesnakes and vipers!

"How about I teach you about those?" I questioned.

"No, thanks. I'm not interested in rattlesnakes or vipers," he calmly pointed out.

"Yeah, but you didn't tell me that, and I prepared it, and you don't know it, so how about I teach it?" I insisted.

"No, thanks."

His being polite about it or not, I was on the verge of a tirade about all the time and energy I put into the unit study, and by golly, my artist son was going to learn about rattlesnakes and vipers! But then, I had an idea, and turned the learning experience from him to me. Something urged me to go ahead and teach him one concept about what he didn't want to learn. Just one. I decided to teach him why a pit viper is called a pit viper. My artist son listened, and then we went on our merry way through the day.

Before he went to bed, I asked him why a pit viper is called a pit viper. He couldn't remember. I explained the reason again. My artist son then initiated a long discussion about all the things I never wanted to know about cobras, pythons and constrictors for a good 30 minutes. The next day, I asked him why a pit viper is called a pit viper. Couldn't remember. Repeat, try again. Repeat, try again. All to no avail. And yet, a month later, a year later, that boy could tell you all the types of cobras, what country they lived in, if they were venomous, how they gave birth to their young, etc. All about constrictors and pythons, too.

Lesson for Mom: I can put lots of energy and time into preparing "the perfect lesson," and if he's not interested in learning it, it's all for nothing. I'd chosen to raise a large family with children close in age, so time was valuable. This is the point when unschooling became the way my artist son pursued learning. Fast forward thirteen years to my retelling this story more formally and sharing it with others: "So, why is a pit viper called a pit viper?" queries an acquaintance.

"Are you kidding me? Do you think I would remember?" I reply good-naturedly as the former teacher of the information.

So, I look it up on the Internet, where I find this definition:

In addition, the pit vipers have developed special organs of heat reception that help them to sense warm-blooded animals, an ability that is especially useful at night, when many of them hunt. These organs consist of pits, for which the group is named, located just behind the nostrils and covered with a temperature-sensitive membrane. Some pit vipers may also use these organs to find cool refuges from inhospitable daytime temperatures.[2]

I also seek out my then 19-year-old firstborn son and ask him if he remembers our snake unit study when he was 6.

"Nope," he states matter-of-factly and without interest.

I give him the Reader's Digest version of this story and then probe, "So, do you know what a pit viper is?"

And showing that my son's ability to gather information continued to exceed mine, my artist son proceeds to correct me, "I think pit viper is a classification, Mom."

"Huh?"

Sure enough, in that same spot on the Internet where I found the definition, it states rattlesnakes(!), the fer-de-lance, water moccasins, bushmasters, and copperheads are all pit vipers! So, I guess his learning about snakes continued after that initial "failed lesson" way back when. The bigger point is that my artist son remembered it well and accurately when he wanted to know the information.

Snakes are a common boy interest.

Right-brained children love to learn, hate to be taught. **Resistance is often a natural response to being taught in a manner not conducive to how they learn or not connected to a meaningful need or desire to know.** That said, when the right resources and timing are utilized, a right-brained learner is actively and eagerly engaged in the learning process. In fact, they are often insatiable learners.

Left Hemisphere	Right Hemisphere
reality	*imagination
*word based (symbolic)	*picture based (3-dimensional)
*sequential	global
part	whole
memorization	association
logical (mind)	intuitive (heart)
compliant	**resistant**
external perfectionism	internal perfectionism
product	process
time	space

*Universal gifts

Compliant vs. Resistant

These two words—compliant and resistant—are often misused when it comes to children and learning. Left-brained children tend to be more compliant. Why? Because their brain processing preferences are met with the right resources and timing. Right-brained children tend to be more resistant. Why? Because the right resources and timing that match their brain processing preferences are *not* being used. I hesitate to even include this core trait, but until schools, teachers, and parents provide a well-matched learning environment, right-brained children will consistently resist. For the *highly* right-brained child, complying with a mismatched environment isn't even an option. Resistance is a tool often used to communicate something isn't working.

149

Mismatched Teaching Style

For some children, resistance means, "You're not teaching me in the way that I understand." A funny thing happened while helping my daughter with math. I have a houseful of right-brained learners, but my daughter is more whole-brained, which means she chooses right-brained strategies for some activities and left-brained strategies for others. For math, she likes to learn in more of a left-brained fashion, with an additional need to write down information to process it. As you're aware, I'm left-brained as well and this processing style is how I naturally do any math needed. However, because my other children taught me how to help them differently, I started using the alternative method first! For example, I would start to explain fractions to my daughter with, "Pretend we have a pie..." Inevitably, she ran for the hills, and jokes with me to this day about that mismatched teaching method. In her case, she simply went to her father, who gave it to her like she wanted it; straight up. She wasn't being resistant because she was unteachable. She was resistant to my mismatched teaching style.

Mismatched Teaching Time

In the same vein, resistance can mean, "You're not teaching me during my optimal learning time frame." Most right-brained children begin to learn to read between the ages of 8 and 10 years old. I've found builders tend to gravitate to the latter end of the time frame; my builder son was no different. At age 8, I tried *Teach Your Child to Read in 100 Easy Lessons* [3] with him. After just a few lessons, it was evident he didn't "get it." Along with that, he showed some early signs of frustration which was my signal it wasn't the right resource or time. Had I continued, I would have earned resistance. At age 9, I tried another strategy to introduce reading. The same thing occurred as before. At age 10, I offered him *Bob Books®* [4] with a brief explanation as to how

150

the books were arranged, and he was interested in exploring them on his own. Voila! No resistance and eventual reading. Right resource; right timing.

Bob Books® *were the right resource at the right time for my builder son. (Image[5])*

Undeveloped Skills

For some children, resistance can mean, "I don't have the skills necessary to accomplish the thing you are asking of me." My oldest son is the classic example of a right-brained person's tendency for a messy, seemingly disorganized room. When he was younger, we had come up with a plan together to tidy up bedrooms on a weekly basis. However, I met with resistance constantly. As intelligent as he was, I couldn't understand why he was defiant. Well, intelligence has nothing to do with organization! He truly didn't have the skills necessary to clean his room in a way that made sense to him. Once I offered him suggestions of various ways to clean a room, he chose one that sparked his desire and found that it worked fairly well for him. Over time, he added another element or two that added to his ability to organize and clean his room.

Inexperienced Communication Skills

Again, along the same lines, resistance can mean, "I don't have the communication skills necessary to let you know what I need to make this work for me." During the 11 to 13 year old stage, I noticed my children transitioning toward more formal schoolwork and goals. Because I start slowly with supports in place, applying the good information on how they learn that I gleaned from their previous stages, the first part goes fairly smoothly. However, when it's time to transition to a workable system that encourages more independence from my direct supports, I find that resistance can occur as they let me know something isn't working for them, and they don't know how to adjust it to make it work. I found my children still weren't versed at verbalizing a need to brainstorm or troubleshoot areas not working for them. They needed a mentor to come in, recognize the need or the lack of workability in a system, and put words to the resistant tool being used.

My fifth son doing some formal work out on the porch.

When my fifth child navigated this stage, I remember suggesting a system that might work for him. A week or so into it, he lamented, "I just can't *do* this!" Since I recognized the resistant tool he was using, I asked, "You were doing it well during this time frame. What's changed?"

"I don't know!" And he really didn't. He needed my communication model.

"Is it too much at one time? Is it too spread out? Do you still need help?" We started to nail it down and discovered he *did* need less at once, and he needed it condensed into one area, and he didn't even know he could ask someone for help by seeking out people!

Inability to Delete Information

For some children, resistance means, "Your advice or ideas may interfere with my own process because I can't delete information well." I remember when my artist son was an older teen, I often hung out with him in his room late at night to connect. He'd often share life situations with me and I'd offer advice or a different perspective. One season, he began resisting our normal interactions and I asked why. He explained that he wanted to start making his own decisions and conclusions without my input unless he specifically asked for it. I apologized and suggested that if I accidentally did that to just ignore it. He explained that it's hard to "delete" or ignore information from his mind once it's placed in there (the negative flip side to the highly visual mind). My artist son then gave me this analogy to help me understand.

> Suppose I was cooking a soup and I knew what type of soup I wanted to create and I was busy putting in various ingredients. Let's say you come up behind me and throw in some rosemary, but I don't want rosemary in my soup! So, I quickly scoop it out. However, there's still a hint of rosemary in my soup. Now it's permanently altered and can no longer be the soup originally planned.

Right-brained people can come up with amazing visual analogies to depict their perspectives! Our key word after that to remind me to withhold my comments was "rosemary."

Lacking Personal Relevance

For some children, resistance can mean, "I don't know why this is important in my life right now." Right-brained learners are often the first to ask, "Why do I need to know this?" It has to have meaning to them or they just won't put in the effort, or they seem unable to remember. I recall when my builder son was at a peak interest stage in progressing with his piano playing ability. For several years, we had focused on the spatial music reading and ear rhythm playing, which were his gift areas. Although his piano instructors consistently pointed out various tempo notations and other interpretations of symbols used, my builder son took minimal interest in them. Suddenly, he was interested in writing his own music. This meant he needed to know more about the symbols in the sheet music. I noticed that my builder son still hadn't taken particular note of the time signature, so to support him I sat down with him and shared what the time signature means. He nodded in acknowledgement, and I felt he had a new piece of information to use in this latest expanded interest in music. A few days later, this builder son excitedly approached me, to show me something he'd figured out while creating his own sheet music. I followed him to the piano, and he shared that he'd figured out what the time signature symbol represented. Swallowing any sense of "but I told you" from my reaction, I simply smiled and enthusiastically recognized his ability to learn when there's meaning and purpose to do so.

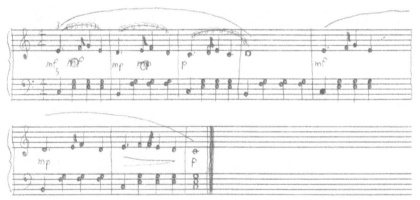

My builder son taught himself time signature when he wrote his own music.

Resistance is a communication tool often used to express something isn't working for a person. I shared some of the ways the resistance tool manifested itself with my children. Resistance isn't a negative attribute when a parent or teacher recognizes it as a communication tool used by unskilled and less experienced little people. Our children need a facilitator who knows when to adjust resources or time frames. Our children need a mentor who puts a voice to what they are feeling or experiencing. Our children need a wise counselor who shares personal stories that shows she understands fear and trepidation along the way to hopes and dreams. Many people use resistance to some level. Hopefully, when an attentive facilitator recognizes and addresses a young person's resistance, this leads to effective communication tools used later when maturity and supported practice prevail.

Left Hemisphere	Right Hemisphere
reality	*imagination
*word based (symbolic)	*picture based (3-dimensional)
*sequential	global
part	whole
memorization	association
logical (mind)	intuitive (heart)
compliant	resistant
external perfectionism	**internal perfectionism**
product	process
time	space

*Universal gifts

External Perfectionism vs. Internal Perfectionism

The two different brain processing preferences tend to favor two different types of perfectionism. [6] A left-brained person tends to exhibit external perfectionism. This is when she wants to exact perfection on everything she does and others do because she thrives on accomplishment (products). An external perfectionist might think, "I want a perfect product; I'm frustrated because I want it to turn out right." A right-brained person tends to exhibit internal perfectionism.

155

This is when he wants to exact perfection on everything he does and others do because his creative expression (process) is an extension of how he feels about himself. An internal perfectionist might think, "Why am I so stupid? Why can't I get this right? I'm no good!" Because many right-brained learners tend to be highly sensitive, [7] this tendency to internalize the effect of their actions or products makes sense. Interestingly, both perfectionist acts can look similar to one another; the difference is in the motive and inner effect.

Perfectionism Support—Mistake Coaching

Parents and teachers of perfectionist children have to become good "mistake coaches." Mistake coaching can include these strategies:

 ➢ Modeling healthy self-talk (or internal dialogue)
 ➢ Using the word "practice"
 ➢ Linking back to previous successes
 ➢ "Gentle pushing"
 ➢ Trying

Modeling Healthy Self-Talk. Perfectionism for the right-brained child shows up clearly in the creative outlets or academic work. One reason stems from the amazing ability to visualize. A right-brained learner sees what he wants to produce in his mind first. In his mind it's in its perfect state and can be scrutinized from every angle. When in the early stage of development, the produced creation often doesn't match the envisioned product. I found I had to provide lessons for my perfectionist right-brained children in how to deal with this temporary discrepancy.

I remember when my artist son first began to draw at 3.5 years old, and for a year or so would draw for hours each day. One time, his father began playing drawing games with him. My artist son would share what he would like his father to draw, and my son would try to recreate the picture. After a

156

few months of playing this game, I noticed my artist son stopped drawing altogether. (After he drew for hours a day, one notices such a change.) I asked why he wasn't drawing any more. Fortunately, I have a verbal-oriented son who seemed fairly connected with his feelings, and he replied, "I'm afraid of making mistakes." Upon further inquiry, he added, "Dad never makes mistakes when he draws with me."

When my 4-year-old perfectionist artist son noticed a discrepancy between his and his father's drawing ability, he stopped drawing.

I quickly sought out his father and informed him to start making deliberate mistakes and talking out loud about his process. He began using a pencil and talked out loud, "Oh, that's not quite how I want it to look. There, that's better." I was into knitting at the time, so when I dropped a stitch or messed up the pattern, I talked aloud about my process: "I could fix it and keep going and no one would know, or I could take out the last hour's work and redo it so it's perfect. Hhmmm, what should I do? I think I'll take it out even though that means I'll lose a couple of hours by the time I'm all done, but it will make me feel better even though no one else will know. I've decided it's worth it to take it out." It's *so* important to include the self-talk *out loud*, since internal perfectionism stems from inside.

Practice Makes Perfect. At the same time, I explained to my artist son that his father had been drawing for years. With much practice, he would also get better, and certain types of drawing would be simpler for him. The word *practice* seems to

157

be fairly important to the perfectionist right-brained learner. If they can view it as "not the real deal," then it doesn't have to be perfect. It takes the pressure off. I also found old drawings from when his father was younger and showed him how his father wasn't always as good as he is now. I took out my artist son's first drawings at age 3 and showed him how much he'd improved in just over a year. These comparisons seemed to reassure him that certain skills have a process that moves toward excellence. Shortly after receiving these supports, my artist son began to draw voraciously again.

Reconnect with Previous Success. Right-brained learners often use their great visualization skill when learning a new skill or joining a new activity. I call it the "watch, then do" strategy. A right-brained learner would rather watch others do something for a while, visualize it in his mind, visually switch out the watched person with themselves, troubleshoot all the possibilities, watch the person fail and correct, incorporate that knowledge in his mind, and then try it for himself; often with near perfect results.

My artist son was one year behind all the other little boys as it pertained to riding the various bicycles. When all the other 3-year-olds were trying out tricycles, my artist son would run alongside them or watch. Because of this, he rode a tricycle fairly well the first time he tried, at 4 years old. Then, when all the 4-year-olds were converting to bikes with training wheels, my artist son continued on his tricycle. He wasn't keen on trading his fast pace and ease of motion for the clumsy process of transitioning he watched his peers experience. Why should he convert to a bike with training wheels when his tricycle was working just fine for him?

I used a "mistake coach" strategy that works well with the "why should I try something new when I'm comfortable" situation. I call it reconnecting with previous successes. After respecting his normal waiting period of one year, he appeared emotionally ready at 5 years old to transition to the training wheels. To implement "reconnecting with previous successes," I reminded him how he'd started off slow and clumsy when he first started riding his tricycle, but was now zooming around.

158

I reassured him that the same result would occur when he transitioned to the training wheels. I let him know I noticed when he was up and zooming around on the training wheels after the initial transition stage. The same thing happened when he transitioned to a two-wheel bike. I gave value to his "watching" strategy, then "doing" by observing his peers for a year. Then I utilized the reconnecting with previous successes as he transitioned to riding a two-wheel bicycle.

My artist son was generally a year behind his age mates in bike riding transitions because he liked to "watch, then do."

Gentle Pushing. In a similar vein, if a right-brained child can't visualize an opportunity a parent or teacher offers, the child may resist trying the new activity. An external perfectionist might think, "I can't do that; I wouldn't know what I was doing. I wouldn't do it right." An internal perfectionist might think, "I might look stupid because I don't know what I'm doing. Others will think I'm an idiot." One helpful strategy is to discuss all of the information available so the child can begin to create a visual. Further, all the potential variables that might transpire could be brainstormed to prepare a holistic viewpoint. After this visual preparation, I often instituted what I call "gentle pushing." It has to be gentle (these are highly sensitive individuals), yet a little push is usually needed.

I remember when a summer art program was offered through our local city. After looking into it, I felt it would be a perfect fit for my artist son. I introduced the idea to him and awaited the expected "nope" in response. It came, so I talked about what I knew about it. The most important aspect of this stage is that we as the parent or teacher have pure motives in our intent. I felt strongly that my artist son would enjoy this;

159

there were no ulterior motives to the offering. Through my gentle pushing stage, I helped him understand the "outs" available to him. I encouraged him to try at least a half hour, and told him I would stay in the building until he gave me the okay to leave. He went to the program, and waved me away within the first ten minutes.

On the flip side, I remember signing up this same artist son for tee ball when he was 5 years old, because "everyone else signs their children up at that stage." Because the motive was societal conditioning, the activity didn't last long. After his first practice, while we watched him play with a stick in the sand out in the field as he waited his turn with the coach, we asked him how he felt about tee ball. His reply, "Oh, it was fine, except the coach kept interrupting me when I was playing with the ants." Okay, lesson learned.

Give It a Try. A right-brained child may resist a particular resource, such as a read-aloud book or a learning tool. My perfectionist artist son never read a Dr. Seuss™ book [8] because he felt they were "below his intellect." He didn't like "dumbed down" resources, preferring instead real depictions of his interest. For instance, during his dinosaur phase, he rarely checked out children's books from the library. He haunted the adult and non-fiction sections, instead, sifting through books until he found resources that portrayed "real," not cartoon-based dinosaurs. On the other hand, this same child voraciously utilized comic books and manga during his pre-fluency stage of reading, and enjoyed video game storylines. In other words, he accepted or rejected various resources based on his particular perfectionistic and subjective viewpoints for his various genres, not on any real objective criteria. His perfectionism appeared to be a criticalness of resources based on outward appearance. "That looks stupid" was a consistent mantra, particularly when I chose our family read-aloud books. I encouraged him to listen to two to three chapters before finalizing his opinion. He inevitably got hooked with the storyline, in part because I took the time to find great books to read aloud.

160

Because my theater son likes "real" drawings, when he colors, he always uses the "correct" color choices.

Living with Perfectionism

With effective strategies implemented, perfectionism as it pertains to learning can often be circumvented. However, perfectionism also finds its way into day-to-day living, which is a whole other venue. It can appear as:

➢ Criticalness of self
➢ Criticalness of others
➢ A strong sense of fairness
➢ Constant negotiations
➢ A strong sense of right and wrong (and they are always right)
➢ Inflexibility (it's my way or the highway)
➢ All or nothing thinking (if I can't do it right, I won't do it at all)
➢ Holding themselves up to impossible or even unhealthy standards (I'm not good enough unless I'm the best)
➢ Skewed thinking (if I don't look good enough; I better change it)
➢ Depression and anxiety

I call these some of the high maintenance temperament traits that affect "living with" the right-brained person versus "learning with" the right-brained person that I discuss in this book. I always say that once you figure out how a right-brained child learns, that's the easy part; living with them can be a constant learning experience as these same traits affect the relationship department. But when seen through the lens of the highly sensitive nature of most right-brained people, you can implement effective skills and strategies to minimize any negative impact in their learning lives or their various relationships. Explaining living with the right-brained person would take another book.

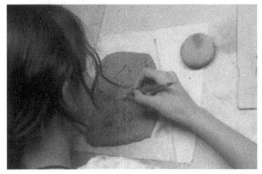

The positive side of perfectionism is creative excellence.

One of the more common complaints I hear from teachers and parents is, "I have a resistant learner." It's my opinion that this resistance is earned. Resistance and perfectionism are sources of contention if not understood in the context of the right-brained learning style. It appears when we're not providing the well-matched learning environment right-brained children deserve. I propose that we feel pride in these "resistant" right-brained children who hold tightly to their right-brained gifts and won't trade them in for the weakness-centered approach that a mismatched learning environment creates for them. Through resistance, right-brained children demand better. We need to demand better, too.

References and Notes

[1] Unit studies are a form of teaching that uses one topic or literary selection to incorporate the majority of school subjects.

[2] The Columbia Encyclopedia, 6th ed. "pit viper." *Encyclopedia.com,* 2011. http://www.encyclopedia.com/doc/1E1-pitviper.html (accessed June 1, 2012).

[3] Engelmann, Siegfried, Phyllis Haddox, Elaine Bruner. *Teach Your Child to Read in 100 Easy Lessons*. Touchstone, 1986.

[4] Maslen, Bobby Lynn. *Bob Books.* Scholastic, 2006. There are currently Sets 1-5, plus additional specialty resources.

[5] Image: Ibid.

[6] I was cued into this idea of different types of perfectionism from the book: Braund, Ron L. and Dana Scott Spears. *Strong-Willed Child or Dreamer?* Nashville: Thomas Nelson Publishers, 1996.

[7] Aron, Elaine N. *The Highly Sensitive Child.* Three Rivers Press, 2002.

[8] Theodor Seuss Geisel, an American author, often wrote his children's books under the pen name, Dr. Seuss™. Although my gifted son wasn't drawn to these well-known, favorite rhyming books, many right-brained children will enjoy these books filled with imaginative creatures.

Chapter Nine

Creative Results

Shift Begins with Me

I clearly remember the moment I made a life-changing decision about my perspective on adulthood. I was a freshman in college in a human relations class. I saw college and being away from home for the first time as an opportune time to begin my metamorphosis into an Adult. Cue dramatic music. I would leave behind my silly persona of humor I developed in junior high and high school that served as a way to get people to laugh and lighten up. I'd begin to develop my serious side because that's what adults do to be taken seriously. I was having inner voice discussions with myself as I slipped behind my desk for class one day.

The instructor wanted us to watch a video of an inspirational speaker. He pushed play. It was Leo Buscaglia[1] and the topic was how adults have lost their child-like enthusiasm for life. I'm sure my instructor thought I was having some kind of personal drama when he noticed me crying in the middle of the video. But I cried at my vivid realization that I'd been cuing up to get rid of one of my best attributes, my bubbly enthusiasm, because I thought that's what it meant to become an adult.

Some examples from Buscaglia's presentation have stayed with me, like when a child notices a duck in a pond at the park, points excitedly, and exclaims, "Look, Mommy, a duck!" Many parents smile sweetly and reply, "Yes, it's a duck." Instead, Buscaglia encourages a parent to remember what it was like to discover something for the first time and emphatically exclaim alongside the child, "I know! Isn't that exciting?! Let's go look at the duck!" How about the first time we tasted ice cream? Have we lost our sense of newness as we watch our child experience it for the first time? Can we be reminded how wonderful eating ice cream can be?[2] This is the type of parent I wanted to be. This was the type of adult I wanted to be. Sure, adulthood brings the opportunity for many experiences that eventually morph into wisdom, but we can also energetically embrace the idea that life is amazing and interesting and wonderful right now. In other words, the journey should be as exciting as the destination. The two processing preferences showcase this perfectly.

Left Hemisphere	Right Hemisphere
reality	*imagination
*word based (symbolic)	*picture based (3-dimensional)
*sequential	global
part	whole
memorization	association
logical (mind)	intuitive (heart)
compliant	resistant
external perfectionism	internal perfectionism
product	**process**
time	space

*Universal gifts

Product vs. Process

A left-brained person tends to enjoy a finished product—reaching the destination. A right-brained person tends to flourish in the creative process of figuring things out—enjoying the journey. These attributes are seen in the facts versus concepts idea that is implied in many of the core traits I've described thus far: sequential versus global, part versus whole, memorization versus association, and logical versus intuitive. Each of these has an aspect of facts versus concepts, or product versus process. These core traits are often revealed in two ways: how learning various subjects are pursued and how projects are pursued.

The Product of Learning to Read

As I mentioned in Chapter Seven, when I was 6 years old, I wanted to learn to read—now! I begged my mother to teach me but she put me off until the first grade teacher could do the honors. It didn't occur to me that I could figure it out myself. I wanted someone to give me the code so that I could quickly reach the destination of being a reader. That was my goal and as soon as I had the information, I was a reader almost instantly. I certainly enjoy the stories told in books. I tend to feel characters as I read versus seeing images. However, it was just as enjoyable to complete a book. As a child, I once decided that my goal was to read every book in the animal section of the young adult section of our small town library. I'd start at A and work my way to Z, more evidence of my tendency toward sequentially completing a goal.

The Process of Learning to Read

As a right-brained child learns to read, the propensity toward process learning is evident. There are two stages of reading: reading instruction (product) and motivation or purpose to read (process). The latter is most required for a right-brained child to become a reader.

Meaningful Purpose. Each of my children received reading instruction at the time and with the resource that honored the right-brained scope and sequence (product), but they didn't take off with independent reading until a meaningful purpose inspired them (process). In his book, *The Power of Neurodiversity,* Thomas Armstrong shared the results of a survey of successful dyslexic adults, stating "interest-based reading was the key to their high literacy levels."

Some of the motivations for my children were reading a particular (adult-level) book, expanding a creative outlet (computer programming), and enjoying a comic book series. I've heard many right-brained children learn to read to be independent and proficient at video game playing. Other right-brained children learn to read because they want to more efficiently read the magazine (or other visual print resource) without having to wait for an available reader. My daughter, who learned to read in a left-brained fashion, did so because she wanted to be a reader (product). My sons, who all learned to read in a right-brained fashion, did so because it served a purpose (process).

My seventh child pressed himself through the reading process in order to read books about his interest in weapons. (Image[3])

Read-Aloud Strategy. The mindset and right-brained attribute is to enjoy the process of hearing a story. Remember, many skills are needed for a right-brained child to read a book: decoding words, translating words to pictures, creating an overall visual from that translation, and comprehending the translation. The hardest skill for an early right-brained reader to learn is the decoding part. What better and easier way to get to the process of hearing a story than by skipping the decoding part and listening to a read-aloud, either from a person or an audiotape? My right-brained children sat for read-alouds long after many might believe they should have been reading more independently. This belief stems from the school mindset and left-brained attribute of independent reading as a finished goal. The product is learning to read, so the goal is to get children doing that as quickly as possible. If they are independent readers, reading aloud to your child is no longer necessary, right?

I gave value to my right-brained children's natural inclination to sit in on read-aloud time after their initial reading acquisition and discovered the following benefits:

❖ Read-aloud time assists in fluency because they are "catching the visual." When they re-read the book themselves, the translation process has already been done once.
❖ Read-aloud time supports the ability to "turn on" the right side of the brain by engaging in a creative activity

168

while listening, such as drawing or building with LEGO®, to better focus on developing a left-brained skill (translating words).

❖ Read-aloud time protects the positive relationship with print during the (up to 2 year) transition from early reader to fluent reader.

❖ Read-aloud time allows the continuation of enjoying the *process* of hearing a story while slowly integrating the newer left-brained skills (decoding words) required for independent reading.

Listening to read-alouds or audio books strengthens the right-brained reading process.

So even after reading fluency is accomplished, joining read-aloud times supports the preference of the *process* of reading, which is enjoying the story. For read-alouds, as the left-brained person, I still prefer to be the reader. It's more enjoyable for me. My right-brained children and husband still prefer to listen to the read-aloud. It's more enjoyable to them. A successful integration of left-brained skills doesn't supersede the ease and preference of the inherent enjoyment from using one's own preferred skill set. Read-aloud time is one strategy that supports the *process* of enjoying a story for right-brained children that leads to a painless transition of the *product* of independent reading acquisition.

The Product of Learning Math

I loved math in elementary school. I got excited when handed a worksheet full of math problems! Why? Because each math problem had an exact answer that I could complete and I had rows and rows of problems to complete. It played right into my product-driven attribute. I felt a strong sense of accomplishment when the worksheet was completed with correct answers all in a row. When I got to algebra, I enjoyed the sense that an incomplete situation was in front of me, and, with the right formula, I could finish it and make it complete. Every loose string was tied. On the flip side, that's why I hated geometry. To this day, I still don't get it. There didn't seem to be finished answers to the process of writing up statements to prove something or other. Proofs made no sense to my mind that liked nicely bow-wrapped packages that moved from start to finish. The product and destination of having everything equal out are the attributes of a good accountant, IRS auditor, or payroll employee.

The Process of Learning Math

Right-brained people who enjoy math love the puzzling out process. My builder son found that discovering the pattern of the nines multiplication facts was far more interesting than being able to say that nine times three is twenty-seven. When he was told that the two sides of a triangle add up to equal the third side, he sat down with a ruler to prove or disprove this idea by trying to create a triangle that is the exception. For hours. For days. These are the minds of people that understand math has a language and become our mathematicians, physicists, and engineers. The process and understanding why are what lead to success in these fields.

The Product of Writing

When I was in college taking a writing class, I decided I'd carefully pay attention so I could learn to write The Perfect Paper. Indeed, the class culminated in writing a paper. I planned to construct each paragraph exactly as instructed with the correct paragraph dynamic. There's the "T" format with the topic sentence at the beginning with supporting sentences. There's an "I" format with the topic sentence at the start, supporting statements, and an ending that repeats the topic sentence. There's an "L" format with the supporting statements first, ending with a topic sentence. Each paragraph needed to flow from one to another. I used all my left-brained attributes and created The Perfect Paper. I was rewarded with an A+. And, it was dry and boring as all get out! I never considered myself a writer before that paper, and didn't consider myself a writer afterward. Somehow I knew my perfectly constructed paragraphs didn't make me a writer.

I didn't consider myself a writer even after my Perfect Paper.

My strength as a left-brained writer emerged in the business world. My forte was business letters, complaint letters, and sales letters. I received my associate's degree in executive secretarial science. This helps show that every brain processing type has its strengths and weaknesses, and that a well-matched niche exists for highlighting the strengths. The business world and sales world is about obtaining a succinct product. It's logical and sequential, based on reality, and uses power words to move people to action. Perfect fit.

Vocabulary and Report Writing

March 8, 1984

The Process of Writing

My right-brained children focus on the process of telling the story. I found it intriguing that my daughter and artist son shared their dreams with each other every morning. Their dreams were high action and adventure themes. Mine were always based on reality. Interesting to witness was the more detail they shared with one another, the longer they described it, and the more open-ended it was, the more exciting they found it. It wasn't about one-upping each other with the coolest dream, but about sharing the experience and savoring the details.

I always wondered how fiction writers knew how the story would turn out. Based on my left-brained needs to first gather all the information, organize it, then write based on formatted patterns, I didn't understand how a fiction writer could gather all the necessary information about the character and the plot to create a story. My fantasy writer daughter helped me understand that as a right-brained person with great visualization skills and attention for visual detail, the story was all in her head in a holistic manner. As she wrote, each detailed scene revealed itself from the whole. Quite fascinating! Observing my artist son's storytelling through drawings, comics, oral, and video (see Chapter Thirteen); I saw how the story's creator gets pulled along the living entity within his mind. This is how storytelling and other creative writing projects exist for a right-brained person. It all begins with imagination and creativity.

The Purpose Is the Creative Process

I often hear parents of right-brained children lament, "They don't finish what they start." I realized the reason for this is that they are process people. It's because of the creative process. A right-brained person needs to feel creative about a project to work on it. A right-brained person is also a highly visual worker. That's why he keeps projects lying around. Creativity has to just happen when it does, so a right-brained person often finds it advantageous to have many projects happening at the same time. Each of them will be in visual sight. In this way, as he looks over the ongoing projects, wherever creativity jumps out for a particular project, that's the one that gets worked on that day, or that week.

My husband's unfinished art piece— from high school.

There's a creative component to most projects pursued by a right-brained person, so it will be more art than science. This means that the project can probably always be better. At some point, a right-brained person has to know when to consider a project "done." Sure, it can always be better. A manuscript can always be improved. A piece of art can always be tweaked. A dance performance can always be sharper. A script can always be more realistic. It can be difficult in the younger years to know when to consider something complete enough. Focusing on an end product goes against the right-brained person's nature as a process person, and it minimizes creativity.

Deadlines—The Left-Brained Way

Schools are focused on products and end results, so assignments, (timed) tests, and deadlines are the means to accomplishing that end. Right-brained children wilt under these pressures to perform on demand, especially in the early years. Their process focus is about creatively figuring things out, unlike the product focus of getting it done. Educators and parents insist, though, that the world is full of expectations of product and a person can't succeed in a career without meeting deadlines or offering something in the form of a product. This is true. And right-brained people *do* learn these attributes—at the right time and in the right way.

Deadlines—The Right-Brained Way

There are two types of deadlines: natural deadlines and created deadlines. Using the strategy of *created* deadlines in the younger years works against the natural bent of a right-brained learner. They are prone to anxiety and pressure shuts down creativity. It's best to create an environment to promote their strengths of imagination and creativity until they're set on a sure foundation. Therefore, I used *natural* deadlines sparingly in the elementary years (ages 5 to 10) for right-brained children to expose them to the idea and opportunity to complete a project. For instance, my artist son often preferred to create his own Halloween costumes (see the picture at the beginning of this chapter). Buying something cheapens the experience for him, because that way the product is more important than the process of creation. The natural deadline for completion was Halloween night. Other natural deadlines might be a science fair presentation, a family reunion, a birthday gift, or an annual portfolio review.

Halloween night is a natural deadline to have costumes finished.

The 11 to 13 year time frame shift is a good time to introduce *created* deadlines in areas of non-creativity. In this way, a right-brained young person experiences goal setting in areas that aren't as emotion-laden as a goal in a creative project would be. For example, we

174

created goals for my artist son in math, grammar, and science because these were areas he hadn't cared much about before this stage. For my builder son, created goals were grammar, spelling, and history because these were areas *he* hadn't cared much about before this stage. After I helped each child troubleshoot a goal-setting system that worked for him/her in areas that weren't emotion-inducing, each child independently applied the knowledge to his/her areas of strength during the 14 to 16 year time frame. Suddenly, my artist son was creating goals for his history, drawing, and Japanese interests that resulted in more products. My builder son was creating goals for his computer programming, science, and math interests that resulted in more products. Left-brained attributes *will* be developed in right-brained children at the stage of development naturally suited to do so. Creativity is emotion; emotion is expression; expression needs space; space promotes creativity...which leads us to the last attributes.

Left Hemisphere	Right Hemisphere
reality	*imagination
*word based (symbolic)	*picture based (3-dimensional)
*sequential	global
part	whole
memorization	association
logical (mind)	intuitive (heart)
compliant	resistant
external perfectionism	internal perfectionism
product	process
time	**space**

*Universal gifts

Time vs. Space

In the unschooling community, it's said that a child naturally picks up an understanding of time simply by abiding by the schedule of our normal lives. A child learns

8:00 p.m. if that's bedtime, or learns 10:00 a.m. because that's time for swim lessons. However, my children were oblivious to time, even with consistent schedule times. I chalked it up to the environment I had created: a happy-go-lucky childhood where they spent days mainly playing and creating and interacting. I decided it was "time" to learn about "time," around the ages of 10 to 11 years old.

Time for Creative Flow

My study of the right-brained learner shed light on the reason my right-brained children didn't notice time in their early childhoods. Further, my own observations validate the idea that the lack of focus on time revolves primarily around the creative outlets. To achieve optimal creative genius, a person needs to enter "the zone," or what athletes call "flow." Flow is a state of timelessness when a person is totally immersed in the present state of being. In the case of a right-brained, creative person, flow occurs with the process of creation. I think most of us can understand this process when we think about a project in which we were particularly engaged. Writing this book was my example. I needed to put all other needs, tasks, responsibilities, or time constraints aside in order to fully engage in writing. Time was of no consequence. In fact, on the days I could work all day, I'd discover I hadn't eaten or used the restroom, and it was already dinner time!

The saying, "Time flies when you're having fun," captures the essence of timeless engagement. To develop a creative outlet, a right-brained learner needs to spend enormous amounts of time immersed in its acquisition. When my artist son was young, he'd spend hours and hours drawing every day. When my builder son was young, he'd spend hours and hours a day building with LEGO®. When my theater son was young, he'd spend hours and hours a day pretending and creating costumes. As each discovered an interest in a career path, the number of hours only increased. My computer son researched and programmed hours and hours a day to create his own computer game. My fantasy writer daughter researched and wrote for hours and hours a day to create a novel. My artist son researched and drew for hours and hours a day to create a visual atlas. It's said that it takes 10,000 hours[4] dedicated to a skill to become a master in it; utilizing timelessness to reach flow has its benefits in reaching that goal.

My builder son had time to clock in thousands of hours on computer programming. (Image[5])

Time for Percolating

I noticed my right-brained children needed "percolating time" to process a concept or idea enough to integrate it into their knowledge base. This occurred in two ways. My artist son liked to percolate on new resources. I'd find an interesting new resource, let him know about it, and leave it for him to investigate. A week or so later, I'd find creations from him reflecting knowledge gained from the resource. Similarly, my builder son liked to percolate on tidbits of information he heard or was taught. When I shared a new piece of information with him, he'd incorporate the new

177

knowledge during his "doodle times" (down time activities, especially in church, when he "doodled" new ideas on paper) over the next few weeks. This is an effective strategy for teaching a right-brained learner: share a resource, skill, or strategy, then allow time and space for the concept to percolate over the next week. Notice how it makes more sense to the child after "percolating time" rather than expecting immediate feedback via worksheets.

Time for Active Thinking

I like to let parents know that, for my children, thinking is an active engagement. Because a right-brained child can see in their mind a three-dimensional, moving image in which they can process information, entertain themselves with imaginative creations, or discover new ideas, they can spend a lot of time in what appears to be "doing nothing." I got an idea of all that's going on in my right-brained artist son's mind and how it works while I was cleaning house one day. I found a notebook lying around and picked it up to discover the owner. I opened the front cover and saw this heading:

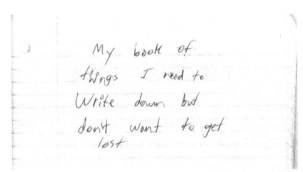

Thinking is an active process for right-brained creative people.

This notebook contained diverse writings. There were lists, story ideas, drawing ideas, character drawings, his role playing game (RPG) development notes, and general notes to self. It helped me realize how powerful his visual mind is and

178

all that is stored therein at any given time. Because right-brained people are so creative, ideas usually abound for many projects at a time and sometimes one might worry that information will be lost if it doesn't get jotted down somewhere. Of course, writing things out didn't start until the 11 to 13 year old stage (see Chapter Thirteen).

Time Schedules

As a left-brained person, I'm hyper aware of time. I know when each family member has to be in any given location. Often, I don't even need a calendar to work in perfect synchronization. If I do want to note time needs, I use a calendar or planner to map it out. Because a right-brained person doesn't operate well in time, I find many of them like to use loosely planned schedules by either writing lists of what they need to accomplish or work in block times. Block time refers to taking a larger block or chunk of time, let's say morning hours from 8:00 a.m. to noon, to accomplish a smaller amount of work, let's say an hour's worth, within the larger block of time (so about a 1:4 ratio of work to time allotted). This allows for productivity but accounts for creative interruption. A left-brained time schedule isn't better than a right-brained system; it's just that different strengths are being used.

Where Am I?

A right-brained person operates best in space as opposed to in time. My explanation of how my builder son plays piano is a perfect example of how he easily perceives the notes in space. This is his strength area. As a child, this same builder son could identify buildings we passed although he could barely see out the window. He was so young and tiny he only saw the building tops, yet knew what and where it was. This builder son, at a very young age, could also direct my way home from most locations. He instantaneously knew, and let me know, when I'd taken an alternative route home.

Barely big enough to see over the top of the seat, my builder son often accurately directed me while I drove.

Me? I inevitably walk out of a mall shop and turn the wrong direction. I've learned to walk out of the shop, stop, look both directions, get my bearings, and then determine in which direction I want to walk.

Helping vs. Changing

As delineated in the past several chapters, there are as many traits to process information in a left-brained fashion as there are to process information in a right-brained fashion. Both are valid, but the current scope and sequence in our schools revolves around the traits of a left-brained learner; thus, our society values those educational resources and time frames. However, because we chose to homeschool in a way that honored each child's learning style, including both preferred resources *and* time frames, I was privileged to see what the right-brained approach looks like. This book offers parents and teachers the opportunity to decide to stop trying to **change** our right-brained learners, and instead **help** them make the most of the amazing traits of a right-brained learner, creating space that allows them to flourish.

I Needed to Change

From my experience, there's very little in my children's learning lives or their education department that needed my help. Most of the **help** needed in this arena was for me! **I** needed to become educated about learning styles. **I** needed to question my conditioned reactions and responses to various methods and time frames. **I** found myself becoming intrigued and excited about what was unfolding before me through my children. (I call it becoming an anthropologist of sorts.) Some of the things I remember letting go of: Why not count on your fingers? Why can't drawing be considered an act of writing? Why do "show me work"? Why can't learning happen orally? Why not watch ants for science? Why can't reading comic books be valued? Why does handwriting have to be from the top down? Why can't a child have dinosaurs as his core curriculum? Why not play LEGO® all day? Why can't he teach himself?

Using fingers is a kinesthetic tool some children use in the early years.

A Little Bit of Help

However, there were *some* times that my children needed my unconditioned wisdom and perspective. My oldest needed "gentle pushing" at times because

181

he's prone to resisting new things—even things I was sure he would love. The biggest criterion I had to learn was to use this strategy only on activities I truly felt he would enjoy, and I didn't want him to miss a wonderful opportunity for his own growth and learning. Every time I pushed gently using this criterion, my oldest ended up loving the activity. This helped him learn to trust my encouragement and to be open to new experiences, and not reject them outright simply because they were new (see Chapter Eight).

This same child also needed my intuitive wisdom in his transition to reading—but not because he was 8 years old and a non-reader. It was because he was showing me that he was ready, but I could see his perfectionism trait that needed to do something well immediately was interfering with his acquisition process. His learning style had always been to observe first, then do, and that wasn't working for him in the reading department, so he wasn't going to do it at all—another common trait of a right-brained learner (I'll do it well, or not at all!).

You notice so far how I'm not *changing* who they are, how they learn, when they are ready to learn, or what should be important to them. I'm recognizing when something isn't working for them and *helping* them find a way to continue to develop their gifts and talents in a way that allows their love of learning to remain ignited. Those of us who are raising right-brained learners must make the distinction between *changing* a person into someone she isn't and *helping* our intense and creative children prosper in their gifts, talents, and unique perspectives. It's not about applying a person's theory to our child to "improve them," like helping a right-brained child "get better" by teaching him left-brained thinking. That just disguises *changing* them with the words "*helping* them improve." It's about observing their lives, understanding the value of their perspective, and becoming true advocates of their particular life journey. We do this by *helping* them navigate their own personal and particular pitfalls. I believe our children show us what they need.

You're Daughter Isn't Sick, She's a Dancer

The story of how Gillian Lynne, the "Cats" choreographer, came to discover her talent, as told by creativity expert, Sir Ken Robinson,[6] highlights this well. The public school she attended in the 1930s informed her mother that she was not fitting in well there, and maybe she had some problems that needed attention. Her mother took Gillian to a psychiatrist, and after a briefing, he asked the mother to step into the hall with him while he left Gillian in his office with the radio on. When they looked back into the room, Gillian was dancing around the office. The psychiatrist simply stated to the mother, "Your daughter isn't sick, Mrs. Lynne; she's a dancer. Put her in dance school." The rest is history as she's renowned for her talent in dance and choreography.

Our right-brained learners aren't sick; they aren't broken; they aren't a problem. Our right-brained learners are dancers; they're artists; they're musicians; they're actors; they're architects; they're video game programmers. This is who they are. To **change** that is, at best, to "squander away their talents" according to Sir Robinson.[7] And at worst, it's to "psychologically destroy them," to quote my oldest son. I want neither for my amazing right-brained children! Does that mean they're perfect the way they are? Of course not, as we all have our weak areas and difficulties. However, because of our conditioning to value left-brained traits, we think the very traits of right-brained thinking *are* the weak areas and difficulties. If we intervene in these areas because they go against the grain of conditioned societal thinking, then we are **changing** who our children are. If we can educate ourselves about how right-brained children learn and combine that with strong advocacy efforts to effect change in our schools, the result is a collaborative process that will liberate thousands if not millions of creative minds that improve our world!

References and Notes

[1] Leo F. Buscaglia, Ph.D., became famous for his messages of love developed from a course he taught on the same subject for the Department of Special Education at the University of Southern California in the late 1960s. As a dynamic speaker that led to popular television appearances, he was considered "the granddaddy of motivational speakers."

[2] Material by Leo Buscaglia can be located at http://leobuscaglia. org/.

[3] The book in the image is: Fowler, Will, Anthony North & Charles Stronge. *The Illustrated Encyclopedia of Pistols, Revolvers and Submachine Guns.* Anness Publishing Ltd., 2011.

[4] Ericsson, K. A., R. Th. Krampe and C. Tesch-Romer. "The role of deliberate practice in the acquisition of expert performance." *Psychological Review, 100,* 1993: 393-394.

[5] This is one of my builder son's senior pictures. The photo is taken by grown homeschooler and professional photographer, Jennifer Pinkerton. You can find her website at http://jennimarie.com/.

[6] As shared on his Ted Talk found here: Robinson, Sir Ken. "Ken Robinson says schools kill creativity." *TED Talks.* June 2006. http://www.ted.com/talks/ken_ robinson_says_schools_kill_creativity.html.

[7] Ibid.

Section Three

Common Subject Differences

What We Believe.

Learning to read is difficult and lots of problems can occur if experts aren't involved.

Shifting Perspective.

There's a natural continuum to learning to read, just as there is for learning to walk or talk. If each person's method and time for learning to read is honored, reading can be attained painlessly by most children.

Chapter Ten discusses the reading fallacies that affect how and when a child learns to read. Different styles of budding readers influence the type of reading material to have available. Additionally, genetic and temperament attributes affect reading time frames. Examples of how children learn to read using both formal and informal reading resources that are meaningful for all types of readers are shared.

What We Believe.

All normal children will learn to read by second grade.

Shifting Perspective.

Children are "normed" in school by measuring against the left-brained way of learning. There is an equally valid way of learning to read using right-brained strengths and patterns. There's a right side of normal!

Chapter Eleven lays the framework for the right-brained way of learning to read. There are three stages during which attributes are developed that promote reading. Here you'll discover how the attributes are linked to the way the right side of the brain functions.

What We Believe.

Everyone has to learn their math facts to be good at math.

Shifting Perspective.

Schools concentrate attention mostly on arithmetic, or the manipulation of numbers. On the other hand, right-brained children are "natural mathematicians," very good at recognizing patterns and proving theories about them.

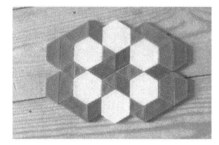

Mathematics involves the recognition of patterns. (Image[1])

Chapter Twelve details the two right-brained paths to math skill development: a spatial approach and a visual approach. Here the right-brained approach to math is explained, the stages for right-brained math development are denoted, and appropriate resources are presented.

What We Believe.

The ability to express yourself through writing is an essential skill.

Shifting Perspective.

Being able to express your ideas *is* important. The reality is that the medium and timing of expressing those ideas vary based on brain processing preferences. Visual, kinesthetic, and oral expressions come first for right-brained children, followed by the written format.

Chapter Thirteen demonstrates an artist path to writing, starting with pictures, moving to oral development, on to using technology, such as computers and video cameras, then culminating with the written. An example of mentoring with "copying" is provided.

What We Believe.

Research papers are the most important type of writing.

Shifting Perspective.

Left-brained learners work well with facts and are adept at organizing them into presentable chunks. Because schools value the left-brained scope and sequence, reports are at the core of writing experiences. Right-brained people work well with creative expression, so creativity reigns at the core, replacing reports with poetry, fantasy writing, lyrics, scripts, and visual books.

Chapter Fourteen celebrates the various types of writing expressions right-brained children enjoy. Giving value to technology resources, the utilization of props and interest-based items for inspiration, and mentoring through reading the work of real writers are illustrated.

What We Believe.

Poorly written communication demonstrates a lack of intelligence, especially one's handwriting, spelling, vocabulary, and grammar, so teaching these skills should be emphasized at a young age.

Shifting Perspective.

Since doctors are infamous for their poor handwriting, we know intelligence doesn't have anything to do with performing the act. In actuality, brain processing preferences impact the optimal timing to learn all of the skills mentioned. Left-brained learners pick up these skills as they learn to read at a young age. But right-brained learners acquire these same skills best *after* they learn to read at a later age than their left-brained peers.

Chapter Fifteen shows how each of these skills unfold for right-brained learners when developed in their optimal time frame. Right-brained and temperament differences are discussed, along with how these may impact skill development in handwriting, spelling, vocabulary, and grammar. Meaningful right-brained teaching options are suggested, and resources are shared.

What We Believe.

Reading, writing, and arithmetic are foundational subjects to learn in the early years.

Shifting Perspective.

Foundational subjects are those topics that strengthen and promote the universal gifts of a person's brain processing preference. From this foundation, all other subjects come more easily and make more sense to that learner. Reading, writing, and arithmetic strengthen and promote the left-brained universal gifts of symbols (words and numbers) and sequencing. Completely different subjects are required to strengthen and promote the right-brained universal gifts of imagination and three-dimensional pictorial thinking.

Nature study is an early subject strength for right-brained children.

Chapter Sixteen expounds on the early subject strengths of right-brained children—history, cultures, geography, mythology, animals, nature, and science—and explains how these subjects strengthen and promote their universal gifts. These are different subjects than the left-brained subject strengths on which schools concentrate in the early years—reading, writing, and arithmetic. This chapter reveals what it looks like when these early right-brained subjects are honored while teaching our right-brained children.

References and Notes

[1] The resource in the image is pattern blocks. I bought mine years ago from Learning Resources®. It can be found at their website at http://www. learningresources.com.

Chapter Ten

Reading Fallacies

Shift Begins with Me

I was the bookworm in my family of birth. Two siblings were considered not good at reading, and the other didn't bother. One year, the only fun Christmas gift we each received was a label maker. Mine was a bookworm. My other gift was a sheet set for my bed. Needless to say, we weren't blessed financially as I grew up, so I greatly appreciated both gifts.

My mother enjoyed books as much as I did. We had two bookshelves spotlighted in our living room, on either side of the television. I remember my mother purchasing a set of World Book® encyclopedias.[1] This purchase must have been quite a sacrifice for my parents. I enjoyed lovingly turning the pages of those books. Around fourth grade, I began receiving books as Christmas presents. I meticulously displayed them on my own little bookshelf in my room. I was the only child in the family with books in my room. I still have every one of those books.

As much as my mother loved books herself, she wasn't the type to read aloud to any of us. She didn't teach me to read, either, as noted in Chapter Seven. I don't remember her specifically sharing her joy of books with me. I remember seeing her read, though, and she brought me to the public library from time to time. I vividly recall the sensory experience of walking through those doors: the smells, the rows and rows of books of all styles and sizes, the hushed tones. It was sacred ground.

When I became an adult, the first thing I desired was a houseful of books. The books I subscribed to receive through a classics book club were the first items I placed in my hope chest. After I married, and as we began our family, I knew I'd share my love of books with my children. Children's books were first on my agenda when decorating the nursery. Unlike my mother, I read to my children from the beginning. There are many facets to the enjoyment of books, and each of my children has developed his or her own relationship with them. They've taught me that there are several conditioned aspects to reading.

Different Types of Readers

The idea that a bookworm is one who reads a lot for pleasure only is a false one. When my artist son began to read at 9 years old, his first book was Michael Crichton's *The Lost World.*[2] Why? He loved dinosaurs, felt the movie version was too graphic for his tastes, so wanted to gain the information from the book.

Information Reader

My artist son loves books for the information he gains from them. Starting as early as two years old, he insisted on looking at our extensive collection of non-fiction books. He preferred and enjoyed books such as Dorling Kindersley's *Eyewitness Books*, atlases, animal books, dinosaurs, etc.

Visual books with captions under the pictures are great book choices for right-brained information readers. (Image[3])

He reads books for pleasure from time to time; yet, such reading still seems to be about gaining information from the book. For instance, he loves *The Lord of the Rings*[4] series, but I wonder if it's to get information about fantasy characters, which he develops on his own by drawing. Throughout his childhood and to this day, scads of books reside next to and in his bed for researching, looking, and scanning (see the picture at the start of this chapter).

Pleasure Reader

My second-born writer daughter is your stereotypical bookworm. When around age 5, she kept stacks of Dr. Seuss™ books next to her bed. Soon thereafter, I would discover she could read. Since then, my writer daughter always had a fiction book going.

Instructional Reader

My third-born builder son has always been a creator—LEGO®, K'NEX®, Popsicle® sticks, anything he could get his hands on. He never enjoyed reading for pleasure, hardly ever looked at books for research, but was always drawn to instructional material, like LEGO® books and how things work-type[5] books. He learned to read at 11, and still reads for instructional purposes.

I wondered if he limited himself to this style of reading because he hadn't acquired enough reading practice as compared to the other two children. I put my conjecture to rest after he began pursuing his interest in computer programming at 13. He carried around programming books like they were bibles. At 15, he trudged through an adult programming book called, *Programming Windows: The Definitive Guide to the Win32 API.*[6] I didn't worry anymore.

Having a variety of books that support reading for information, pleasure, and instruction gives value to the diverse types of readers.

With my first three children, I have an instructional reader, a pleasure reader, and an information reader. Each style of reading is valued, and I consider them all bookworms in their own right. I have to wonder if my siblings, who didn't read for pleasure, may have enjoyed a different style of reading if it had been recognized and valued in their environments. As for our home, we have ten five-shelf bookshelves and ten three-shelf bookshelves filled with books. There are at least two bookshelves in every bedroom. They're filled with pleasure books, information books, and instructional books. Visual books such as comic books, manga, pictorial science experiments, pictorial cookbooks, atlases, and Dorling Kindersley's *Eyewitness Books* adorn the shelves. We have traditional books, too: classics, novels, Joy Hakim's *A History of US*,[7] biographies, computer programming, interactive math stories, and more. I carefully chose resources with attributes I knew were important to each child to complement each child's learning style. I like to think the variety of material each child led me to purchase, our book-enriched environment, and redefining what constitutes a bookworm all contributed to my children successfully finding their niche with books.

Joyful or Hard?

So many people think that learning to read is supposed to be hard. It doesn't have to be. The process is meant to be joyful. We choose to make it difficult. There are exceptions out there, but the majority of humanity, when guided on their particular path to reading, can do so seamlessly. It seems we'd rather believe we can *make* it happen to assuage our own fears or to meet the school's time frame. It's harder to trust that gentle support, facilitation, and attuned observations lend themselves to each person's natural unfolding process.

9 ⁵ 10 ⁴ 7 14* 12*

The ages at which my children have learned to read (*estimated).

It's not about preferring earlier; it's not about preferring later. It's about preferring that each child gets to pursue reading exactly when it's right for him and exactly in the way that works for her.

Different Learning Patterns

By observing and being attuned to each child's learning patterns, I was able to predict when my first (at 8 years old), fourth (at 4 years old), and fifth (at 7 years old) were ready to learn to read—and how. My second child (at 5 years old) learned on her own, so I missed that partnership, which is perfectly fine! With my third child, I offered help two different times (at 8 and 9 years old, respectively), but the third time was the charm (at 10 years old) to experience the right moment with the right process. It clicked for him. Each time I offered him something that I thought was a good guess about what he needed, his struggle was immediately apparent. I dropped it and waited until I felt it was time to offer again, with something different or similar. Again, it was immediately apparent he wasn't ready. Just as apparent as it had been that he wasn't ready, it was equally apparent when he was. He took off.

Individual Readiness

We could have started with my first offering, when my son was around 8 years old, and continued plugging away at it, but what would've it accomplished? He wouldn't have learned to read any sooner than he did. I've heard story after story about working away at a program for several years before it suddenly "clicked" (see the story at the beginning of Chapter Eighteen). It only "clicks" several years later because it was finally time, not because the program was "miraculous." If successful reading is achieved by instruction with a particular resource alone, then we should be able to predict a guaranteed time frame. But we can't, because individual readiness *must* be a factor.

In today's atmosphere of expecting children to read between 5 and 7 years old, some children learn within months, some by the end of the school year, some by the next school year, and some end up in remediation. Once remediation starts, some children may need the "special program" for months, others until the end of the school year, and still others a few years. Do we notice a pattern here? It has nothing to do with the instruction or programs used, special or not! It has to do with individual readiness meeting preferred resource and method. It's the push of instruction as most important that creates "hard." The secret to joyful learning is in recognizing the important role of individual readiness.

A friend tells the story of her younger son's path to reading that validates this idea.

> *Last year when he was 5, my son became very interested in learning to read. After doing some lessons in* Teach Your Child to Read in 100 Easy Lessons,[8] *it became apparent that he really wasn't ready. He loved the lessons but they weren't sticking and I could see that he just wasn't getting it. I stopped suggesting that we "do reading." My son didn't notice or remind me. We continued doing what we normally do—read and talk about reading and letters.*
>
> *This fall, he again became interested in learning to read so I decided to give* Teach Your Child to Read in 100 Easy Lessons *another try. The difference is incredible! He totally gets it. And remembers it. He reminds me to do his reading. It's coming very easily for him.*

I've witnessed the ease of learning to read over and over again in my own home because of the right resource *at the right time.* Why do so many parents and teachers have a hard time waiting for the individual readiness factor? I believe the reason is the enormous pressures in our society surrounding reading. We truly believe that some people need years of work before they are ready to read, and some only need a little nudge. I've had personal experience with children that "should have" needed a little nudge but actually needed more time, children that did just need a little nudge, and children who could have been given years of "practice" but didn't need it because we accepted and valued different time frames for learning to read. Each and every one of them simply needed to be given time to reach personal readiness, and then given the nudge to find themselves learning to read joyfully.

It's not the program alone that makes a reader; it's the right resource at the right time. (Image⁹)

How do we know when a child is ready to learn to read? Some people have enough faith to wait until their children pursue reading on their own. Admittedly, I'm the type that will offer opportunities through reading programs on a consistent basis, usually starting somewhere between 8 and 10 years old, depending on the reading readiness signs I observe in each particular child. This means that some of my children were offered many different programs over years before their readiness met opportunity. This is what happened to my friend's son from the story above. Although he took off in his reading learning compared to his previous exposure to the program, he still didn't leap into reading fully after using the resource. The difference is that neither my friend nor I press the issue of reading, or pursue it as a remediation to fix something, or stress about it. It's presented as an opportunity. As long as easy progress is occurring, I continued. If not, I dropped it.

What happens when we don't honor the individual time frame or push children into years of remediation? A recent survey by advocacy and research group People for Education has uncovered a significant decline in those children who like to read: 50 percent, down from 76 percent ten years ago.[10] It's unfortunate what's happening in the field of reading instruction, considering all the research and global evidences pointing in the right direction (see Chapter Four).

Reading Time Frame

Because of the left-brained scope and sequence found in our schools, as a society we are conditioned to believe that the "correct" age to learn to read is in the 5 to 7 year old age range, a range that includes first grade at its center. We even use the comparative descriptions "early reader" if a child learns in the 3 to 5 year time frame and "late reader" if the skill is attained between 8 to 10 years. This is false conditioning. The truth is that it's within the norm to learn to read anywhere from 3 to 12 years old. The age time frame of 5 to 7 years is simply the average norm for a left-brained learner and the age time frame of 8 to 10 years is the average norm for a right-brained learner.

Typical Right-Brained Time Frame

As mentioned in this book many times (and probably more times before the end of the book), there's an "age of shifting" for the right-brained learner regarding how they view information. Up until the ages of 8 to 10 years, the right-brained learner is amassing a library of pictorial images in their brain's filing system (see Chapter Five). These are three-dimensional images, able to be seen from all angles. Their brain is wired to process messages from their eyes to view everything from a three-dimensional vantage point (see Chapter Seven). When a right-brained child learns to read, he translates every word into a picture. When a child has had plenty of time to gather these images, it eases the process of learning to read (see Chapter Eleven). However, the brain of this creative learner isn't ready to shift from three-dimensional viewing to two-dimensional viewing until between 8 to 10 years of age (see Chapter Four).

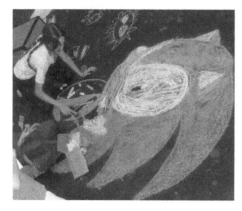

Right-brained children enjoy the expression of three-dimensional activities until ages 8 to 10. (Image[11])

Typically, a child who is right-brained dominant will *begin* to learn to read between the ages of 8 to 10 years old. My artist son was a prime example of that time frame. He *began* reading lessons at 8 years old. I picked up some signals from him that let me know he was ready, but he needed some facilitation. The most accurate signal was when he stopped looking at print books as often as he normally did. I intuited this to mean he was ready to be able to get more out of them, but something was interfering. I felt it had to do with his perfectionism. Now I realize that when a right-brained child who doesn't like to fail fears he can't do something well, he stops doing it to avoid that failure. I was right. As I matched the correct resource to his need of feeling supported in figuring out the reading pattern, by getting him reading real things as quickly as possible, he picked up the skills easily. Through my work with thousands of parents, I've seen this time frame for learning to read for right-brained children apply over and over again.

Verbal Ability Exception

A few exceptions are worth noting regarding the average time frame for a right-brained child to learn to read. Female right-brained learners sometimes learn to read more like a left-brained person due to the gender factor. Because girls are more verbal, some apply that attribute to reading and are ready before 8 to 10 years old. However, some female right-brained learners still learn with their peers beginning between ages 8 and 10. Similarly, highly verbal male right-brained learners may also be ready to read before the ages of 8 to 10 years old because of their verbal attribute. It's the word-based attribute of being verbal that contributes to reading during the earlier time frame of the left-brained learner since one of the foundational traits is a word-based focus.

Spatial and Energy Exceptions

Another exception on the opposite end of the reading time frame for the right-brained learner pertains to builder-types (those who like to build things, like LEGO® or are into electronics). Builders often begin to read at the latter end of the 8 to 10 year time frame. Thus, they tend to *begin* reading closer to the 10 year old mark. This is because their focus is primarily spatial (an awareness of space) which has little to do with words. Further, the builder child exposes himself to wordless print material, like diagrams and maps. On the flip side, builder-types are more apt to excel in math earlier than their other right-brained peers for the same reasons they may learn to read later. This could also translate to a musical inclination. A talent including spatial ability equates to a focus on subjects that utilize that gift, with a later shift of readiness for word-based activities.

My high energy, risk-taker son needs to spend a lot of time outside to balance his physical needs.

In this same vein, another type of right-brained learner who may acquire reading later is the high energy, risk-taker type (described as dynamos in the book, *Dreamers, Discoverers, & Dynamos,*[12] discussed in Chapter Two). Like their builder peers, these children focus on non-reading pre-skills during early development. It's important to this dynamo type to concentrate on centering the body and emotion balance which is a preface to including the mind balance. My high energy son was either playing sports, working in the yard with his dad, or being physically active with his play outlets (like wrestling, bouncing on the trampoline, or riding bikes) through the 8 to 10 year time. Once my dynamo son's high energy needs were satiated, and he had enough experience understanding how those physical impulses affected his emotional actions, only then was he in balance enough to focus on his mind development. It all interconnected. Thus, I find that this type also begins to learn to read at the latter end of the 8 to 10 year mark and may reach fluency between 12 and 14 years of age. This has been true for my young dynamo son.

Resources vs. Curriculum

An interesting Bible story in Second Kings, Chapter Five,[13] tells of a captain of the host of the king of Syria who is encouraged to seek a cure for his leprosy. He eventually presents himself to the prophet who directs he wash himself seven times in the Jordan River to be cleaned. The captain becomes angry by the cure's simplicity, having expected something grander to be needed. His wise servant reasoned with the captain asking, "If it had been some great thing, would you do it? So why not this simple thing?" I often feel we have the same false thinking about reading acquisition as the captain in the story. We're led to believe a person must be qualified and certified to teach it. We think some great and well researched curriculum must be purchased and meticulously followed to achieve reading fluency. This isn't true for the great majority of people.

Meaningful Reading Opportunities

The right-brained child wants to learn to read by reading. Learning with actual books or programs that use book or passage reading is best. Reading programs with a bunch of bells and whistles, separated from real, meaningful stories, will be confusing and ineffective. Further, the right-brained child doesn't like to fail, so she watches others do what she wants to do. Listening to read-alouds, audio books, and hearing books re-read help right-brained children feel comfortable attempting the reading process.

In his book, *Reading without Nonsense*, Frank Smith agrees:

> *Most people who can read have a "sight vocabulary" of at least 50,000 words; they can recognize 50,000 words on sight, in the same way that they can recognize cars and trees and familiar faces, without any sounding out. How did they learn those 50,000 words? 50,000 flashcards? Were there 50,000 occasions when they stopped to figure out a word letter by letter, sound by sound? Or even 50,000 occasions when they asked a helpful adult to identify a word? Words are learned by reading, just as speech is learned through an active involvement in spoken language. No formal exercises are required, simply the opportunity to make sense of language in meaningful circumstances.* [14]

The right-brained child enjoys reading "real" material of substance and/or with a substantive storyline. Graded readers, phonetic readers, or even sometimes Dr. Seuss™ type of material isn't tolerated. When our family visited the library, my artist son headed straight for the adult non-fiction section. As an information reader, he loved picture-based books about his newest interest usually based in science, animals, or history. Sharks, ancient Egypt, snakes, or crystals might be his newest spark and there were always

colorful, picture-based books with captions to choose from to feed his curiosity.

Reading real books for a real purpose encourages learning to read.

Be aware, though, that it's easy to fall into the trap of looking for "teaching moments" when a pre-reader asks for help with reading. I remember my artist son approaching me with one of his favorite books at the time, a Dorling Kindersley *Eyewitness Book*, as a pre-reader. He pointed to a picture caption and requested, "Can you read this? And *just* this!" He anticipated my potential reflex of providing more information than was requested. This prompt helped me refrain from "teacher mode" in the future to remain his trusted reading resource.

Make the Resource Work for You

I seemed to inherently understand Smith's philosophy that "a teacher's responsibility isn't to instruct children in reading but to make it possible for them to learn to read."[15] I knew my artist son needed a resource to help him know he could figure out this reading thing. Most importantly, he had to *read* quickly to achieve this realization. I knew a drawn out process, or separated lessons with flashcards or skill drills, wouldn't work. He needed a "watch, then do" way to begin reading real words in stories. I found that in *Teach Your Child to Read in 100 Easy Lessons*, by Siegfried Engelmann, Phyllis Haddox, and Elaine Bruner.[16] For my builder son, it was *Bob Books®*.[17] Each of these resources enabled that particular child to learn to read in a way that worked best for him.

Programs that introduce learning to read by reading are ideal for right-brained learners. (Image[18])

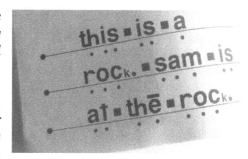

The instructions found in the manual, *Teach Your Child to Read in 100 Easy Lessons,* warn its readers that a student must complete each and every exercise found in the book or it won't "work." However, I'm here to attest that not only *will* it work if you skip things or change them up, but you may not even have to go through 100 lessons! The most important aspect of this book was my artist son reading by lesson 8. The second important aspect was the ability to skip exercises I felt he'd deem "stupid." I didn't *make* him do it the way the system was laid out; he could read it any way that worked for him.

Since my artist son used this resource as his tool to figure out reading, he shifted it from a phonics program into a sight word program. We simplified the resource to my son's learning style, so learning to read *was* simple! We only made it to about Lesson 50 in six months. We stopped when he had enough "tools" to read when he was ready to take off. Six months later, he did. Because we used the book as a guide rather than an instruction manual, we "individualized" it by making changes that made sense for us.

Each right-brained learner has his own perspective. That's why there are as many ways to learn to read as there are readers. Though *Teach Your Child to Read in 100 Easy Lessons* worked well for my artist son, it didn't work for my builder son. And though my artist son rarely read a Dr. Seuss™ book on his own, my writer daughter learned to read with them. And even though my builder son loved mnemonics, my artist son hated them. Even as my builder son loved *Bob Books®* and learned to read with them, my artist son would have rejected them for not being "real."

My builder son appreciated the literal pictorial translations of the words in *Bob Books®* employed to create absurd humor, similar to the function of mnemonics. He especially enjoyed the independence of using the *Bob Books®* to crack the reading code, as they're purposefully user-friendly. The same could be said for *Teach Your Child to Read in 100 Easy Lessons*. Once a pattern of going through a lesson and preferred activities is established, a pre-reader can easily proceed independently with the guidance of a mentor. It's advantageous for a right-brained-friendly learning environment to maintain a variety of reading resources, particularly those that can be used to self-teach.

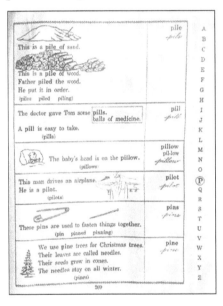

Providing access to a visual children's dictionary is a good resource for self-teaching reading. (Image[19])

Types of Visual Reading Resources

Another area in which we've been conditioned is how we value various resources that turn children into readers. Current good information is a powerful remedy to these onslaughts of value judgments and conditioned reactions ingrained in each of us.

Right-Brained Criteria

There are two criteria for good reading resources for right-brained children. They have to be meaningful and interesting,

208

and highly visual. Many reading programs contain dry and stilted material barely bordering on a storyline. Because reading is all about the visualization for the right-brained person, such material doesn't capture the imaginations of these highly creative learners to entice their efforts. As if that wasn't bad enough, many reading programs separate learning words from the context of reading. Some reading programs even leave out visuals to prevent "cheating." Because right-brained learners are whole-to-part people, they want to capture the big picture and they use story and visual context to do so. Separating words from context cripples their learning process.

Beware of Fitting In

Educational philosophies that espouse preferred methodology or superior resources, such as Charlotte Mason's[20] preference for "living books" versus allowing "twaddle," can undermine parents' and educators' confidence in a child's natural inclination toward certain materials. Let's review Charlotte Mason's definitions. Twaddle is considered dumbed-down literature, absent of meaning. Living books are well-written and engaging, absorbing the reader with narrative and characters that come alive.[21]

The most popular interesting and visual reading choices for right-brained readers are comic books, manga, and magazines. For our creative learners, comic books provide the visual component that brings *the narrative and characters alive.* Because the visual aspect is of utmost importance for these learners, it helps *immerse the reader* into the world of reading as they decipher the semantics of the symbols. If a parent or teacher looks at the vocabulary, the character development, and the plot line of some of these resources (through both picture and word), they'll find *well-written and engaging material.* Comic books are often associated with twaddle because of the predominant left-brained educational value system created by our schools. However, closer

209

inspection shows that comic books clearly fall under the definition of a valuable and effective resource for the creative learner. (See the next chapter to understand why comic books are a good choice for the right-brained learner as he becomes a fluent reader.)

Comic books, manga, and magazines are great first reading material for right-brained readers. (Image[22])

As one who loves to read, my personal goal was to have all of my children love books. As one who loves reading, you'd think I'd have been a prime candidate for reading panic with my children. Yet, I instinctively knew that to meet this lofty goal, I needed to employ more than one path or educational philosophy for learning. Just like the various misinterpretations and stereotypes involved in the word "twaddle" as outlined in Charlotte Mason's ideals, each of our children is unique and won't always benefit from the educational approach we are drawn to ourselves. The reason my children flourished as they have is because whatever each child found valuable received the credibility necessary to make an important contribution to their learning needs. With so many right-brained children in my home, learning about and applying my research about how and when they learn to read greatly contributed to the success we've achieved. So far, so good...five down, two to go.

References and Notes

[1] World Book® encyclopedias can still be purchased. Their website is here: http://www.worldbook.com/.

[2] Crichton, Michael. *The Lost World*. New York: Alfred A. Knopf, 1995.

[3] Image depicts a random collection of a series of children's reference books called *Eyewitness Books,* published and ©2012 DK Publishing, 375 Hudson St. New York, NY 10014. There are currently over 100 titles in the series.

[4] *The Lord of the Rings* series, written by J. R. R. Tolkien, includes: Part I: Tolkien, J. R. R. *The Fellowship of the Ring.* Boston: Houghton Mifflin Company, 1982. Part II: Tolkien, J. R. R. *The Two Towers.* Boston: Houghton Mifflin Company, 1982. Part III: Tolkien, J. R. R. *The Return of the King.* Boston: Houghton Mifflin Company, 1983. A companion to this series is Tolkien, J. R. R. *The Hobbit.* Boston: Houghton Mifflin Company, 1966.

[5] One of my son's favorite books in this category was: Macaulay, David. *The New Way Things Work.* Boston: Houghton Mifflin Company, 1988.

[6] Petzold, Charles. *Programming Windows: The Definitive Guide to the Win32 API.* Microsoft Press, 1998.

[7] A ten volume American history series written by Joy Hakim, published by Oxford University Press in New York, 1994. Book One: The First Americans, Book Two: Making Thirteen Colonies, Book Three: From Colonies to Country, Book Four: The New Nation, Book Five: Liberty for All? Book Six: War, Terrible War, Book Seven: Reconstruction and Reform, Book Eight: An Age of Extremes, Book Nine: War, Peace, and All That Jazz, Book Ten: All the People.

[8] Engelmann, Siegfried, Phyllis Haddox, Elaine Bruner. *Teach Your Child to Read in 100 Easy Lessons.* Touchstone, 1986.

[9] The resource being used by my high energy son in the photo is the Tag™ Reading System created by LeapFrog®. Products can be found at http://www.leapfrog.com/tag/.

[10] People for Education. "Reading for Joy." December, 2011. http://www.peopleforeducation.ca/wp-content/uploads/2011/12/People-for-Education-report-on-students-reading-enjoyment-Reading-for-Joy.pdf.

[11] The creative young girl is chalk drawing a picture of Sonic the Hedgehog™, a video game character first debuting in 1991 for SEGA®. The drawn picture found in this body of work is not intended to challenge any copyright but was the innocent artistic expression of a young creative child.

[12] Palladino, Lucy J. *Dreamers, Discoverers & Dynamos: How to Help the Child Who Is Bright, Bored, and Having Problems in School.* New York: Ballantine Books, 1999.

[13] As found in the King James Version of the *Holy Bible*, published by The Church of Jesus Christ of Latter-day Saints, 1979.

[14] Smith, Frank. *Reading Without Nonsense.* Teachers College Press, 2006.

[15] Ibid.

[16] Engelmann, Siegfried et al. *Teach Your Child to Read in 100 Easy Lessons.*

[17] Maslen, Bobby Lynn. *Bob Books.* Scholastic, 2006. There are currently Sets 1-5, plus additional specialty resources.

[18] Image is an inside view of a lesson from: Engelmann, Siegfried et al. *Teach Your Child to Read in 100 Easy Lessons.*

[19] Image depicts an inside view of my old picture dictionary given to me as a child that I loved and cherished. Watters, Garnette and S. A. Courtis. *The Picture Dictionary for Children.* New York: Grosset & Dunlap, 1972.

[20] Charlotte Mason, an only child and mostly schooled at home by her British parents, became a teacher who developed her own ideas in helping children learn. Those ideas are often used by some homeschoolers. A site dedicated to promoting her ideas is Simply Charlotte Mason found at http://simplycharlottemason.com/.

[21] These summarized definitions of twaddle and living books comes from the blog, The Original Simple Mom, written by Deborah Taylor-Hough, in the blog post entitled, "Recommended Children's Literature by Grade Level." It can be found here: http://thesimple mom.com/bookstores/recommended-reading/recommended-childrens-literature-by-grade-level/.

[22] The comic book featured in the photo is Volume 1 in the *Bone* series. Smith, Jeff. *Bone: Out From Boneville.* New York: Scholastic, 2005.

Chapter Eleven

Reading Stages of the
Right-Brained Learner

Shift Begins with Me

I smile knowingly as my fourth child (then 8 years old), who has been diagnosed with autism, skips past me in the hallway clutching his favorite book, Dr. Seuss' ABC. *My husband is unaware of the diversion heading his way as he enjoys a sports event on the small TV. He's always the willing participant, however, and creator of this popular little interaction. I soon hear emanating from the bedroom with a rousing beat—"Big A, little a, what begins with A—Aunt Annie's alligator—A, a, A."[1] I listen as my husband's well-orchestrated rhythmic sounds intermingle with my son's peals of laughter as a result of my husband's tickling fest. By the time they reach the letter C, the now long-lasting tradition reaches the ears of my then*

213

youngest son (6 at the time), who runs up to join the fun and his father's tickles. The boys patiently await their turns between letters as the beat increases and the physical interaction becomes wild.

The Dr. Seuss' ABC interaction is just one of the reading relationships my fourth son enjoyed over the years. It's a result of his perseverative interest in letters and numbers. One of the common symptoms of autism is that a child will perseverate, or have an intense focus on, an interest—sometimes exclusively, sometimes in an odd manner, and sometimes on something apparently useless. This son spent hours a day with alphabet puzzles, alphabet books, and alphabet toys. He knew his alphabet before he was two years old. The same was true of his numbers. He seemed to positively respond to the predictable pattern of letters and numbers. On the other hand, hearing words spoken to him was confusing, unpredictable, and frustrating. Books with patterned letters that created words were a source of comfort, pleasure, and predictability.

My fourth son was four years old when it occurred to me. I'd been trying to help him learn to speak and understand the spoken word, but it was slow going. He often misunderstood what he heard because of poor auditory input processing. Why not see if he could learn to read? If he could better understand the written word, would that help him understand what he was hearing of the spoken word? We could write things down as we spoke them. I saw that letters made sense to him, so maybe words would also. I bought a new flap book alphabet book and made picture flashcards of the words in the book.² Matching was his favorite way to learn, so I helped him learn these words separate from the book. He picked them up quickly. There were five words per letter, and I taught him through the letter H. Then I showed him the book containing his flashcard words and had him start *reading it with his new knowledge. His eyes lit up as he realized he could learn to read his alphabet books without someone having to read to him. His reading took off using these learning strategies.*

So many of us assume high intelligence (IQ) equates to early learning. And yet, this fourth son's IQ tests in the mentally retarded domain. It wasn't his intelligence factor that helped him learn to read at age 4. It was his strength in patterns and his love for letters. These strengths—and his readiness based on those strengths—helped him learn to read at age 4. His oldest brother has an IQ in the gifted domain. His strengths are in imagery and creativity. These strengths and his readiness based on those strengths helped him learn to read at age 9.

Right-brained children are often very bright and inquisitive learners. The strengths and interests often associated with this brain processing preference require a different time frame for learning to read than found in our left-brained-centered schools. I have identified three stages to reading fluency for the right-brained learner: the pre-reading stage (5 to 7 years old), the learning to read stage (8 to 10 years old), and the pre-fluency stage (9 to 11 years old).

Pre-Reading Stage (5 to 7 Years Old)

All learners develop pre-skills specific to their brain processing preference that makes it easier to learn in the appropriate time frame. Right-brained children build pre-reading skills during the 5 to 7 year time frame in preparation for learning to read during the 8 to 10 year time frame. The pre-reading skills are:

✓ Building a library of pictorial images
✓ Developing strong visualization skills
✓ Enjoying a positive relationship with print

Building a Library of Pictorial Images

The first pre-reading skill is building a library of pictorial images. This is best accomplished through the use of visual resources and real life experiences. Visual resources have images that can be seen and filed away in the right-brained, picture-storing mind. Real life experiences have live images that can be seen and filed away in the right-brained, picture-storing mind.

The creative outlets (see Chapter Six) all require a real interactive experience. Theater is a live picture. Dance is a live moving picture. LEGO® is a real spatial picture. Photography, cooking, video games, puppetry, sewing, gardening—all involve live images. Because there's a creative element to these activities, it more directly opens the right-brained, picture-storing mind.

Each step of creating this doll involved a visual or spatial picture.

Books, computer software, and certain educational material are all great sources for visual picture input for the young right-brained child. We began our book collection before children arrived. With our firstborn came the enlarged collection of board books, then picture books, then intellectually engaging visual books like *Eyewitness Books*, *Kids Discover®* magazine, *Zoobooks®*, atlases, Aliki, *Magic School Bus*, visual experiment books and more.[3] My artist son amazed me with what he gleaned from the pictorials in these resources. When he wanted to know more, he asked for assistance. His inability to read didn't infringe on knowledge acquisition because he had access to an available parent. Educational computer software, such as *Encarta®*, *GeoSafari®*, and *JumpStart®,* as well as educational videos, were favorites. There are plenty of materials available that contribute to learning to read by combining visuals with print. These include children's picture dictionaries, picture flashcards, word magnets, *Boggle*™ and other word games, turning on the television's closed captioning, *Bob Books®*, and *Leap Frog®* videos. Above all were lots of discussions and conversations—a main staple for a highly intelligent person. Each of these venues was part of the scaffolding toward the acquisition to reading for each of my children.

Developing Strong Visualization Skills

The next pre-reading skill is the ability to visualize. After the translation process from word to pictures is complete, visualizing the individual pictures as a whole unit is key to comprehension. In fact, right-brained people often share that reading can be translated into a moving picture like the big screen movies! Strong visualization skills are important to a right-brained child's learning process.

I can't stress enough the importance of creative outlets in the lives of right-brained, creative people. These activities inherently develop and showcase the strengths of the right-brained person (see Chapter Six). Creative outlets help visualization skills develop naturally. When a right-brained child creates a new LEGO® model, he visualizes. When a right-brained child creates a piece of art or drawing, she visualizes. When a right-brained child creates a dance routine, he visualizes. When a right-brained child creates a cooking concoction, she visualizes. Visualization is essential for the right-brained learner to become a fluent reader.

Developing pre-skills for reading should include a well-matched activity that includes books themselves. Listening to

read-alouds and audio books is that activity (see Chapter Nine for read-aloud benefits to right-brained children).

Listening to read-alouds develops important pre-reading skills.

Read-aloud times with my two oldest children revealed how well this activity develops the visualization skill. During or after a reading, my two oldest children frequently talked to each other about the characters in the story and compared their drawings and visualizations. They asked me what I thought various characters looked like and offered to draw them for me. I realized how visual my children are, down to minute details they can replicate on paper. I "feel" characters with more of a fuzzy visual image, which I can connect to another visual character or person I've seen before, because I can't conjure a visual image for myself. Once, during a read-aloud, I shared a visual representation of a character, and my artist son was shocked. According to him, my rendering was completely inaccurate of the author's original description. *I* was shocked when he searched for and found the character description in the book series, two books earlier, within about five minutes. Now that's amazing visual memory!

Enjoying a Positive Relationship with Print

The last pre-skill needed is developing and enjoying a positive relationship with print. As parents and teachers feel pressure surrounding reading acquisition for their children in the 5 to 7 year time frame, right-brained children can inadvertently be exposed to unpleasant experiences with books. Right-brained children are highly sensitive individuals and they are the first to turn on themselves ("I'm stupid") or on the activity ("I hate reading"). Each of these reactions can result in avoiding books and reading altogether (if I can't do it well, I won't do it at all). By understanding the concepts found in this book, right-brained children can be supported in enjoying positive relationships with print.

As noted consistently throughout this book, listening to read-alouds and audio books is a key skill-building activity for right-brained children. But, it has to be done their way. Initially, I thought read-aloud time meant my children sitting in my lap or next to me on the couch and looking mesmerized into the book as I read each page. This wasn't typically true of my right-brained children. My children always drew, colored, or built LEGO® as they listened to the reading. I could never do that! I have to concentrate when I listen to someone read. What I discovered is many right-brained learners need to "turn on" their creativity (housed on the right side of the brain) to attend to a passive (listening) or left-brained (translating words to pictures) activity. Their independently chosen creative pursuit engaged the right side of the brain so they could be at peak focus. Right-brained children are simply using their best assets to create a positive relationship with print.

Another popular resource that helped my children enjoy a positive relationship with print was a book about how to make books, *Read! Write! Publish!,* particularly featuring visual-based books.[4] Each of this book's two-page spreads showed a visual and pictorial type of book, and how to create it alone or with minimal adult preparation. (The book contains forms that can be copied to make creation easier.) Another common activity for my children was making their own comic strips. Visual and pictorial book making, with words added extraneously, was a legitimate way to value a right-brained path to enjoying a positive relationship with print material. This approach also exposed the children to reading opportunities through creative writing (see Chapter Thirteen).

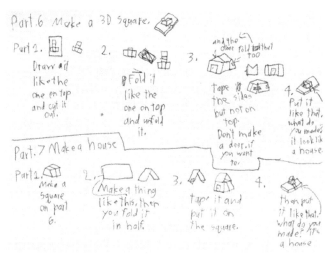

Visual and pictorial book making is one way to build a positive relationship with print. This is a page from my builder son's book about how to make a pop-up book, inspired by the resource, Read! Write! Publish!

Learning to Read Stage (8 to 10 Years Old)

Every learner uses the strengths specific to their brain processing preference to learn a skill. Right-brained children typically begin to learn to read during the 8 to 10 year time frame. (See Chapter Ten for some common exceptions.) The strengths for right-brained children that will be relied on in the reading acquisition process are:

- ✓ Word-to-picture translations
- ✓ Picture and story context
- ✓ Sight word base (with phonics "behind" it)

Word-to-Picture Translations

Right-brained children use the pre-reading skill strengths of strong visualization and a large mental picture library to assist them in learning to read. Since right-brained people think in pictures, every word is translated into a picture during the reading process. Because of word-to-picture translations, several unique traits are revealed.

Right-brained children typically read large, visual words before little, non-visual ones. Why? Because a word like "encyclopedia" is easily translated to a picture, but a word like "the" isn't. Examples of other large, visual words are "comforter," "giraffe," and "restaurant." Each of these words conjures up an immediate image. Dolch[5] words (see chart below) are many of the smaller, non-visual words that are difficult for right-brained children to read because it's hard to produce an image—words such as "has," "is," "of," and "been." Yet, schools *begin* reading instruction with the Dolch words, figuring the shorter the word, the easier to remember, right? That's based on the strength of the left-brained learner who often uses memorization to learn (see Chapter Seven). Instead of learning these smaller words first, right-brained learners often learn them last, usually about a year after reading commences.

a, about, after, again, all, always, am, an, and, any, are, around, as, ask, at, ate, away, be, because, been, before, best, better, big, black, blue, both, bring, brown, but, buy, by, call, came, can, carry, clean, cold, come, could, cut, did, do, does, done, don't, down, draw, drink, eat, eight, every, fall, far, fast, find, first, five, fly, four, found, four, from, full, funny, gave, get, give, go, goes, going, good, got, green, grow, had, has, have, he, help, her, here, him, his, hold, hot, how, hurt, I, if, in, into, is, it, its, jump, just, keep, kind, know, laugh, let, light, like, little, live, long, look, made, make, many, may, me, much, must, my, myself, never, new, no, not, now, of, off, old, on, once, one, only, open, or, our, out, over, own, pick, play, please, pretty, pull, put, ran, read, red, ride, right, round, run, said, saw, say, see, seven, shall, she, show, sing, sit, six, sleep, small, so, some, soon, start, stop, take, tell, ten, thank, that, the, their, them, then, there, these, they, think, this, those, three, to, today, together, too, try, two, under, up, upon, us, walk, want, warm, was, wash, we, well, went, were, what, when, where, which, white, who why, will, wish, with, work, would, write, yellow, yes, you, your

The Dolch words are often the last words learned by right-brained readers.

How can a reader understand what's read if he doesn't know many of those Dolch words? Knowing how and why a right-brained learner reads answers this question. Right-brained people are "skim readers" who glide across the top of words enough to "catch the visual." In the early stages of learning to read, a right-brained learner may skip a third of what he reads because all he needs is enough to "catch the visual." He can effectively develop reading style and fluency without knowing all the little filler words until later. To illustrate, my right-brained son's first reading effort was *The Lost World*, an adult novel. He read this book within weeks of learning reading basics, so I asked him, "Are you understanding that book?" to which he replied, "Enough." That's often all that's required while they're in the pre-fluency stage.

Picture and Story Context

Right-brained people think in pictures. If pictures are removed, could that be likened to making a right-brained person blind? Does removal "disable" his process? Pictures are how a right-brained learner makes sense of his world.

Pictures need to be part of a good reading program. Many programs, including *Teach Your Child to Read in 100 Easy Lessons*, recommend covering up the pictures to see if the child comprehends what he read. However, that's removing a right-brained learner's best asset! At first, I obeyed the instructions and covered up the picture, but my curious artist son kept pushing my hand out of the way. He was too distracted to read without first seeing the pictorial image that enhanced the experience for him. I easily conceded and gave value to his own instinct to honor his learning style.

Teach Your Child to Read in 100 Easy Lessons presents stories with visuals right away. Therefore, all of the first words learned are in the context of a picture. Since the system is about creating stories, the book starts off with easy-to-visualize words important to the story. Filler words that are difficult to visualize were brought up in context. The book clearly shows that there are some words (particularly those Dolch words like "the," "of," and "has") that just have to be memorized: they make no phonetic sense, and no visual sense, either.

Bob Books® are laden with pictorial imagery to highlight the reading material's words and content. Even the mini phonics lessons at the beginning of each book are illustrated. Sadly, I've seen programs use nonsense sentences to make sure a child isn't using picture context to "cheat." Given what we know about how a right-brained child learns to read, this negative conditioning about using pictorial context as a legitimate tool to learning to read is unfortunate.

Mac ran to Ruff.

Mac, Muff, and Ruff tug.

Visual context, such as in Bob Books®, *is an important part of the reading process for right-brained children. (Image[6])*

As with word-to-picture translations, a couple of unique traits arise from the picture and story context skill. Sometimes, right-brained children appear to guess at words. This is because they're trying to read by context as well as knowledge. This "word guessing" will correct itself through context and practice if the visualization skills are working and they are concentrating on comprehension and not semantics.

Another unique variation for some right-brained children is substituting a synonym for a word. For instance, the child reads the word "couch," translates the word to a picture in his mind, places the word "couch" under the picture in his mind's visual filing system, and moves on. The right-brained child then encounters the word "sofa" as he reads. As he translates the word into a picture in his mind, he chooses to use the one already created and stored in his mind. He looks at the word "couch" filed under the picture in his mind, and reads "couch" instead of "sofa." In actuality, substituting "couch" for "sofa" doesn't change the context of the story. This phenomenon confirms that context is more important than semantics for right-brained readers.

Sight Word Base

As outlined, the strengths-based way for a right-brained person to read is skimming across the top to "catch the visual," translating words to pictures, and using picture and story context to capture the meaning of the story. Due to these traits, combined with the whole-to-part core trait of a right-brained learner, a sight word based learning method is best on the front end, with some general phonics information either interspersed throughout, or included during the pre-fluency time. *Bob Books®* are a good example of this as they're set up as sight word base instruction using picture context while throwing in short phonics lessons to support the material.

An ongoing debate surrounds phonics versus sight word, but when the way people read is analyzed, a strong sight word base prevails. In *Reading without Nonsense*, author Frank Smith reminds us that it's even difficult for computers to be programmed for text-to-speech. Smith illuminates the reason:

> *Here are 11 common words in each of which the initial HO has a different pronunciation: hot, hope, hook, hoot, house, hoist, horse, horizon, honey, hour, honest. Can anyone really believe that a child could identify these words by sounding out the letters?*[7]

224

Smith clarifies when he says, "Phonics will in fact prove of use—provided you have a rough idea of what a word is." This is why I advocate what I call a "phonics program behind a sight word approach." Though *Teach Your Child to Read in 100 Easy Lessons* is considered a phonics program, we converted its contents into a sight word base review. For instance, we didn't follow the scripts, skipped most repetition, and converted each exercise to a sight word foundation. Interestingly, the visual phonetic cues utilized in this system appear to support children learning the words more easily as sight words. My artist son used these visual prompts to more easily view the word as an entire chunk because it enabled him to see at a glance how a word should be pronounced (or what should not), particularly in context of a story. The visual cues continue well over halfway through the lessons enabling a right-brained learner to visualize the words as part of their sight word repertoire before the visual prompts disappear.

Pre-Fluency Stage (9 to 11 Years Old)

Left-brained learners become fluent readers by starting with early readers, then systematically advancing through "graded readers." A right-brained reader becomes fluent in a completely different way. The key to fluency is interest—through highly visually appealing and creative plot lines that are readily visualized. There are three ways to support this criterion:

- ✓ Use visual resources to help concentrate on semantics
- ✓ Use a book series to help predict visual and semantic patterns
- ✓ Use silent reading to "practice"

Visual Resources

The types of reading materials our creative learners most gravitate to while they are in the pre-fluency stage are highly visual materials such as comic books, magazines, and manga. Why? Remember, the most important aspect of their reading is "catching the visual." If they have to master the semantics of reading *and* catch the visual, it's difficult because they have to have a certain level of fluency to catch that visual. If you read material that already has the visual captured for you, then you can concentrate on the semantics! This is also why our creative learners still want you to read aloud to them or bring in books on tape. These offer additional ways for them to catch the visual before reading the material themselves so they can concentrate on working out the semantics when reading the words.

Some right-brained children use Calvin & Hobbes *comics as their primary reading program. (Image[8])*

My creative learners moved away from highly visual material when around 11 to 12 years old (after the pre-fluency stage at around 9 to 11 years old). Does that mean they'll discard these resources completely? No. They often continue to prefer the visual medium of comics and magazines, but they will have gained enough competence and confidence to begin reading non-visual material as well.

Book Series

I always assumed the reason for a book series is to provide more of a good thing—readers enjoy the series so make more! Through my right-brained children, I discovered another important use for a book series that supports the way right-brained children become fluent readers.

As just discussed, it's difficult for right-brained children to simultaneously translate words *and* visualize the story. Reading a book series helps ease both of these jobs for the right-brained reader. When I read a book series aloud first, my right-brained reader was pre-exposed to some of the rhythm, visuals, and words involved in the story. Prior exposure to the book's attributes during the read-aloud made it easier for that child to "catch the visual" and predict the storyline as he tried to read it himself. Some popular book series for right-brained children are *The Boxcar Children, American Girls, Captain Underpants, Junie B. Jones,* and *Magic Tree House.*[9]

In the same vein, I might choose a more difficult series, one that my child might not feel up to tackling on his own. Once his appetite was whetted, he was motivated to continue with the series on his own and could generalize the particular rhythm, visual, and words associated with the series without the need for a "pre-read." *Redwall, The Borrowers,* the *Tennis Shoes Adventure Series,* and *Harry Potter* are some book series I used in this way.[10]

Silent Reading

As a left-brained learner who was more than eager to painlessly learn to read in first grade, I'd often be the first to volunteer to read out loud in the classroom. I also saw those who would slink down in their seats, avoid eye contact, dreading the idea while expecting the laughter as they painfully struggled through the request to read aloud. Most likely, these reluctant readers were right-brained dominant. We're conditioned to believe that reading aloud well proves a person is a proficient reader. Actually, all it shows is that a person is at a fluent reader stage.

As discussed previously, a right-brained pre-fluent reader may skip words, replace words, or guess at words. If right-brained children are asked to read out loud during the pre-fluency time frame, it can cast a spotlight on these fluency differences and make the child feel incompetent. During silent reading, fluency differences won't be noticed because "catching the visual" masks them until they're worked out over time. Most important, silent reading matches the right-brained learning style. Some people ask, "How do we know if a child is learning to read if a parent or teacher doesn't require him to read aloud?" I asked my children questions about what they were reading—legitimate questions—because I wanted to share in their reading choices. If they can answer questions about what they're reading, then the skill must be developed enough to fill its role: comprehension.

One of my children illustrates the right-brained pre-fluency reading path well. My fifth child chose to read out loud as a way to socially connect as he was learning to read. At 7.5 years old he would skip or slaughter the small Dolch words as well as periodically interchange a synonym for a word. I tried to carefully correct him and saw him stare at me in confusion. He didn't know what I was talking about and he didn't see the point at the time. I let it be as he enjoyed reading aloud and was unaware of "mistakes" at this point. About 9 to 12 months later, I was listening to him read aloud again. He was a fluent reader: no skipped words, no substitutions, nice rhythm.

I observed my electronics son work out his right-brained fluency differences on his own without my intervention since he was my only child who initiated reading aloud.

When we honor and value the natural process to reading fluency for each learning style, reading acquisition occurs painlessly. When we interfere with the preferred process to reading with our conditioned requirements, such as reading aloud, reading every word, not using context, and sounding out every word, stilted reading can occur. In a workshop about the right-brained learner, I spoke of this natural process for the right-brained child for acquiring reading fluency. One adult woman raised her hand and declared she now understood what happened to her in college.

Because of her schooling experience in learning to read, this woman was a painfully slow reader. Upon entering college, she was required to take a speed reading class as a study skill prerequisite. She lamented the silliness of a poor reader learning how to speed read. Lo and behold, upon completion of the class, she could read normally! She now understood that somehow she relearned in that time frame, using those techniques, the way she was naturally meant to read to begin with (skimming across the top of words to "catch the visual"). She was a right-brained learner.

Creative learners are often highly sensitive as well as perfectionists. They like to watch, and then do it well the first time. If there has been any type of "testing," such as asking them to read aloud during pre-fluency (when they may not yet pick up every word just right), or asking them questions without allowing them to use their best strategies (like visual materials to help "catch the visual"), or making them sound

229

out words (which bogs them down in the semantics), you may have a resistant creative learner (see Chapter Eight). The best way to counter these roadblocks is to understand and honor the natural learning path for right-brained, creative children found in this book. We need to value the right-side of normal in our learning environments.

References and Notes

[1] Seuss, Dr. *Dr. Seuss' ABC.* Random House Beginner Books, 1991.

[2] The flap book I bought to teach my son with autism to read was: Tucker, Sian. *A Is for Astronaut (My First Lift-the-Flap ABC).* Little Simon, 1995.

[3] The resources listed in this sentence are as follows: For the *Eyewitness Books,* see reference #3 in Chapter Ten. For *Kids Discover®* magazine, visit their website at http://www.kidsdiscover.com/. For *Zoobooks®,* visit their website at http://www.zoobooks.com/. Aliki is an American children's author and illustrator with at least 80 titles to her credit. One such book we had was Aliki. *Dinosaurs Are Different.* Collins, 1986. The *Magic School Bus* series is a highly visual, almost comic-style of storytelling that integrates facts within a storyline. One that we had was: Cole, Joanna. *The Magic School Bus Inside the Human Body.* Scholastic Press, 1990.

[4] Fairfax, Barbara and Adela Garcia. *Read! Write! Publish!: Making Books in the Classroom Grades 1-5.* Creative Teaching Press, 1998.

[5] Dolch words are the top 220 high frequency sight words that can't be learned by pictures or phonics.

[6] This is a two-page spread from within Set 1, Book 8, of the *Bob* Book series called "Muff and Ruff." Maslen, Bobby Lynn. *Bob Books.* Scholastic, 2006.

[7] Smith, Frank. *Reading Without Nonsense.* Teachers College Press, 2006.

[8] The resource used in this image is: Watterson, Bill. *The Indispensable Calvin and Hobbes.* Kansas City: Andrews McMeel, 1992, p. 183.

[9] The resources listed include: Warner, Gertrude Chandler. *The Boxcar Children* series. Albert Whitman & Company, 1924-1976. The first 19 in the series were

written by the original author. There are 111 other books in the series written by various authors. About half of the *American Girl* series books were written by Valerie Tripp. Each girl has a set of six books. There are currently eleven girls: Addy, Felicity & Elizabeth, Josefina, Julie & Ivy, Kaya, Kirsten, Kit & Ruthie, Marie-Grace & Cecile, Molly & Emily, Rebecca, and Samantha & Nellie. Pilkey, Dav. *Captain Underpants* series. The Blue Sky Press, 1997-2006. There are currently eight books in this series, with two more slated. Park, Barbara. *Junie B. Jones*. Random House, 1992-2007. There are currently 27 books in the series with two other specialty books. Osborne, Mary Pope. *Magic Treehouse* series, Random House, 1992-2012. There are currently 28 books in the first series, and 20 books in the second, with another slated.

[10] The resources listed include: Jacques, Brian. *Redwall* series, 1986-2011. There are 22 books in the series. Norton, Mary. *The Borrowers* series, 1952-1982. There are five books in the series. Heimerdinger, Chris. *Tennis Shoes Adventure Series*. 1989-2012. There are currently twelve books in the series. Rowling, J.K. *Harry Potter* series, 1999-2009. There are seven books in the series.

Chapter Twelve

Building the Road
to Math Competency

Shift Begins with Me

I was in third grade. Learning came easily to me in elementary school and I was content. Maybe it was the teacher who noticed I was the first one done—without breaking a sweat—every time we did math. A boy in my class was in the same boat. Back then we had no gifted and talented programs, but apparently the teacher felt that we should be more challenged. She decided to get the next grade level textbook, move us to the hallway, and let us move ahead in our math proficiency. Though the two of us had an easy time with math in the classroom, we didn't know how to figure out for ourselves how to learn new material from the book. I think we studied in the hallway for about two weeks before everyone knew it was ineffective.

Once I reached junior high where each student chose individual classes to attend, the administrators encouraged me to skip ahead a grade level in math. I remember it was more challenging, but I also remember thinking it was nicer just to glide through easily. I stayed in the higher level class, though, because I was an obedient student. Eventually I took algebra and enjoyed that quite a bit, but next came geometry. I squeaked through that class with the average score needed to pass. I valiantly utilized my standard strategy of plugging in formulas to get the neat, packaged answer, but geometry didn't operate that way. It was application and concept based, and that style of math thinking was foreign to me.

Next I was back in second level algebra in high school, and again in my comfort level in the math domain. At that same time, I was carving out a greater social and athletic school life. By the time I hit third level algebra, I was losing interest in developing any kind of talent I might have in math. Plus, it was first period and it was difficult to stay awake. I had a young new teacher, too, who tried hard to give problems that made you apply the knowledge you were learning. Being stretched that way, I was lost. Even though I was an A/B student, I flunked this class, the only time ever.

I still consider myself proficient in math, but I also recognize my particular math skill limitations. As a left-brained learner, I enjoyed manipulating numbers, and I found an accounting class in business college interesting and enjoyable. I seemed to instinctively understand I was skilled for this style of math. I now realize there are different types of math proficiency, each valid in its own right, but often misunderstood.

Parents and educators everywhere are most concerned about skills related to memorizing one's math facts and learning to read. These are the most talked-about topics on my e-mail support list about right-brained learners.[1] In the previous two chapters, I've delineated the right-brained learner traits that explain why a right-brained child comes to reading "later" than the prescribed time frame in public institutions of learning. I shared the optimal time frame and procedure to help a right-brained child learn to read joyfully. This chapter reveals the same for learning math facts, and math in general, in a right-brained fashion.

I uncovered two ways right-brained children pursue math. Those most likely to have a gift in math will take a hands-on, spatial approach to learning it. Those most likely to simply want a competency in math will take a visual, mental math approach to learning it. Let's look at the journey my builder son took for learning and loving math (appears under "The Spatial Approach"), and the journey my artist son took for being competent in math (appears under "The Visual Approach"), along with general right-brained math learning information.

Math Pre-Skill Development (2 to 4 Years Old)

As mentioned in Chapter Six, pursuing creative outlets strengthen the right-brained learner's gifts. These gifts naturally strengthen the universal traits of the right-brained learner in the early years and prepare him for left-brained based academic tasks down the road. Often, a right-brained child discovers these creative endeavors between the ages of 2 and 4, and really delves into them between the ages of 5 and 7. At this stage, a creative child may engage in these creative pursuits four to six hours a day in a way that others tend to view as "play." It's not; it's serious business and the foundation of their gift development. It was through the creative outlets I noticed my right-brained children begin developing math pre-skills.

The Spatial Approach

My builder son was able to flourish in his gift of math because he was able to develop his strong spatial awareness, pattern recognition, and visual attunements through the creative outlets that encourage it. Puzzles/mazes, building/ electronics, and music/dance are the creative outlets most conducive to developing these skills.

Puzzles/Mazes. Like many preschoolers, my builder son enjoyed puzzles. He started around 18 months old after taking notice of his older siblings' alphabet puzzle. While visiting, my mother was impressed that he could do it (upside down at that time she watched him). I think he used the shape of the puzzle to find its match, while working upside down, showing early spatial ability. My builder son moved on to 50 and 100 piece puzzles by age 4, worked on "expert level" three-dimensional puzzles by age 9, and periodically completed 1,000 piece puzzles by age 11.

Three-dimensional puzzle building relies on spatial gifts. (Image[2])

Similarly, he enjoyed the dot-to-dots I introduced to him between 5 and 6 years old. Online I found and printed mazes I thought he'd like. During this time, I showed him how tracing paper works. He used this to trace the mazes I gave him. This sparked ideas, as you may recall from the free-drawn mazes in Chapter Six.

Compared to my older right-brained artist son's "normal" interest in puzzles and mazes, I knew my builder son's interest was deeper. It was obvious, in hindsight, that he gained a lot of spatial, visual, and pattern experiences that later would translate into a math gift.

Building/Electronics. When thinking of childhood building, LEGO® immediately comes to mind. My builder son certainly gathered a huge collection of LEGO® through his building stage, but he showed the building domain has many facets. As shared in Chapter Five, building track configurations for trains takes spatial ability. Spatial ability is a foundation for math skills. We moved a lot while my older children were growing up, and my builder son always established a train building area in each new house.

My builder son always had a "corner" of a room for train building.

All types of building material were fair game for my builder son to explore and develop his spatial skills. There were specialty sets, such as a screw and nail building set, a car ramp and road building set, and a road and train mountain set. There were traditional sets, such as Tinkertoy®, Lincoln Logs®, and even paper and tape. I remember receiving a big surprise when I walked into his room and found that he had taken the Lincoln Logs® pieces and laid them out to represent all the single digit numbers. He was about age 4.5 years. I guess that was my first indication that he would naturally be drawn to math!

A right-brained child will explore and experiment with building tools.

It was only a matter of time before LEGO® entered the scene. My builder son started dabbling with it around 4 years old, and continued to around 14 years old. Besides traditional LEGO® blocks, he enjoyed TECHNIC™, LEGO® Studio, MINDSTORMS®, and K'NEX® (see Chapter Six). He always built with the actual directions the first time, and then he'd build his own creations. It takes great visualization and spatial ability to create novel LEGO® designs.

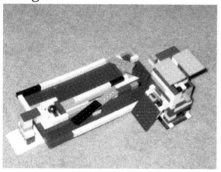

A novel LEGO® contraption built by my builder son.

My son's building focus, beginning at 18 months with trains and continuing to age 14 with LEGO®, were the foundation for mathematical thinking. These activities developed the visualization and spatial skills that would serve him well both for math and computer programming. He spent at least 6 to 8 hours a day building during this time frame.

Music/Dance. Research indicates that listening to music can promote better mathematical ability, sometimes referred to as the "Mozart Effect." My experience with my builder son is noticing that the gift and skill needed to be competent in math, and the gift and skill needed to be naturally gifted in playing a musical instrument, is the same. That needed skill is a strong spatial awareness.

My builder son taught himself to play the piano at age 9 using his strong spatial ability. Although he eventually learned the names of the notes (probably around 12 to 13 years old), he still plays spatially. He sees that a particular note found on the paper falls on the piano in a particular location. He can do this with large groups of notes. Playing an instrument is an extension of strong spatial awareness. (See Chapter Six for the difference in playing verbally versus spatially.)

The Visual Approach

My artist son improved the gifts he needed to be competent in math because he was able to develop his strong visualization skills, symmetry recognition (noticing two opposite sides of an object are mirrors of each other), and auditory attunements through the creative outlets that encourage it. Art/photography, video games/computers, and dabbling in the puzzles/mazes and building/electronics side of things are the creative outlets most conducive to developing these skills.

Video game skills have been linked to good math ability.

Puzzles/Mazes. My artist son grew competent with puzzles in his toddler years. His interest in the visual picture he was piecing together was central to determining where each puzzle piece went. He often referenced the puzzle cover as he put it together, too. Puzzle construction continued through the 2 to 4 year stage for my artist son, with some dabbling with 100 piece puzzles at my request during the 5 to 7 year range.

Building/Electronics. During this pre-skill development stage, my firstborn artist son began our eventually extensive LEGO® collection. He was mostly interested in the castle line, and easily deciphered the visual directions that accompanied the sets. Completed sets became fodder for elaborate imaginary play scenarios in which he often engaged (see Chapter Five), assisting in developing his high level of visualization skills.

Drawing/Photography. Chapter 11 outlines how pre-reading stage activities are conducive to developing visualization skills for the right-brained child. This same visualization skill helps a visual learner like my artist son hone the skills needed to attain math competency. For this son, these activities included drawing, looking at visual books, and listening to read-alouds.

Video games/Computers. As soon as our family purchased computers and video games, my artist son took advantage of their benefits. He especially liked role-playing games (RPGs). RPGs require high levels of problem-solving abilities, spatial visualization, and math calculations and estimations. Chang Suo Hui of the National Institute of Education at Nanyang Technological University in Singapore confirms the connection between these types of computer games and math ability in his study. Hui chose "three different types of computer games namely, simulation, role-play and quest or adventure...for the study." He discovered that "pupils who are normally uninterested in mathematics stayed on task in games that required tedious computations and problem solving."[3]

Conversations. I haven't written much about the benefit of conversation, especially for the gifted, those with strong auditory skills, and those with high verbal ability. Conversation more fully develops all of these attributes at the same time it provides additional opportunity to practice visualization by translating spoken word to pictures and back

again. Conversation was a staple in my oldest son's learning life and an important catalyst for his engaging in mental math.

My artist son and builder son engaging in visual activities.

My artist son's ability to draw pictures, play RPG video games, and have many conversations were physical representations of his particular right-brained skills and gifts. My builder son's ability to complete puzzles and mazes, play piano, and construct using various building materials were physical representations of *his* particular right-brained skills and gifts. Due to growing and learning in an environment where all types of activities, play, and experimentation were valued, the skills and gifts that were my builder son's and artist son's areas of expertise were accessed.

Beginning Mathematics (5 to 7 Years Old)

There's a difference between arithmetic and mathematics. Here's how I differentiate the two in this book. Arithmetic is the act of manipulating quantities (facts); mathematics is the science of finding patterns, coming up with theories about it, and proving its existence (concepts). Elementary schools primarily focus on arithmetic. Learning one's "math facts" is arithmetic. Even most of high school "math" would be

240

considered arithmetic because of how it's presented (formulas to be plugged into problems). Right-brained learners are natural mathematicians. Left-brained learners are most comfortable with arithmetic. One way to tell if you're right-brained or left-brained is to ask: Did I do better at geometry or algebra? If geometry, then you're most likely right-brained; if algebra, then you're most likely left-brained.

The current scope and sequence found in our schools prefers to teach math facts (arithmetic) sequentially, and move toward learning math concepts (mathematics). Our right-brained learners prefer to understand math concepts in the early years, while they're still focused on three-dimensional, hands-on interactions, and move toward learning math facts. In actuality, it's often a right-brained child's desire to know the purpose of mathematics (big picture thinking) that inspires him to learn the details of arithmetic (see Chapter Seven). For right-brained children, early math development should begin with focusing on mathematics, not arithmetic.

The Spatial Approach

Between the ages of 5 and 7 years old, when school introduces arithmetic with addition and subtraction facts, a right-brained learner is more ready for mathematics. Without knowing this, I recognized this was the path that my builder son took to learning and loving math. At this stage my builder son started dabbling in areas our society recognizes as "math." The first resource my 5-year-old builder son found on my shelf was a book called *Geometry Puzzles*.[4] This math manipulatives book contains pattern challenges using two-dimensional pentominoes. He spent hours "puzzling" over the challenges found therein (as seen in the photo at the beginning of this chapter). I could see that math intrigued him, so I started introducing other spatial-oriented activities. From ages 5 to 7, my builder son discovered manipulative-based logic math experiences using pentominoes, tangrams, geoboards, pattern blocks, 100 boards, linking cubes, scales, and more. When a companion book can be found for these math manipulatives that offers challenges, pattern creations, and thinking skills, it can spark even more in-depth math concept exploration and understanding.

Because right-brained learners are creative as their foundational trait, encouraging self-exploration and discovery can be the best strategy in promoting a hands-on learner to understand early math concepts. Manipulatives can be used to "build concepts" of beginning arithmetic such as addition or subtraction as well as depict story problems. My builder son showed me how the concepts of math and arithmetic patterns can be applied to learn a new skill. The following example was how he used addition to do a multiplication problem using patterns for a shortcut:

$$
\begin{array}{r}
23 \\
\times 18 \\
\hline
\end{array}
$$

23	1
+23	1
46	2
+46	2
92	4
+92	4
184	8
+184	8
368	16
+46	2
414	18

Right-brained builders are pattern-finders. My builder son used an addition pattern to solve a multiplication problem.

The Visual Approach

Just as my builder son preferred the spatial focus that math manipulatives provide, my artist son steered toward visual resources and mental imagery. He preferred mental math games and activities in the 5 to 7 year range that utilized his advanced visualization abilities and strong verbal skills. Math histories and math literature are good sources (and read-alouds) for this style of right-brained learner because they tap into his natural love of a good story along with strong visualization skills. Many visual-based concept-centered math stories are on the market today.[5]

Beginning Arithmetic (8 to 10 Years Old)

The right-brained learner is most ready to learn arithmetic starting between the ages of 8 and 10 years old, after the "age of shifting" from primarily viewing everything from a three-dimensional perspective, to the ability to include two-dimensional, symbolic processing. Right-brained learners remember best by using long-term memory. Long-term memory works best with learning by association. This is why math concepts (mathematics) are the foundation for the right-brained child learning math. Left-brained learners remember best by using short-term memory. Short-term memory works well with learning by memorization. This is why math facts (arithmetic) are the foundation for the left-brained child learning math. However, our schooling system primarily uses short-term memory strategies for learning all information, including math. Right-brained children need to use long-term memory to learn arithmetic, and that requires its own set of strategies for learning math facts.

Exploration through Percolation Time

For the right-brained child to learn arithmetic, one must tap into the math concepts explored during the 5 to 7 year time frame that are stored in long-term memory. My right-brained children learned arithmetic utilizing "percolation time" (see Chapter Nine) and short-teaching moments hooked to their learning style. To ease the transition from a math concept focus to applying and understanding where math facts fit into the big picture, "short teaching moments" were instituted. Short teaching moments were 10 to 15 minutes approximately three times a week. I gave a child one piece of information at a time utilizing his preferred learning style (hands-on or visual input), and then allowed "percolating time." Percolation time allows time for the brain to access similar information stored in long-term memory, then link the new information to it to make sense (big picture thinking).

The Spatial Approach. I might show how addition works with linking blocks (hands-on and spatial), write out what the "symbols" look like, then provide access to other numbers (math facts) to play around with and figure out during the week. Exploration and experimentation, especially for builder types, tap into the right-brained learner's natural gifts of puzzling out, imagination, and creativity to promote retention and understanding.

As an example of a short teaching moment with percolation time, I shared "math tricks" with my builder son. For instance, as he explored addition and subtraction, I would explain the idea of doubling to get to a fact more quickly. "Did you know that if two numbers are close together, like 7 + 8, you can either double the 7 and add 1 or double the 8 and subtract 1?" He got so excited over the discovery that he created a "Math Trick Book," drawing out the concepts and making his own "now you try it" section. This worked well because my builder son was making these types of "how to books" for his train drawing. He linked this type of information to his stage of wanting to share "tricks of the trade." I noticed and capitalized on it. As is typical of a right-brained learner, upon learning new concepts, he often took the information back to a creative outlet to play around with the idea in a creative context and/or expression (drawing and building, in this case).

Opportunities regularly arose that showed my builder son how his amazing spatial skills related to real life situations, such as numerous trips to science museums where math and science often interplay with hands-on puzzles and maze creations.

Science museums are great places for right-brained builders.

The Visual Approach. I used percolation time and short teaching moments to learn arithmetic with my visual son, too. (Remember, it's usually at 8 to 10 years old for addition and subtraction facts and 11 to 13 years old for multiplication facts.) Visual tools can be effective in linking to long-term associative memory. Visual tools are those resources that can be visualized, such as a multiplication chart; or for addition facts, a number line, abacus, or a hundred chart.

I gave my visual, right-brained learner three to five math facts to complete *using* the visual tool. After doing this daily for about three months, suddenly my right-brained learner knew the answers from the sheer visual repetition of looking them up. Often, the visual tool becomes a visualization recall and a permanent tool within right-brained learners' minds to pull up and access. A calculator may not be as effective because the answer suddenly appears, so a right-brained child can't visualize the process of getting to the answer. A math problem can be "calculated" inside a right-brained child's mind on a visualized abacus.

A storyline and characters hooked to the numbers and answers are another visual resource similar to mnemonics (see Chapter Seven). *Times Tales*™ is an example of this type of resource.[6]

Common Myths about Right-Brained Math Processes

During the 5 to 7 and 8 to 10 year time frames, a variety of societal conditioning needs to be addressed.

A Spatial Example. Hands-on learners may need to touch manipulatives to learn and understand math. Fingers are handy and may be used to calculate. We're taught to consider this cheating or infantile, but it's simply utilizing what's available to process the information *in a way that works for the learner.* An abacus, number line, dominoes, hundreds charts, tens frames, and other manipulatives can all serve the same purpose.

A Visual Example. Another societally-conditioned math myth involves the implication that there's "one right way" to do something. Adding and subtracting numbers from right to left is a popular example of this. Schooling practices play on the strengths of the left-brained learner and establish a sequence to be meticulously followed to get an answer. Someone decided that the "formula" for adding and subtracting large numbers was to add from right to left, creating a borrowing formula for those numbers subtracting below zero, and a carry-over formula for those numbers adding up to more than ten. As a society, we now see this as the "one right way." One reason this came about is that if you add or subtract from left to right (which is logical since we read left to right), when an answer adds up to more than ten or subtracts less than zero, then you're in trouble. Not so for a right-brained concept learner!

Right-brained children understand higher concepts like negative numbers. It confuses them when an educator or parent tells them that adding or subtracting left to right "can't be done." A right-brained child will prove you wrong. See what my friend's right-brained child showed her (a left-brained parent). Interestingly, the method makes it easier to do horizontal problems. Take the addition problem 567+172. Adding left to right, 500+100=600, 60+70=130, and 7+2=9. So, 600+130+9=739. When a person adds this way, each number can be added to the previous number as he goes versus waiting until the end to add all of the numbers together. Now let's take the subtraction problem 567-172. 500-100=400, 60-70=(-10), and 7-2=5. So, 400-10+5=395. Again, you could subtract as you go. Those with visual mental math abilities find this "easy" and sensible.

$$
\begin{array}{rr}
567 & 567 \\
+172 & -172 \\
\hline
600 & 400 \\
130 & (-10) \\
+\ 9 & +\ 5 \\
\hline
739 & 395
\end{array}
$$

Adding and subtracting can be done left to right.

Just like highly verbal, right-brained learners may learn to read beginning at ages 5 to 7 instead of the traditional 8 to 10 time frame for most right-brained learners, a builder-type, right-brained learner may be able to begin arithmetic-style learning starting at ages 5 to 7 instead of the traditional 8 to 10 time frame. (An interesting side note, I notice it's usually either one or the other; it's rare to find a right-brained learner who starts both reading and arithmetic well in the 5 to 7 year time frame.) Knowing that math's "puzzle challenge" intrigued my builder son, I exposed him to simple addition and subtraction with short teaching moments from ages 5 to 7. However, I utilized the concept base with manipulatives (as explained in this section) to honor his three-dimensional time frame stage.

Formal Math Resources (11 to 13 Years Old)

It may seem counterintuitive—or outrageous—to delay formal mathematics instruction until 11 to 13 years old. However, a classic research study [7] showed that playing around with math *concepts* and *thinking skills*, as well as using math manipulatives to understand numbers in the early years, can promote better mathematical understanding and application leading to a faster learning curve in the later years. When was formal math introduced in this study? Sixth grade, or 11 to 12 years old. Most of my right-brained children started formal math learning at around 11 years old knowing the basics of addition and subtraction and the concepts of multiplication and division, yet by 14 were ready for algebra.

The Spatial Approach

As noted in the previous section, because of my builder son's interest in numbers, math concepts, and math manipulatives as one of his creative outlets and gifts, he wanted a more in-depth and formal math program at 8 years old. I experimented with the math series recommended by an admired unschooling friend. The series is called *Real Math*™.[8] Sponsored by the National Science Foundation, it takes the learner through pre-algebra. It highlights patterns in math and thinking skills with story problems, games, and other strategies; thus, it's a concept-based math program (the strength of a right-brained math learner). Unfortunately, it doesn't appear to be in print any longer. My son continued with this series until he was 14 years old. Other math programs good for builder math types are *Singapore Math*® and *Math-U-See*®.[9]

The Visual Approach

When it's time for formal resources, there are some elements to look for, especially for visual math people. Right-brained learners can become distracted with too many extraneous attention-grabbing visuals, so "clean pages" can be useful. Watch for resources with only a few problems on each page. This helps keep the learner focused without feeling overwhelmed sensorially or creatively. A resource that promotes real applications, experimentation, or game play taps into the natural learning style of the right-brained learner. My visual right-brained learner also enjoyed the *Real Math*™ series for its story problems and math games. A verbal/visual right-brained learner may also enjoy the *Life of Fred* series[10] that utilizes a humorous story to teach math concepts.

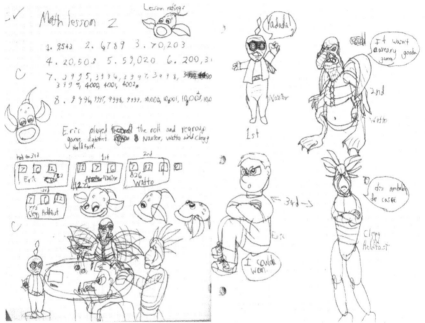

My artist son's math lesson with a dice game. No one was around to play with him, so he made up his own competition! A good math program utilizes concepts and creative thinking. (Image[11])

Career Path and Gift Development (14 to 16 Years Old)

As mentioned in Chapter Six, when the creative outlets are encouraged and valued, and the natural progression to learning various subjects is honored, our right-brained learners often choose a career path related to one of their passions. My builder son is no exception.

At around age 13, my builder son wanted to learn computer programming. We found some great books that kick-started him, and from ages 14 to 16, he programmed about 6 to 8 hours a day. At 14, he wanted a formal algebra program, tried a left-brained-oriented math series, hated it and asked for "a program that gives it to me straight." He switched to *Math-U-See®* and loved it. He "wanted it straight" because he naturally knows how to apply math to real activities. In fact, he was already using various math aspects in his programming (like graphing).

At 17, he took trigonometry at the community college, working up and through calculus and differential equations. He literally received 100% on his exams! He said that "when the instructor explains a concept, it's as if I already knew it." Math is "natural" to him. I often claim that math is his primary language, English his second.

I believe by honoring my builder son's natural progression through math, his creative outlets in the young years, and by feeding this gift that revealed itself in his middle years, together they created his passion for computer programming that filled his teen years and directed him to pursue it as a career. Because computer programming is so math based, he also intends to minor in math.

Was it memorizing math facts that helped my builder son excel in math? No. Was it his early manipulation of numbers that made me believe he was going to be proficient in math? No. It was his early interest in challenging himself with math manipulatives in pentominoes that got me thinking he might be proficient in math. It was his early drive to challenge himself to develop spatial skills with mazes, track configurations, and puzzles that made me believe he might be proficient in math. Mathematics requires the drive to puzzle out the challenge.

My builder son showcased the "likes to be challenged" attribute perfectly while in community college. When studying physics for the first time, he came home after class and declared, "Physics is the application of math." He immediately sat down and for hours experimented with physics concepts—outside of the homework required—for the challenge of it. His successful foray into math was an extension of his natural early interest in the informal conceptual skills and activities that precede the formal learning.

The Spatial and Visual Approaches

In his research paper, Hui states, "A typical mathematics classroom in Singapore, driven by quarterly summative formal assessment and tight syllabus coverage, predominately consists of chalk and talk as well as drills and practices. Although attempts are made to infuse more pupil-centered and engaging pedagogical ideas, they are reserved mainly for the lower primary pupils (i.e. Grade 1 and 2). As such, pupils from the upper primary (i.e. Grade 3 to 6) often perceive mathematics as boring."[12] American schools approach math much the same way. By concentrating on arithmetic instead of mathematics, problem-solving, and other innovative-rich attributes, schools present the "boring math," as my friend's right-brained son calls it. The "fun math" (as described by this same boy) brings into play the right-brained way of learning: the spatial and visual approaches to math skill development. Hui accidentally stumbled on video games as one positive contribution to math ability. This chapter outlines many more. We owe it to our right-brained learners to make room for the right side of normal that adds interest, involvement, and success for *all* students.

References and Notes

[1] My *Homeschooling Creatively* e-mail list advocating for the right-brained learning environment can be found at http://groups.yahoo.com/group/homeschoolingcreatively/.

[2] The puzzle my son completed in the photo is the Star Wars® Millennium Falcon™ 3-D puzzle. It's listed as "Super Challenging."

[3] Hui, Chang Suo. *Learning Mathematics Through Computer Games.* Singapore: Mathematics and Mathematics Education, National Institute of Education, Nanyang Technological University, 2009. http://atcm.mathandtech.org/EP2009/papers_full/2812009_17199.pdf (accessed June 13, 2012).

[4] Wells, Alison. *Take-Home Math: Geometry Puzzles, Grades 2-3.* Oak Lawn: Ideal School Supply Company, 1995.

[5] The website www.livingmath.net is a fabulous place to find visual-based, concept-centered math resources. The Living Math® site was created by Julie Brennan, CPA and homeschooling parent, from San Diego, California.

[6] Eggers, J. von, M. J. Flanagan & Dena L. Wood. *Times Tales.* Trigger Memory Systems, 2003. www.TimesTales.com.

[7] Benezet, L. P. "The Teaching of Arithmetic: The Story of an Experiment." Originally published in *Journal of the National Education Association* in three parts, 1935/1936: Vol. 24, #8, pp 241-244; Vol. 24, #9, p 301-303; & Vol. 25, #1, pp 7-8.

[8] Willoughby, Stephen S., Carl Bereiter, Peter Hilton, and Joseph H. Rubinstein. *Real Math.* La Salle: Open Court, 1991.

[9] A math series developed for students in Singapore, the Singapore Math® program can be found at their website at http://www.singaporemath.com/. Steve Demme, a former math teacher and homeschooling parent, created the Math-U-See® program after his popular math class for homeschoolers resulted in parents asking for his methods for their own use. The Math-U-See® information and products are found at their website at http://www.mathusee.com/.

[10] Schmidt, Stanley F. *Life of Fred.* Polka Dot Publishing, 2002. Ordering information can be found at this website: http://www.stanleyschmidt.com/FredGauss/index2.html.

[11] The characters my son drew as his "competitors" were those found in: Lucas, George. *Star Wars®: Episode 1 – The Phantom Menace.* Lucas Film, Inc. and Twentieth Century Fox, 1999. He said he was especially inspired by the video game for Nintendo 64 called *Star Wars® Episode 1: Racer,* produced by Lucas Arts and Nintendo® in 1999. The other images drawn by my artist son were

characters from the Pokémon fad. Pokémon and its many characters are registered trademarks and ©Nintendo. The drawings shown here are not intended to challenge any copyright but are used to demonstrate the creative enhancements an artistic, right-brained child brings to left-brained subjects.

[12] Hui, Chang Suo. *Learning Mathematics Through Computer Games.*

Chapter Thirteen

The Art of Writing

Shift Begins with Me

My oldest son has a remarkable talent for drawing. Oftentimes as a child he would draw 3 to 4 hours a day. Alas, since I was public schooled myself, the "drawing-has-no-value" mentality emerged and I wondered if I should encourage more meaningful pursuits from him. Thankfully, my husband was one of those children constantly told to "stop doodling" in the classroom. He pointed out that our son should have the opportunity to explore his God-given talent to the extent that he desires. He reminded me that this was one of the many reasons we chose to homeschool. My doubts quickly dissipated after this simple reminder.

Many young children draw and/or color as their first experience with a writing instrument. It begins as soon as they can hold a crayon, marker, or pen. The enjoyment they glean from this art form is enhanced as they get older—until they enter school. At this time, their recreational time is greatly reduced, and often the arts isn't a core subject in the classroom. Those children who enjoy drawing for pleasure's sake quickly drop the habit as there's too little time to dabble in something "just for fun." Those children who continue drawing because they have a talent for it are harassed by the teacher to "stop doodling" during class time. Drawing often regresses into a "spare time" hobby the children find little time to pursue.

Since my artist son had free rein to draw, I discovered that he relies on his drawing to make sense of the world around him. Many children utilize the drawing and/or coloring medium in their early years in a similar manner, as I've seen with my successive children. However, artistic children need to incorporate their drawing instincts into more advanced and diverse areas as they grow. My artist son approached and investigated subjects from geography to mythology to history via the drawing medium. His freedom to pursue his artistic nature also led to his ability to write using his own learning style.

In Chapter Four, I delineated the time frames of three stages of learning (5 to 7, 8 to 10, and 11 to 13) based on processing preferences. For the left-brained learner, two universal traits—a word-based, symbolic focus and sequential ordering—work together, enabling this learner to begin exploring writing with words between the ages of 5 and 7 years. The right-brained learner is also focusing on his two universal traits between 5 and 7 years—three-dimensional pictorial thinking and extraordinary imagination. This learner doesn't explore writing with words until 11 to 13 years old.

However, writing with words is simply one method of expressing one's ideas. The left-brained learner often prefers expressing herself with written words. A right-brained learner favors other ways to express ideas. Drawing a picture

255

expresses an idea. Creating a movie expresses an idea. Acting in theater expresses an idea. These examples are visual expressions of ideas, while writing with words is a symbolic, verbal expression of ideas. Each venue of expression is valid, yet only one is valued in our current school system.

I was able to create a learning environment that valued diverse avenues of idea expression. This environment allowed my creative children to express themselves visually until their natural progression brought them to produce written work. My artist son's path to written work is one example of what that process can look like.

Pictorial and Oral Expressions of Ideas (5 to 7 Years Old)

Like many parents, I began to read to my son when he was 1 year old. And, like many children, he loved to be read to by his parents. Typically, he favored several books I had to read over and over again. My son also sat and looked at books by himself one to two hours each day. Whether I was reading or he looked at the books himself, he concentrated on the pictures. He never picked up a crayon, marker, or any

writing tool until he was 3 years old, but he drew a real picture the first time he put pen to paper. (See Chapter Eight to learn more about this "watch, then do," trait.)

One of my artist son's first drawings.

It wasn't until I raised more children that I realized this was unusual. My second writer daughter picked up a pen rather early and drew little circles or long straight lines over and over again. After about

256

a year of this practice, she also began to draw pictures when around 3 years old.

My insight tells me that drawing is a child's first attempts at telling a story. Most first children's books are pictorial, portraying characters and events with large and colorful images accompanied by few or no words. After months of "reading" picture books, a child's drawing represents first attempts at using images to express ideas. The child experiences the wonderful feeling that his "picture is worth a thousand words." If asked to explain one of their drawings, children may give a lengthy description, or tell us in one or two words. However complex or simple the verbal explanation, the pictures express their ideas in their entirety and serve as an early form of communication.

Advancement through Copying

My artist son was about 5 when he reached the next stage. He discovered he could trace pictures. When I first stumbled across one of the tracings, I thought it was free-drawn. I exclaimed, "Son, did you draw this?" Of course he said he did, and then showed me how. When my initial response was a less-than-impressed, "Oh," I witnessed the fire fade from his eyes. I quickly repented my invalidating response. I encouraged this drawing technique by purchasing tracing paper (which he loved) and praised his ability to trace (which is a talent all its own).

Several years later, my eyes opened to tracing's benefits. I noticed that after he repeatedly traced a certain type of picture, he incorporated the new technique into his own drawings. For instance, maybe he traced characters with fists. Eventually, I saw more accurately drawn fists in his drawings. Or maybe he traced animals with hind legs drawn correctly. Before long, the hind legs on his animals were also more life-like. Tracing enabled my son to develop technique! The more refined the technique the better he was able to recreate the adult image of a story.

Hind legs before practicing through tracing, age 7.

A drawing traced with hind legs depicted. (Images[1])

258

Hind legs free-drawn after practicing through tracing.

Mirroring a Story Line

Up until the time he was around 6 years old, my artist son basically drew solitary pictures. Then the movie *Jurassic Park*[2] came to theaters. We knew he'd be inspired to see it because of his passion for dinosaurs, but we also knew his fear of scary things (see Chapter Five). My husband went to the movie alone to determine the extent of frightening parts. Upon his return, he honestly depicted its scariness to my son, especially when viewed on the big screen. We recommended he wait to see the movie until it came out on video, and he readily agreed. My son's fascination with the movie didn't dissipate because he hadn't watched it. His father had viewed it, so he pumped him for details part by part. My artist son then recreated movie scenes on paper with as much detail as possible. Then, he'd have his father review the pictures for accuracy. This continued for 1 to 2 hours a day or until his father grew bored of it, whichever came first. He did this for 4 to 5 days until it was complete. Then he started over and did it all again.

Creating stories begins without words for many right-brained children. (Image³)

Inspired by this technique, my artist son did the same thing after watching *The Lion King®*. (This time he didn't have to ask his father about it since he watched the movie himself.) Recreating the movie part by part, he now spent 4 to 5 hours per day since he never grew bored of it. With no reference except that one visit to the theater, with startling accuracy he recreated the scenes and depicted the characters. He mimicked this technique with his favorite cartoons as well, engaging in this process for at least a year.

This mimicking was much like his tracing pictures. By duplicating existing story lines, my son could *feel* how they were created so he could make his own. And he did. First, he created original story lines about those he'd mimicked. I remember stories involving *The Lion King®* characters and others with characters from *Jurassic Park*. He gained experience and confidence to venture into his own character and plot development. Near the end of this time period, my artist son's own adventure series starring him and his sister evolved. Original adventure stories containing great humor, consistency, and depth, my son created a new one at least 2 to 3 times a week for a good year or more!

His sister squished on a T-Rex foot while he and his younger brother panic.

Oral Storytelling

My husband began telling diverse, original oral stories to the older children as part of their bedtime routine about the same time my artist son was recreating story lines. One story line combined two easy readers: *Morris Goes to School* and *Amelia Bedelia.*[4] The initial character was Nooffy MaDooffy, the stupidest person in the world. Later, Nooffy got relatives such as Scruffy MaDuffy, the dirtiest person in the world, and Raffy MaDaffy, the weirdest person in the world. My husband told some stories with a moral, usually involving animals, like a fish that always swam in the opposite direction as all the others. He told adventure stories, like "The Purple Parrot" and

261

"How the Raptor Got Its Name." (My husband is a very talented storyteller and could create stories from his head. The children loved them.)

Such great stories should be captured on tape for posterity, I decided, so I set up a tape recorder for bedtime. The venture was successful and he eventually filled both sides of a tape. It didn't take long for my artist son and my writer daughter to ask for a blank tape so they could record their own stories. At first, my son told stories similar to his father's using Nooffy MaDooffy. Eventually, he ventured into completely original story lines. (They went through blank tapes as if they were water and it wasn't long before they accidentally taped over my husband's stories, so there go my future earnings from his storytelling!)

Now that my artist son was integrating story lines and plots into his skill set, the next stage was moving the still pictures into book format. As he explored this way of expressing ideas, he kept the visual and pictorial aspects of story making as the foundation.

Bookmaking

As mentioned in Chapter Eleven, my son stumbled across a resource on our bookshelf called *Read! Write! Publish!*[5] Most of the books in this "how to make books" book were visual and pictorial by nature. My artist son was inspired to make books because this book promoted his natural way of expressing himself at that stage. From there, he easily moved into making his own books and considering himself a "writer," because *writers* create *books*, right? He didn't know there might be a different level of value for a visually-based book versus a word-based book. After all, in our adult society, we do value authors of both types (e.g., Eric Carle and Charles M. Schulz as well as Agatha Christie and J. K. Rowling). He dabbled in this resource for up to two years, roughly from ages 5 to 7.

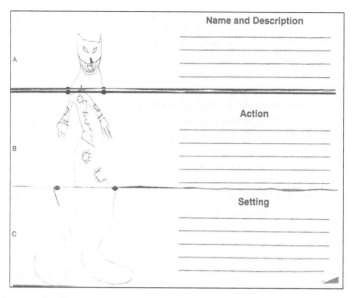

A book made by my artist son from the resource Read, Write, Publish![6] *in which you draw different creatures on each page. The instructions state to create the head on the top part, the body filling the middle section, and the feet in the bottom area. After completing the number of creations desired, each section is cut. By turning the various sections to different drawings, as shown above, even more funny-looking creatures result. Note he did not want to add words yet.*

Recognizing and honoring the natural pictorial and oral stage of expressing ideas is crucial to your child developing a positive relationship with writing. These are simply the visual and spoken word versions of expressed ideas. Julie Bogart, creator of the Brave Writer program,[7] invites parents and educators to "jot down" these ideas expressed by children during this stage. Utilizing adult scribes isn't cheating, but they're effective tools for hooking a young child's drawn or spoken ideas to the written format. When a child realizes that an adult feels what he has to say is worth writing down, it helps that child to develop a positive relationship with writing. As noted through my example with my children in this

263

chapter, however, it's not necessary to be a scribe for your child during this stage in order for your child to develop into a competent writer. I agree with the Brave Writer material[8] that this stage marks the beginning of a child's creation of his own "voice," which is so important to good writing later. Bogart emphasizes that this pictorial and oral storytelling time frame is a natural stage of growth toward successful writing.

Visual and Technological Expressions of Ideas (8 to 10 Years Old)

My son naturally progressed from creating diverse visual books as previously described to the next stage of writing development: combining written or spoken words with visuals. Inspiration for this stage came from comic books, his favored reading material (see Chapter Eleven), video games, computer animation, and movies.

Comic Books

Because of his pictorial nature, my artist son didn't begin reading until he was 8 years old. He started working out his reading fluency at age 9, and his favorite thing to read was comic books. To create his own comics inspired by the books he read, he simply had to make the next leap of adding words to his visual story line from the previous stage. My son had two great friends who lived next door with whom he played almost daily. One of their favorite focuses of play was the newly adopted fad of Pokémon®. My son began a never-ending comic story line depicting himself and his two friends as the main characters on a Pokémon® adventure.

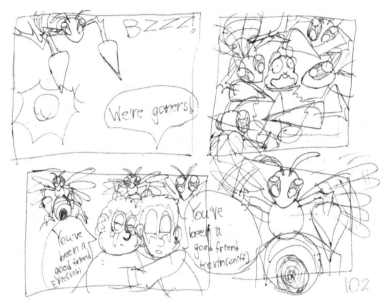

Original comic book making is a common story writing activity for many right-brained children. (Image[9])

As noted in Chapter Nine, right-brained children are process people. Writing comic books is a perfect example of a profession that doesn't require a "finished" product; the product continues until the market is saturated for that particular comic strip. My artist son began his comic book project between 8 and 9 years old. He would lay it down and pick it up from time to time until he was around 11 years old. He wrote nearly 550 pages. Some people complain that a right-brained child doesn't "stick to" projects, but continuing that project for three years took incredible tenacity.

Computer and Video Games

When my son was around 8 years old, a state-of-the-art computer became an additional tool for everyone. At this point, my artist son was incorporating more words into his stories. However, although my son liked to spell correctly and wrote neatly, he easily tired of writing words by hand. Remember, because every child has a unique method to approach a subject, parents have to be open to allowing their children to utilize the medium that most enhances the child's method. In our case, I encouraged my son to use more words with his stories by suggesting he use the word processing package on our computer. I felt his creativity would flow more easily if he typed, rather than enduring the tedious process of hand writing (see Chapter Fifteen). Able to work more comfortably with words with the medium that best suited his strengths, he enjoyed more experimenting with the written word.

Because of the interactive nature of computer software, my artist son became creatively engaged. For instance, this computer came prepackaged with a *Spider-Man*® animated cartoon-making program on which he could create an original cartoon.[10] Through this medium, my son further explored his creative capacities in a simple "moving picture" manner. During the time frame of 8 to 10 years old, we were inspired to purchase many educational software programs for his use. These included *GeoSafari*® (history, geography, etc.), *The Oregon Trail*®, *JumpStart*®, *Encarta*® (visual encyclopedia), *Simtown*®, *Dinosaur Adventure 3-D*, and others.[11] In addition to these visual resources was his deeper foray into video game playing, especially his interest in role-playing games. Each of these provided inspiration for an artist to bring a moving picture into a story line.

Movie Making

From the time my son was 8 years old until he was 11, he had two friends living on either side of us who happened to be perfectly matched in personality and temperament to my son, enabling his next stage of idea expression to occur. Both boys worked well under my son's direction in producing movies as a way to express their ideas.

Most of the movie themes centered on *Indiana Jones*™, *Star Wars®*, *Alien®*, and an original character named Spudnus. My son incorporated camera tricks (learned through 4-H) and three-dimensional angling as well as thinking outside-of-the-box to create believable backdrops. For instance, he recorded clips of shows from television to use as part of a particular scene. This moving visual picture avenue continued from about age 9 until 11. A big reason this stage occurred was giving my creative children access to technology, even when accidental damage could occur (see Chapter Fourteen). We have about ten VHS tapes of priceless creative expression and friendship collaboration thanks to this stage of writing development—a moving visual story line with the spoken word.

Abigail & her friends
Abigail and Sonic went to the hoatsvile park & Tails came running up to them & told them that the cosmic nyras of the golden river have been arrested by the evil boss Silver Sonic of Boncorääniasè in the cosmic rogue. And she sent several of her friends to the cosmic rogue.(including Abigail and Faith.)And she decided to let Vanila (whitch is creams mom) to stay and guard Wii land.

Video games are common inspiration for right-brained writing. Creativity is evident even in their use of technology. (Image[12])

Recognizing and honoring the use of visual technology to encourage and inspire the written word in short increments enhances this stage of writing development. Comic books, video and computer games, and favorite television shows and movies are all popular fodder for early right-brained writing themes. Julie Bogart, in her Brave Writer program, introduces short writing opportunities during this stage that she calls Friday Freewrite, [13] a time set aside for everyone, including the adult mentor, to sit and write whatever comes to mind for 15 minutes. It's perfectly acceptable for the adult to still be scribe or to help with stuck moments by asking leading questions. (Do you want to write about our trip to the nature center? How about your latest LEGO® you built?)

Bogart also expands a child's interaction with diverse writing genres (such as poetry) on Tea Tuesdays (or any fun drink—don't forget the food). She had poetry books of all kinds on hand and everyone picked one to read to the family in attendance. Again, helping a child read, or reading for him is acceptable. Make it fun! The key benefit of this idea is nurturing a positive relationship with writing through powerful and moving words that poetry evokes. The Brave Writer program has these ideas and more that are conducive to supporting the natural right-brained writing process (though it's not a program created specifically for right-brained learners). [14]

Written Expressions of Ideas
(11 to 13 Years Old)

My artist son used video games to inspire and transfer his visual enjoyment into the written format. As mentioned in Chapter Six, he wrote a 35-page, single-spaced typewritten novel based on his then current favorite video game, *The Legend of Zelda®*. Most fascinating was how clever and talented he was at writing, with little to no formal instruction.

At about that time, our family moved away from his two friends in Kentucky to a new home in Pennsylvania. We moved in May so I arranged to have his two friends come for a two-week visit at our new home in June. Before we left Kentucky, the trio was still heavily immersed in movie making endeavors, so anticipating another venture when they visited, my son prepared material to save time. Among his preparations was a handwritten 100-page script! Although handwriting wasn't his favorite task, his creative drive compensated for the tediousness of any individual skill when it's for a meaningful project. His handwriting was legible and a means to an end.

Script writing is a creative form of expression.

As a left-brained learner, I'm drawn to the framework of writing. It's systemic and formulaic, and utilizes the strengths of the left side of the brain. Since schools follow a left-brained scope and sequence, they focus on the *parts* of writing, and I did this well. Yet, I didn't consider myself a writer until adulthood because I never found my voice until then, nor did I understand I had something exciting to write about (see the story at the beginning of Chapter Fifteen).

Recognizing and honoring the natural path to writing confidently is accomplished by first encouraging our children to find their voices, inspired by their interests and real experiences. This chapter shows my artist son's path to just that. Julie Bogart of Brave Writer attests that the best writing in these early stages is interest-led. The writer's voice must come first and then the framework of writing can enhance writing ability. It's from this foundation that the elements of grammar, spelling (see Chapter Fifteen), research, and higher level thinking through writing will evolve.[15]

269

I notice in retrospect how my son's path to writing reflected the timeline of humanity's path to communication. Historically, expressing ideas began as visual communication through mediums such as cave painting, hieroglyphics, and pictographs. My artist son started with single pictures, and then moved to sequencing these pictures into story lines. He intermixed this with oral storytelling, which was a tradition for centuries. Later, the alphabet and written words expanded on the original picture form of communication. My son also added the written word to his pictures when making comic books and other forms of visual books. And now, in the era we find ourselves in today, we've embraced the next progression in the realm of higher level moving visual communication avenues such as photographs, digital imagery, and interactive words/audio/video on the Internet. My son mirrored these stages using those same mediums to express his ideas. The natural process humans took as we progressed along our path to communication was the same organic process my artist son took in learning to express his ideas.

Thus, an artist's road to writing began with his preferred creative outlet of drawing utilizing the two universal gifts of a right-brained learner: picture-based thinking and imagination. This was his foundation for learning to write. None of this required formal classes or resources. In fact, when my artist son took college writing classes, he had no trouble transitioning and receiving high marks. In the end, children with each processing preference will be capable of using words to write, in their proper time frame, utilizing appropriate resources matched to their learning style. Most noteworthy, our right-brained children will be more proficient at using our current forms of technology-based communication since they utilize their strengths. These technology skills should be encouraged since they match the needs of our current civilization. In the end, it's all about valuing the individual process.

References and Notes

[1] The Lion King® is a registered trademark of Walt Disney Pictures registered in the United States Patent and Trademark Office. All images and characters depicted in the movie are copyright © 1994 and 1995 the Walt Disney Company. The drawings found in this body of work based on The Lion King® characters are not intended to challenge any copyright but were the innocent reflection of a young child's enjoyment of a children's movie.

[2] Spielberg, Steven. *Jurassic Park*. Universal Pictures, 1993.

[3] My artist son's inspiration for this story was: Ibid.

[4] Wiseman, B. *Morris Goes to School*. Harper Collins, 1983. Parish, Peggy. *Amelia Bedelia*. Greenwillow Books, 1992.

[5] Fairfax, Barbara and Adela Garcia. *Read! Write! Publish!: Making Books in the Classroom Grades 1-5*. Creative Teaching Press, 1998.

[6] Ibid. This depicts one of the pre-made forms at the end of the book one can use to make this particular style of book.

[7] Julie Bogart, professional writer and editor and homeschooling parent, was asked by her fellow homeschoolers if she could help them teach their children to write. She realized that learning to write from a writer's viewpoint versus from a teacher's viewpoint was very different. Bogart was inspired to start to share her love of writing with others, and Bravewriter was born. For more information about her philosophies, classes, and products, visit her website at: http://www.bravewriter.com/.

[8] This information was gleaned from a workshop given by Julie Bogart during The Organization of Virginia Homeschoolers annual conference during the year 2012 held at the Cultural Arts Center at Glen Allen. A handout is referenced entitled, "Natural Stages of Growth Notes."

[9] The images drawn by my artist son were characters from the Pokémon fad. Pokémon and its many characters are registered trademarks and ©Nintendo. The drawings shown here are not intended to challenge any copyright but are used to demonstrate the creative talents an artistic, right-brained child brings to writing endeavors.

[10] *Spider-Man Cartoon Maker*. Windows 3.1, Knowledge Adventure, 1995.

[11] I'm referencing when my children played with them, which was run on Windows 95, but most of these have current versions of the software. *GeoSafari Multimedia Game: History, Geography, Science*. Educational Insights, 1995. *Oregon Trail II*. The Learning Company, 1995. *JumpStart*. Knowledge Adventure, 1995. *Encarta '95*. Microsoft, 1995. *SimTown*. Maxis Kids, 1995. *Dinosaur Adventure 3-D*. Knowledge Adventure, 1995.

[12] The story features the characters, Sonic the Hedgehog®, a video game character first debuting in 1991 for SEGA®; Tails®, a sidekick video game character to Sonic the Hedgehog®, who debuted in 1992; and various other Sonic the Hedgehog® characters, such as Vanilla and Cream. The story found in this body of work, including these characters and other elements of the video game, is not intended to challenge any copyright but was the innocent storytelling expression of a young creative child.

[13] Julie Bogart, creator of the Brave Writer program, credits Peter Elbow with the term "freewriting." Elbow, Peter. *Writing with Power: Techniques for Mastering the Writing Process*. Oxford University Press, 1998. Julie discusses her Friday Freewrite days at her website at http://www.bravewriter.com/bwl/friday-freewrite/.

[14] Julie Bogart, creator of the Brave Writer program, encourages a "lifestyle" of writing. She has the ideas discussed in this section and more found in her "Brave Writer Lifestyle" section at http:// www.bravewriter.com/bwl/.

[15] This information was gleaned from a workshop given by Julie Bogart during The Organization of Virginia Homeschoolers annual conference during the year 2012 held at the Cultural Arts Center at Glen Allen. A handout is referenced entitled, "Natural Stages of Growth Notes."

Chapter Fourteen

A gaggle of geese glide from within the treetops and fly toward the sky. "There's my dinner!" Brave Jojo exclaims joyously. He swiftly nocks an arrow and lets it soar.

Writing Traits of the Right-Brained Learner

Shift Begins with Me

I watched as my 12-year-old daughter read one of the American Girl *books. [1] She began reading the series when she was 7 to 8 years old. She probably read each book about 100 times, without exaggeration. A lot of thoughts ran through my head. Should I be discouraging her from reading the same book over and over again? I rarely re-read books, whether as a young girl or now as an adult. I'm a "feeler" when I read, so once I felt the emotions and character of a book, it wasn't as interesting to read it again because there was no surprise. What was the attraction for my daughter? I decided to ask. She and my artist son both shared with me that, as visual readers, with every reading they collect more visual details to add to the picture formed in their minds. In other words, more clarity is acquired.*

Something else I wrestled with as my daughter read the American Girl *series: it seemed "below her level." It wasn't stretching her in content or vocabulary, let alone in depth of writing. If it were just one series, maybe I could excuse her devotion, but it was the same with other books and series, like* The Magic Treehouse *and* Dear America.[2] *I chose to accept the idea that there may be value being gained that I couldn't understand. If she was attracted to this style and level of book, I needed to trust in her natural bent.*

Fast forward to my daughter's mid-teen years when she suddenly took off as a fantasy writer. She spent many hours each day writing her novel. And what was her writing focus level? It was near the same level that she'd read voraciously for years: the 8 to 14 year old reading range. Had all of that reading and rereading prepared her for her life career? What if I had intervened and steered her away from her instinctual focus?

As noted throughout each of these subject chapters, each one of us often has numerous conditioned ideas about learning: how it looks and when it should be accomplished. As also noted throughout this book, it's because of the left-brained focused schools most of us attended. We maintain an educational and learning value system based on the time frames and processes we experienced there. The same applies to the writing process. Watching my right-brained children naturally unfold and succeed helped me change my thinking. Further, it's been informative to witness how truly unique and individual every person's process to learning and acquiring particular skills really is.

Copying: Mentoring or Cheating?

Schools dredge up a lot of attention on plagiarism and cheating through copying. In my opinion and from my perspective, that applies to the adult world and to a system that highlights jumping through hoops versus learning to know. Why do young people plagiarize? Do they feel incompetent as writers? Do they feel the main purpose is to receive a passing grade and move on? Do they not see the relevance in writing? The answer may be in another question. Would imitating successful writers lead to feeling more competent as writers themselves? I found that, for my children, copying meaningful writing is a highly useful strategy. It serves as a form of mentoring, which is when a more experienced person teaches another person a desired trade or skill.

Drawing takes talent even when a how-to-draw book is used to learn.

As outlined in the previous chapter, my artist son utilized "copying" with such acts as tracing for drawing and understanding pictorial storylines by reproducing popular movies. My writer daughter copied a storyline using her own learning style. She's a fantasy writer today, but it all started when she copied word for word from some of her favorite books when she was 5 to 7 years old (see Chapter Five). She imitated short stories and poetry a bit at that time as well. When in the 8 to 10 year old range, as noted in the beginning story, she often read books over and over again while "reading below her level," staying at the 8 to 10 year old book level even as she grew into the 11 to 13 year old time frame. Again, in hindsight, I see how she was "researching" story patterns for this age group for which she now writes novels. How else does someone learn about good writing, but by reading and mimicking good writing?

The idea of mentoring crystallized when I attended a conference hosted by *Growing without Schooling*[3] where I listened to a panel of unschoolers grouped by twos: a parent and a teen. One set's description of how the teen learned essays both fascinated and shocked me. The mother, proficient at this skill, would sit side by side with her son, telling him what to write and why. Slowly, over time, he began to fill in more and more, relying less and less on her input. Eventually, he shared with her that her services were no longer needed. I was shocked because of how I was taught to view "cheating" in school, but my newfound understanding of how real learning takes place overruled this institutional viewpoint. With this example of modeling and mentorship, my husband and our son did the same thing in his junior year of high school. It worked beautifully for my son as he gained more and more confidence navigating a language that has always been a struggle for him.

A mentor is when a person who is more experienced helps another person gain better ability through the act of modeling.

From each of these successful

examples, I came to realize some learning truths. Having a mentor is using someone else's expertise to gain better techniques through modeling, copying, or tracing as a form of learning. Julie Bogart of Brave Writer recognizes that "hijacking the words of parents or books while learning how to think for themselves" leads to the creation and confidence of one's own writing voice.[4] Right-brained learners tend to like to observe first, and then do, because the desired act is first processed through their visual mind to become comfortable with the attempt. Copying is just plain smart for them as they use their best asset to learn how to do something new. Plagiarism is for profiteering; cheating is for institutions; copying *can* be mentoring.

Creative Writing Outlets

My writer daughter presents as whole brained, leaning to the right. This means she was able to learn many subjects in a left-brained fashion, but some subjects were expressed creatively in a right-brained manner. For instance, most of her writing was right-brained writing genres.

Color Inspiration

My writer daughter used coloring as her earliest form of art expression. She rarely used the "correct" colors and I often complimented her on her imagination. The more colorful the result the better she liked her picture. For about a year, many of her pictures and papers sported various "rainbow swatches" along their bottoms. At a very young age, she gifted me a paper with one of her creations with what I deem the first indication of her talent with poetic words.

Poetry is a creative expression of writing.

My writer daughter's strong interest in color introduced her to poetry when she was riveted by the book, *Hailstones and Halibut Bones,* by Mary O'Neill. [5] With its highly visual imagery, it makes sense that poetry is a right-brained writing medium. Many of my writer daughter's gifts to me for birthdays and Mother's Days were poetry personally written for me. She also picked up the guitar at 10 years old and wrote lyrics, another right-brained writing venue. She can still remember a childhood song she and a friend created about...color.

Computer Graphics Inspiration

Once the Internet and graphics programs made the visual and color medium more accessible via the computer, my writer daughter married her enjoyment of writing and color to engage in a variety of projects. She went through a season of creating her own greeting cards, utilizing her poetry skills. Her ease with words and fun stories resulted in original gifts for her four younger brothers based on their current interests.

She made alphabet books for her brother with autism who enjoys this genre.

Creating visual books using Internet images is a well-matched right-brained activity. (Image[6])

278

She made personalized books for her two little brothers. She took photographs of them in various positions, and inserted those pictures of her brothers into background images from the Internet to depict their specific interests. She then wrote stories to go with them. One brother's Indian stage is depicted at the beginning of this chapter, and the knight interest for another brother is shown below.

Fiction writers can find creative ways to express themselves visually. (Image[7])

Knight William prepares to
depart immediately!
for part of his long, long journey,
he will ride his knight horse,
Snow White,
to help him reach the dragon's lair quicker.
"Good girl!" Knight William says nicely.

Creative, fictional writing comes very naturally to a right-brained person. Many school writing assignments are report format. While these rely on factual, dry information lacking creative interest (the framework first format), a fictional story with fascinating characters and unexpected plot twists and turns (the voice first format) appeals to the right-brained learner's imaginative foundation (see Chapter Thirteen). My writer daughter wrote many short stories as a child, particularly about animals, but they never made it past a half page to a page in length. Many topics were copied from another storyline in those early attempts.

When my writer daughter and her older brother described their "dreams" to one another, they became fodder for her eventual fantasy writing. She clarified that sometimes they were actual dreams (stories lived out in her night sleeping), but other times they were ideas she constantly explored in her mind throughout the day. By orally sharing her creative story ideas with her brother, who had many of his own for her to listen to, she had catalysts to character development and plot explorations. One day, in her mid-teens, she sat down to write another story. She suddenly realized it was an original work, and the story flowed easily on to pages and pages. Thus began her fantasy writing passion.

Builder Storytelling

Who tends to write even later than their fellow right-brained peers? Right-brained children with the creative outlet gift of building/electronics. I mention that the typical right-brained learner tends to primarily use words sometime around 11 to 13 years old. A builder child may be 14 to 16 years of age before he's ready to shift because his focus is so heavily spatially based (see Chapter Six). The focus on this creative outlet also often leads to an interest in the math/numbers outlet (with math and computers having their own "language" different from the written word) or a music/dance outlet (which also uses a notation language). The builder child is often less exposed to traditional word-based products and processes than right-brained children interested in other creative outlets. As mentioned throughout this book, all paths are valid because the strengths centered in each gift area are specially formulated to develop the skills needed at the right time for each child.

Because my builder son had an artist older brother as a model, he pursued some traditional early writing outlets, like creating his own comic pages and books. However, he had some drawings that wouldn't be in my artist son's collection. With LEGO® and trains as the focal points of my builder son's interests, and with spatial abilities the focal point of his gifts, his story writing efforts revolved around those.

My builder son's early writing attempts featured LEGO® imaginary friends as characters. Notice how the spelling of "Jack" is slaughtered (see Chapter Fifteen).

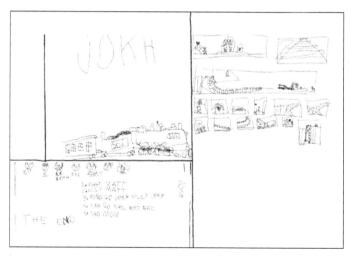

Trains and LEGO® were often characters in my builder son's early storytelling.

Spatial themes turned up in my builder son's early stories.

After building with LEGO® for years, and then moving to TECHNIC™, my builder son naturally gravitated toward other LEGO® products, such as LEGO® Studio. This program uses stop-motion movie-making to create a story with LEGO® figures and other block creations, perfectly aligned with a builder's style of storytelling. A spatial awareness of how everything interplays is required to create a storyline. My builder son enjoyed planning the necessary camera tricks to achieve the visual image of the objects in movement. His strength for spatial details allowed him to plan out synchronized movement of each piece.

Acting Out Storylines

I'm in the middle of discovering what the process of expressing one's ideas looks like for a theater child. Mine spends most of his day in some kind of self-made costume, depicting some character or another from television or books. I created a huge bin into which I toss objects, cloth, and

282

accessories as potential fodder for his imaginative expression. I'm liberal with my contributions, but periodically something piques his creative juices and I'll find him knee-deep in the destruction of something useful to me, as it becomes part of a creation useful to him. The most recent escapade involved my Mrs. Beasley® collectible's bright blue polka dot clothing outfit secretly turned into a knight cloak. Sometimes deep breathing is a staple for the parent of a creative child with impulsivity difficulties (see Chapter Seventeen).

Beware the impulsive right-brained costume creator! (Image[8])

Just as my theater son prefers to be as realistic as possible in his costuming, he also loves *real* things when he's thinking about his stories. To this end my theater son needed visuals depicting real characters or settings from the Internet. Based on the images in the pictures he cut out and glued into his story form, he dictated his stories to a more experienced scribe. It has started simply, but as his ability to express himself grows and his desire to mimic more legitimate storylines increases, so will his interaction with this format.

Make Technology Available to the Young

As can be surmised from these writing chapters, the way a right-brained child pursues the process of expressing ideas looks different than his left-brained peers' pursuits. Right-brained forms of expressing ideas necessitate creating access to visual types of resources, particularly technology. I allowed my young children to use our camcorder, computer, and photography equipment. I instructed them on use and shared how to protect the resources from harm. More importantly, I explained that being careless results in a broken resource which means an inability to use it. My children responded well when they saw they were trusted with meaningful and real equipment. However, children are children and from time to time I needed to gently remind them about care instructions. Accidents did occur periodically, with minimal damage at each occurrence. Damage does add up, ending a resource's functional life, but usually several years' use was enjoyed beforehand. The technology we enjoy today was created by right-brained people, and it's an amazing resource for our right-brained children.

Allowing access to technology provides the best tools for right-brained children to express their ideas.

Each child utilizing each creative outlet has her own individual path to learning, expressing her gifts and her own time frames. In the last two chapters, I've shared the paths of my artist son's strengths, my writer daughter's strengths, my builder son's strengths, and the beginning path of my theater son. Each is valid even as it differs from the others, yet they share a process that utilizes visual, pictorial, and/or hands-on means to express their ideas. Truly, there's an art to the writing process for right-brained learners.

References and Notes

[1] About half of the *American Girl* series books were written by Valerie Tripp. Each girl has a set of six books. There are currently eleven girls: Addy, Felicity & Elizabeth, Josefina, Julie & Ivy, Kaya, Kirsten, Kit & Ruthie, Marie-Grace & Cecile, Molly & Emily, Rebecca, and Samantha & Nellie.

[2] Osborne, Mary Pope. *Magic Treehouse* series, Random House, 1992-2012. There are currently 28 books in the first series, and 20 books in the second, with another slated. There are various authors for the *Dear America* series. They were originally published by Scholastic from 1996-2004 and there were 36 titles in the original series. This series has been re-launched in 2010 with 17 titles so far, with many new titles.

[3] *Growing without Schooling* is the magazine started by the late John Holt founded in 1977 and discontinued in 2001. Back issues are available to be read at http://www.holtgws.com/growingwith outsc.html.

[4] This information was gleaned from a workshop given by Julie Bogart during The Organization of Virginia Homeschoolers annual conference during the year 2012 held at the Cultural Arts Center at Glen Allen. A handout is referenced entitled, "Natural Stages of Growth Notes."

[5] O'Neill, Mary. *Hailstones and Halibut Bones*. Doubleday Books for Young Readers, 1990.

[6] Minarik, Else Holmelund. *Little Bear* series. Harper & Row, 1957-1968. Illustrated by Maurice Sendak, this series originally had five books. Wiseman, B. *Morris the Moose*. Harper Collins, 1991. Wiseman, B. *Morris Goes to School*. Harper Collins, 1983. Use of these images were for personal use and were not intended to challenge any copyright but was the innocent book-making expression of a creative person.

[7] The horse and background were found on a general Internet search. Use of these images were for personal use and was not intended to challenge any copyright but was the innocent book-making expression of a creative person.

[8] Mrs. Beasley® is a registered trademark of Viacom, Inc.

Chapter Fifteen

The Act of Writing

Shift Begins with Me

It was my first year of homeschooling. I really felt like I was getting the hang of things and learning a lot of lessons. I had subscribed to the magazine Growing without Schooling [1] *and devoured its contents each time it arrived in the mail. There was a "concerns" section that opened up the opportunity for readers to respond to the concerned person in a personal letter addressed to the magazine. The magazine then forwarded it to the recipient. One particular concerned parent piqued my interest in responding. The topic was siblings as best friends and I had some ideas and thoughts.*

I took pen to paper and poured out my experiences, thoughts, and ideas to her, parent to parent. I felt strongly about what I wrote. I sent the letter off and didn't think much about it, though I hoped to hear from her to know if it had been helpful. Much to my surprise, the next issue of Growing without Schooling *contained an excerpt from my letter! Although I knew the magazine staff read the letters before forwarding them in case they wanted to publish them, it never occurred to me that I was a good enough writer to be considered in this way. In fact, I had to sit back and read my response again because when I originally wrote it, I didn't take into consideration any "proper methods" of writing; I simply wrote from my heart.*

In that moment everything came together. Long ago, I decided that my writing—perfectly formulated as taught in school—was too boring (see Chapter Nine), so I concluded I wasn't a writer. It didn't occur to me that the way I'd been taught to write in school wasn't the only way, or even the better way to write. I realized the heart had to come first, followed by the mechanics that helped to express the idea. When I saw my name in print, the way I viewed myself as a writer changed.

Expressing one's ideas using words has two components: the creative process and the logistical products. The creative process entails having something to write about, developing one's voice, and finding a way to share it. The logistical products are the presentation elements, including grammar, spelling, penmanship, and vocabulary. Since right-brained learners are process people, the creative process of writing (telling stories) tends to come more easily. Since left-brained learners are product people, the logistical skills (spelling and grammar, for instance) tend to come more easily. Because right-brained children think in pictures, their ideas and stories are more easily expressed through the creative outlets in the early years using oral storytelling, theater and video cameras, dance and dress-up, art and comic books, showmanship and puppets, and other such venues. Because left-brained children think in words, their ideas and stories are more easily expressed by writing and using words, so early engagement in grammar, spelling, penmanship, and vocabulary enhances their ability to share their ideas.

Currently, the scope and sequence found in schools follows the preferred writing development of left-brained learners. Because they are part-to-whole learners, and they think in words, learning how to construct words in the early years enhances left-brained learners' ability to express themselves. Thus, we see spelling, simple grammar, and penmanship are introduced between the ages of 5 and 7 years old. Vocabulary is often integrated through spelling. Because right-brained learners favor whole-to-part and they think in pictures, learning these logistical parts of using words is often confusing and difficult in the early years. It's best for a right-brained child to learn to read first (whole), which usually occurs between the ages of 8 and 10 years old. The right-brained learner is then ready to be introduced to the logistical parts (spelling, grammar, penmanship, and vocabulary) between the ages of 11 and 13 years old (after reading fluency).

Penmanship/Handwriting

I vividly remember penmanship in second grade. Being left-brained, I was quite good at it and enjoyed trying to perfectly create each symbol. Today, kindergarten is the new first grade, so penmanship begins in first grade, seemingly integrated with spelling. Although handwriting has its place, with all the technological advances of computers, cell phone texting, instant messaging, and e-mail, it may not be as essential a skill to know in the early years as it was in bygone years.

Teaching Methods

My first two children were consistently engaged in learning, so I didn't feel a need to interrupt their focus on other worthy topics (see Chapter Sixteen) in order to follow the prescriptive subject scope found in school, such as penmanship. Each of them picked up a writing instrument by 3 years old and enjoyed playing around with using it in the way that worked for him. In fact, they both taught themselves handwriting, or the act of writing we call penmanship. An interesting thing happened. I noticed both of them form their letters from the bottom up! When I discovered other children who taught themselves penmanship, I saw a high percentage of them form their letters from the bottom up. Although it can be strange to watch, the product looks the same.

Writing samples from two of my children's 9-year-old folders. One child writes from the top down and the other from the bottom up. Can you tell which is which, and does it matter?

My third and fourth children also initiated learning penmanship, but they wanted to teach themselves using some resource. I offered them a simple workbook showing starting position and direction using dots and arrows. Both children write from the top down as instructed in the resource.

Most of my children had no interest in learning cursive handwriting. Two of my children wanted to learn enough about cursive to be able to read it. All of them learned to write a signature as they approached adulthood. In other words, as they've needed to use penmanship, my children have learned whatever was required.

Right-Brained Time Frame

If you observe the needs of each individual child, and respect and give value to that child's particular needs and strengths, you'll know the time to pursue various subjects so that learning will come more easily for the child. By pursuing the different subjects this way, each child is able to progress without added angst from past negative experiences that have their roots in lack of readiness. Learning can be a positive experience. For most right-brained children, 8 to 10 years is the primary *starting* gate for formal handwriting.

I found it fascinating that my oldest son drew meticulous detail in pictures, but balked at writing. Surely if he could concentrate on such fine detail in his drawing, writing would be a cinch. In my research on the specialized skills for the right and left sides of the brain, it was no surprise to discover that word writing processes through the left side of the brain (being that words are symbolic, it makes sense), and that drawing and calligraphy and cursive are processed through the right side of the brain (being that each uses creativity, it makes sense). Thus, before the shift of 8 to 10 years of age happens for the right-brained learner, and even afterward just for sheer fun, it's not uncommon for a right-brained person to play around with writing in mirror image, block lettering, or any other form of "creative" writing.

The creative aspect of mirror writing taps into the right side of the brain.

Letter Reversal

Letter reversal is common in right-brained learners because of their need (before age 8 to 10) and their preference (even at or after 8 to 10) to view objects three-dimensionally. So, if a child can draw a person facing to the left, or facing to the right, why can't a "d" do the same thing? And considering a "d" and "b" simply *are* mirror opposites of one another, thus playing into the natural three-dimensionality of a right-brained learner, why *wouldn't* the right-brained child consistently reverse them? It's the same for "p" and "q." Over the past ten years, researchers have discovered that all of us from infancy create a mirror image of objects. Once we begin to learn tasks that require a two-dimensional perspective, such as reading and writing, we train our brains not to use this feature. In their book, *The Dyslexic Advantage,* the Eides note that "until the age of eight as many as one-third of children continue to make occasional mirror image substitutions when reading or writing." [2] Is it a coincidence that this statistic matches the number of strong right-brained learners in our schools (see Chapter One)? This delayed shift into two-dimensional positioning is associated with high levels of three-dimensional imagery. My artist son reversed "s" and "j" until at least age 10.

Reversing letters is a reflection of three-dimensional thinking.

Settling Down

Along with the picture focus that shifts the time frame for left-brained word tasks to 8 to 10 years old for right-brained children, energy needs may be a factor for some (see Chapter Seventeen). My last child is my risk-taker and active mover. Like many boys, he needs to move around a lot, be outside a lot, focus on big muscle movement (gross motor) a lot, and simply learn to manage his body and energy overall. It wasn't until he reached the 8 to 10 year range that he was body/energy regulated enough to sit still to develop the skill of writing. Here's a sample at 8 years old when he first started some formal work. He mainly wrote his name.

And here is his work six months later after practicing two to three days a week:

The cat is on the mat.

Developmental Differences

Four of my children had a natural hand grip and average or above intelligence. I also have three children who did not have a natural hand grip and who struggled while learning language and other skills that are often picked up imitatively. All three of them have low muscle tone and two of them are diagnosed with autism, both attributes often associated with handwriting difficulty. All three of these children struggled with handwriting. Does this result in dysgraphia? I don't think so (see Chapter Eighteen). These children are also right-brained learners, so the natural later time frame applies. We often want to start sooner when there are obvious differences because parents and teachers figure learning is going to be more difficult, but I disagree (see Chapter Ten). Waiting longer may be the most effective answer!

Let me use my fifth child as an example. He practiced handwriting in the traditional 8 to 10 year time frame for right-brained learners. The practice was too frustrating and the hand grip was obviously problematic. Though at the time I followed instinct, I now know that before the age of 11, children's brains are focused on the concrete. Teaching instruction is done *to* children during that brain development stage. But learning collaboratively can be done *with* children when the brain shifts sometime between 11 and 13 years old. During this brain development stage, young people begin to think more globally and abstractly. We waited until age 11 to begin more formal handwriting practice.

Since my electronic son didn't have negative connotations of handwriting at age 11, and because he could engage in abstract thinking to understand why he might want to learn to write better (global and abstract thinking), he could work *with* me to problem-solve ways to improve.

This is what his handwriting looked like when we started at age 11:

Here is a sample from his 12-year-old folder:

And here is a sample from his 14-year-old folder:

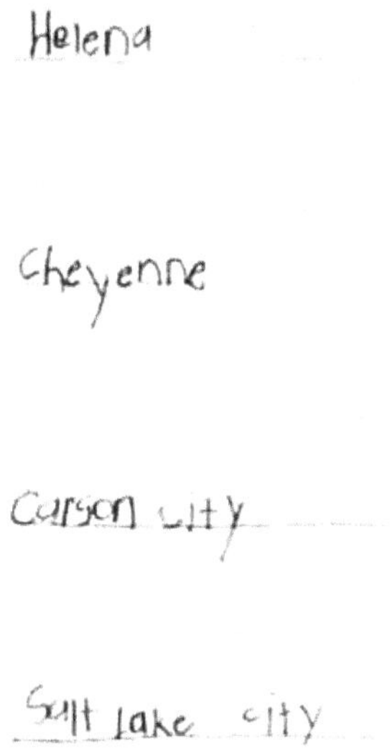

Helena

Cheyenne

Carson City

Salt lake city

Significant improvement occurred over time. I believe he has age appropriate handwriting at this time (17 years old). Although you can't recognize it from a handwriting sample, his hand grip improved and he can write long enough to fulfill the handwriting requirements of today's world. Yes, it's still more tiring for him compared to those who didn't have hand grip differences, but he can push himself if he has purpose for doing so. Otherwise, like most of us, he utilizes the keyboard religiously for big projects. He's written several short stories (mentored by his writer sister), keeps up with a blog (inspired by his mother), and writes daily in on-line forums based on his various interests.

Handwriting will always have its place. I still get a thrill out of receiving a handwritten letter or card, yet e-mails have become the norm. I record events on my calendar next to my landline, yet calendars on phones and computers are commonplace. I revise this book on hard copy pages, yet comment and revision tools on word processing programs make it easier for my editor and copy readers to share their insights with me. I jot down notes in casual meetings, yet colleges and businesses encourage or even require laptops in the classrooms and conference rooms. Having competent handwriting is useful, but prioritizing it for our young children as if it was as prominent in our society today as in the past isn't necessary. Technology makes it easier for parents and teachers to embrace the 8 to 10 year old time frame for a right-brained learner's implementation of handwriting.

Spelling

I've had two naturally good spellers so far in my family of right-brained children. My oldest artist son is one of them. I've also had atrocious spellers. My builder son was one of those. Both incorporated words here and there in the 5 to 7 year age range, and both began adding words to pictures during the 8 to 10 year time frame. Neither extensively focused on words until 11 to 13 years old. Both followed the same right-brained time frame, yet different individual traits impacted spelling.

No Lessons Required

When my artist son wrote a word, he often asked me how to spell it. I believe it was his perfectionism bent prompting him to do this. I grew up with adults telling me to "sound it out" or "look it up in a dictionary." I found myself prone to do the same. But, in some of my studies before choosing to homeschool, an idea I read about—I believe it was in a John Holt book—stated something like this: If a child asks you to spell something, just spell it. Don't turn it into a lesson. Allow yourself to be a trusted resource. In other words, isn't a child using his best resource when he asks a parent or teacher, whom he knows has the ability to spell things, to spell something for him?

Every time my artist son asked me to spell something for him, I did. In this way, he always saw the word spelled correctly. Because a right-brained person has such a vivid visual mind, the word is imprinted more indelibly. Remember in Chapter Eight when I shared the story about how it's difficult for a right-brained person to delete information? This may be particularly important information with regard to spelling skills.

Invented Spelling

Invented spelling became popularized in school some years ago. It seems like a good idea. It encourages young people to get their ideas down without worrying about the mechanics. It helps keep the flow going. For a left-brained person who systematically gets better and better at skills, this may work efficiently. For a right-brained person, however, invented spelling may be problematic as the wrong spelling gets imprinted with the "mind" picture. It takes concerted effort to delete old information and replace it with new information. I knew of a child who took years to spell his name correctly because of the initial incorrect input!

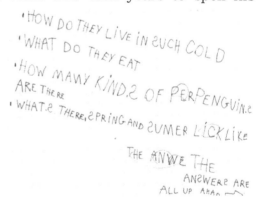

Notice how three words are crossed out as my artist son was about to misspell them, but then he spelled each correctly. I'm sure he sought out a reference for the correct spelling. Notice the S is backward, a common right-brained phenomenon because of three-dimensionality. Last, the word "summer" is misspelled, so his ability to spell perfectly wasn't infallible. Artist son, just turned 9.

297

Since children are going to dabble in spelling words and expressing ideas on paper without access to correct information, what happens when invented spelling does occur? I'll use my builder son as my main example. When I came across his self-initiated comics and other writing during the 8 to 10 year stage, I saw his spelling had become atrocious, yet he hadn't noticed. I felt revealing this fact would be a detriment to his continuing to express himself with words. Further, he wasn't a reader, so I felt that needed to come first. Around 10 years old, he began his reading journey.

I remember my builder son's 11 to 13 year mind shift vividly. He began noticing a lot of his differences as he started to understand his place in the greater world. One of the things he noticed was his poor spelling. This initiated our sitting down together to work a little on spelling. I noticed that if a word was lengthy, he had absolutely no idea how to spell it. He had no skills in breaking a word down into smaller parts. As a whole word reader, he was also trying to be a whole word speller. If it was a small word, he could hang onto the letters that create it. This goes along with the idea that a right-brained person is a whole-to-part learner. He had the whole down (reading sight words), but he hadn't yet delved into what the parts were.

Spelling Words are Like LEGO® Building

I decided it might be advantageous for him to learn word parts, but not individual parts. Examples of word parts are "tious," "anti," "ible," and "tri." I found a good resource that explained word parts through Greek and Latin roots of words.[3] I showed it to him. I explained how each of the word parts had a meaning, and words were formed by putting various word parts together to create longer words. After he played around with it for a while, he approached me and exclaimed, "Why didn't you tell me words were like LEGO®?" It took me a while to realize what he was saying. Just like little individual blocks fit together to create a whole unit, so do word parts. He never noticed the parts of words (verbal strength) like he did the parts of LEGO® (spatial strength). Now he drew the connection. Working through the Greek and Latin root resources helped my builder son make big leaps in spelling. I might even have called him a fair speller at that point.

I knew my son's next hurdle was to figure out how his less reliable auditory input was negatively impacting his ability to spell a word when hearing it. We used the resource *Natural Speller*[4] to help him improve in this area. Like our reading resources, I didn't use the spelling resource the way it was intended. I used it because it contained word lists divided by word parts separated into grade levels. We used *Natural Speller* with me saying the word part aloud for him to hear what it sounded like, and then he wrote it down. He'd listen carefully to how it sounded and how he was supposed to spell it. Then, we'd go through the list of words containing that word part. Most often by the time I gave him the last word in the list, he knew how to spell the word part and all the various words that often used it. This gave him another leap into good spelling.

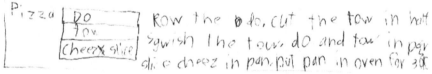

"Row" instead of "Roll," representing poor auditory input. "Do" instead of "dough," representing invented spelling. "Tow" instead of "tomato," representing a complete slaughter of a word of any length. "Sgwish" instead of "squish," representing a letter reversal of "g" instead of "q." "Cheez" is a stereotypical invented spelling for "cheese."

To complete his new spelling skills, we used the *Sequential Spelling* resource.[5] This is yet another resource focused on word part patterns, but in a unique way. Remember the game in which a word is given, then you replace the first letter with another letter to create a new word,

299

then you take off a letter on the end and add a suffix to create another word, and so forth and so on? *Sequential Spelling* uses this idea. It works well for a right-brained person *at the right time* to help improve spelling skills. That's usually in the 11 to 13 year time frame and/or after reading fluency. This spelling skill improvement process worked well for my builder son.

Spelling through Real Writing

My writer daughter took a different approach. She started off as a fair speller. During the 14 to 16 year stage, she really took off writing novels, using a computer—and the spell checker. She improved her spelling by using the application for a real and useful reason. Another way using spell check is an advantage for right-brained children is it minimizes the possibility of visualizing an incorrect spelling because it instantaneously provides the correct spelling.

I've heard from many parents whose children improved in spelling via similar real and useful purposes such as instant messaging friends, writing fan fiction, or using social media. In the same vein, exposure to correctly spelled words through reading books (whether comic books, magazines, or novels), reading video game dialogue, and viewing television with closed captioning on are catalysts for a right-brained person to improve in spelling.

Grammar

All of these same ideas can be applied to learning grammar. When my writer daughter wrote novels on the computer, the grammar application cued her in when she went amiss. Reading a variety of materials exposes a person to correct grammar usage. The need to be taken seriously when writing encourages a person to want to know better grammar. When my artist son wrote his first novel, he already had excellent spelling and grammar skills from reading books and exposure to other print resources with good spelling and grammar. There are as many ways to acquire these skills naturally as there are by using a formal resource.

Grammar is one of those subjects that has a beginning and an end. There's a set amount of grammar knowledge and our learning is complete. Following the left-brained scope and sequence, schools often start with simple grammar principles while children are learning to read and write in the first grade. For right-brained children, learning basic principles of grammar aligns with the readiness factor for symbolization, which occurs during the reading acquisition stage of 8 to 10 years old. Fully learning grammar is best approached at the same time as writing for right-brained children, which is the 11 to 13 year time frame.

To make grammar skill-building palatable, finding a resource that's short, sweet, and to-the-point is best for right-brained learners. (This is a one day assignment.) (Image[6])

Standardized tests often focus on grammar because it's quantifiable. My right-brained children didn't see any use for it until they started to write. To make grammar skill building palatable, I found a resource that kept it short, sweet, and to-the-point like grammar really is. Too many programs and resources for grammar make it more difficult than it needs to be. The resource *Daily Grams*™ cuts to the chase. [7] Interestingly, it's espoused as a supplement, but I found it more than sufficient for the core knowledge.

301

Each page outlines a day's assignment. It relates a principle of grammar, such as a capitalization rule, and gives the student a sentence to capitalize. It incorporates the new rule while reviewing old ones. Each *Daily Grams*™ lesson takes about 10 to 15 minutes. The book series is labeled by grade, starting in third grade, but I ignored those. Again, grammar has a beginning and an end. It doesn't matter if you start in third grade or sixth. In a given amount of time, the knowledge will be attained. I typically started using this resource in the 11 to 13 year range and had my child complete two days' worth. The series was usually completed in 2 to 3 years. Since writing with words became more meaningful at this stage for my right-brained learners, grammar knowledge made more sense with its real application.

Parents of right-brained learners also like the *Editor in Chief*® series[8] for its real application aspect. Produced by The Critical Thinking Co.™, this resource provides sentences and paragraphs for the student to correct as an editor would. Similarly, some parents have their children take real e-mails sent from real people and edit them. In this way a right-brained child who cares about meaningful experiences learns the impact of a poorly written post compared to one that's grammatically well-written. Which is better understood? What impression is made? Which is taken more seriously? Meaningful experiences can create a long-lasting knowledge base.

Vocabulary

Vocabulary development was the easiest and trickiest subject, depending on the needs of my children. How does a person randomly add words into everyday life? The words have to have meaning for a person to incorporate them successfully.

Maturity and Environmental Influences

With most typical humans, vocabulary grows when exposed through the spoken words around them or through consistent exposure to print, whether read silently or listened to during a read-aloud. We speak at our level of intellectual functioning. A 5-year-old speaks at a beginning level. A 10-year-old is developing more sophistication. A 14-year-old mimics adult speech if she isn't trying to fit into the teen-speak world. An adult speaks at the level of his peers in his chosen environment. For many of my children, I didn't see a specific need to incorporate vocabulary outside of the rich vocabulary environment in which they lived and interacted. This made vocabulary development easy.

Use It or Lose It

I do have several children who struggle with learning English due to developmental difficulties. These were the children I felt might benefit from help to expand their vocabulary since it's not natural for them to pick up these things from the environment. My first instinct was that if you don't use it, you'll lose it. I found various lists to work with, but I knew if the child didn't think to use the words in everyday life, the list wouldn't be effective. This is why helping expand vocabulary for some of my children could be tricky.

My builder son was one of these children who benefited from some vocabulary development. A primary goal was to have the meaning of a new word stick in his mind. I knew mnemonics had worked really well as he memorized states and capitals, so when I found a resource using this memory tool,[9] I chose to use it in our initial attempt. My builder son enjoyed the resource immensely. It made it easy for him to remember the meanings of words. However, we still struggled to make the words a part of his everyday conversation. He made good faith efforts, but with minimal gain. We used other packaged ideas from various resources with similar results.

303

Raising the Bar through Mentoring

When my builder son was at the latter end of the 14 to 16 year stage, I realized a person speaks at the level in which he's functioning. In this child's case, his functioning level was at his English-speaking ability. (As a side note, his math, computer, and science skills were sky high, so he had a specialized technical vocabulary working for him.) It occurred to me that the only way to increase his overall vocabulary and speaking ability was through more consistent exposure to words than his math- and computer-centered strengths provided. We holistically determined his comprehension level and chose books for him to read that were just above that. To get the most out of his reading vocabulary-wise, we found the *Total Language Plus* series[10] a great help. My builder son worked through the vocabulary exercises in the book before reading each set of chapters to get the most out of the readings.

At the same time, my husband mentored him in technical writing using a science text as the base resource. In this way, my builder son was consistently exposed to higher level readings while learning to use words to write at a higher level in a subject area he was strong in. In the 17 to 19 year stage he attended community college. He experienced a short learning curve in applying this knowledge to writing college papers. He flourished! I feel strongly that the reason my builder son, with his weakness in English-related skills and ideas, could compensate was because of the strengths-based foundation he stood on before tackling the tougher areas when he was older. My direct experience with several children showed me waiting doesn't cause deficiency. In fact, waiting just may be the reason for the successful compensations and increased competency.

"Any reports on Kitty Bell's whereabouts?"

For a moment, all that Lieutenant Surge can hear on his walkie-talkie is the sharp crackling of static. Then, at first barely audible but growing clearer by the second, the young voice of Officer Pascal shouting, "We have been successful in tracking the girl's body. It's too soon to tell what her condition is so we're preparing now to lower rescue crew members and the stretcher down into the trench."

His brow furrowing, Lieutenant Surge asks, "How long do you estimate it will take to get her out of there?"

More static, and then, "At least twenty minutes, sir. It will take time to safely get in and out of the Sheer Drop, sir."

"That will do."

Setting the walkie-talkie heavily on the cabin desk, Lieutenant Surge leans back in his chair and runs a hand across his face wearily, a toothpick dangling from his lips. Seated before the cabin desk are the extremely anxious parents of Kitty Bell, her father pale, her mother beside herself, worry eating away at them like a <u>herbicide</u> eats away a weed. All three of them are situated in the camp ranger's cabin, <u>anterior</u> of the hiking trails that lead to the Sheer Drop and posterior of the camp's parking lot.

Two of my children who wanted to further develop their vocabulary used their enjoyment of writing a good story as a catalyst. (The underlined words are the new vocabulary words.)

It makes sense that spelling, grammar, and vocabulary are learned during the same stage as learning to express ideas with words on paper. As mentioned in Chapter Five, left-brained learners specialize in words, so learning to write can be instituted at the same time as learning to read. In this way, handwriting, spelling, grammar, and vocabulary are addressed. Right-brained learners begin the translation of their stories and ideas into written words after learning to read and becoming fluent in that skill. Thus, learning to spell, understanding grammar, and incorporating new vocabulary happen at that stage as well, which is the 11 to 13 year time frame. Handwriting can be encouraged when the symbolization stage starts in the 8 to 10 year range.

Just like technology has taken a primary place in our society, words still have a prized place as well. It can be difficult for parents and teachers to consider waiting so long. As mentioned many times in this book, just because a right-brained learner isn't engaging in learning activities like we are used to seeing in school doesn't mean the right-brained child isn't developing skills in that area. As described in Chapters Thirteen and Fourteen, right-brained children express their ideas through oral storytelling, movie-making adventures, and creative outlet endeavors before reading occurs. A lot of verbal communication and collaboration occurs that exposes them to new vocabulary and spoken word rhythms and intonations associated with grammar. After reading occurs, the highly visual mind of a right-brained person subconsciously notices the patterns of spelling and grammar and picks up new vocabulary through context. All the important basic writing elements are learned at the *right* time in the *right* manner.

References and Notes

[1] *Growing without Schooling* is the magazine started by the late John Holt founded in 1977 and discontinued in 2001. Back issues are available to be read at http://www.holtgws.com/growingwith outsc.html.

[2] Eide, Brock L. and Fernette F. Eide. *The Dyslexic Advantage: Unlocking the Hidden Potential of the Dyslexic Brain.* Hudson Street Press, 2011.

[3] The resource I used was Blanchard, Cherie. *Word Roots, Level A, Book 1* and *Level B, Book 1.* Critical Thinking Books & Software, 2002.

[4] Stout, Kathryn. *Natural Speller.* Design-A-Study, 1989.

[5] McCabe, Don. *Sequential Spelling.* AVKO Educational Research Foundation, 2006. This series has seven volumes.

[6] The image is a one day assignment completed by my electronics son from the following resource: Phillips, Wanda C. *Daily Grams: Grade 5*. ISHA Enterprises, Inc., 2002. There are six levels in the series.

[7] Phillips, Wanda C. *Daily Grams*. ISHA Enterprises, Inc., 2002. There are six levels in the series.

[8] Baker, Michael. *Editor in Chief*. Critical Thinking Co., 1995. There are eight books in the series, and each is also available on computer software.

[9] The resource I used was Burchers, Sam, Max, and Bryan. *Vocabulary Cartoons*. New Monic Books, 1998.

[10] Blakey, Barbara. *Total Language Plus*. There are at least 54 titles in the series ranging from elementary age reading material to high school.

Chapter Sixteen

Early Subject Strengths

Shift Begins with Me

"Hey, son, I hear the natural history museum in Pittsburgh is having a special exhibit of a real mummified human." I knew my then 7-year-old firstborn son would be excited about seeing something in which he had shown an interest for several years. I was quite surprised when he started looking at library books about ancient Egypt. *"What 5-year-old is interested in ancient histories?"* I wondered. Of course, I was comparing him to the only person I really knew—and that was me. Throughout my school experience I just didn't get history. Sure, I remembered dates and people and events for tests easily enough. When the backdrop was explained, however, history seemed like a mythical story with no context for me—and that was recent history! Now I had a young

child who seemed to naturally understand how history fit into his world view, especially ancient peoples and customs.

I took my son to the natural history museum where he went from exhibit to exhibit, eager to know what each placard said, able to add some commentary to most ideas. When we reached the mummified human, my son studied it with hushed tones and a reverent attitude. Again I compared to what I knew; my own experience. I went on a few field trips to museums while in elementary school. I anticipated boring experiences and always felt vindicated since everything seemed so disconnected to my current reality. I possessed no imaginative ability to reap any benefits from exposure to historical or scientific ideas.

When we got home from our trip, my son sought out some of the ancient Egypt materials he'd collected. He came across ... a mummification experiment using a chicken. He convinced me we should try it. (I imagined a curious neighbor peeking into our garage to see what homeschoolers are all about. She'd see a dead chicken strung up from the ceiling, body juices dripping into a container below, as we tried to figure out how to prepare the "body" for mummification. It's what horror stories are made of.)

I've since discovered that the subjects in which my firstborn son was interested were not unusual for a right-brained learner. At a young age, he grew interested in ancient history, nature, science experiments, mythology, geography, and social studies. None of these subjects, with the exception of nature, interested me as a young left-brained learner. My right-brained husband, though, says he had similar interests when young and continues to be intrigued in the topics as an adult.

The scope and sequence in schools tend to limit exposure to these subjects in early elementary. This worked for me as a left-brained child because these were subjects in which I was relatively weak. Since schools tend to follow the strengths and learning patterns of the left-brained processing preference, these subjects don't make it to center stage during early skill acquisition. Reading, writing, spelling, and math facts take priority. As noted in the learning time frame charts found in Chapters Four and Seven, a right-brained child has a stronger interest in areas of study that promotes creative and imaginative thinking. History, other cultures, how nature works, diverse animals and living things, and the people and places in our society are prime fodder for these right-brained strengths.

History

The first historical fiction I remember reading aloud to my right-brained children was the newly released *American Girl* series.[1] Although most of my children are boys, female main characters didn't seem to dilute their interest in viewing history from the point of view of their peers. I noticed my very right-brained artist son and right-brained writer daughter both reacted emotionally to the historical events, deeply feeling the human element involved. It was real to them. Whether reading about the mistreatment of slave children or the sacrifices made by families during World War II, each child understood at an emotional, yet concrete level, the reality of living during the era in that main character's shoes.

Next, I observed that both children sought out print resources to further study the historical material. My artist son is an information-based reader (see Chapter Ten). He gathered informational-style books about the historical event to better understand it. For instance, he grew interested in the Underground Railroad after reading about the times of slaves, or he became curious about the customs of Colonial America after a story centered in that era. My writer daughter, on the other hand, is primarily a pleasure book reader. After exposure to an interesting historical event, she sought more historical fiction from a similar era. She wanted information in a story format gathering perspective from diverse characters. After hearing the *American Girl* series, my writer daughter read many of the *Dear America* series[2] to learn more history. Each child sought further learning using their preferred reading style based on brain processing preference.

I also noticed how the pursuit of history revolved around the creative outlet each child enjoyed. My artist son and information reader was always researching and drawing historical material. Because of his strong auditory skills and large vocabulary, he also enjoyed lecture-style resources whether through conversations with his history-buff father or documentaries. My theater son learns about historical events via full body experiences, acting out ideas and events. Because of my theater son's poor processing of auditory input and weak language skills, he prefers attending live reenactments and interactive visual story forms. As mentioned in Chapter Six, subjects are often more fully learned and comprehended using the preferred creative outlet.

Theater-oriented right-brained children may enjoy historical reenactments.

Cultures and Geography

Closely related to history are the different cultures around the world during various eras of time. My artist son's interest in ancient Egypt at 5 years old led to a fascination with Africa, its people, and customs at 6 years old. His love of animals

311

during the same time took him to the land of India and the island of Galapagos to know more about the diverse and unique animals found in each. When the book *Children Just Like Me*[3] came out, it triggered immediate fascination for the lives of peers all over the world.

Another resource about cultures was magazines. I was fascinated that my then 5 to 7 year old artist son examined each newly arrived edition of *National Geographic®*. As an adult and left-brained person less inclined toward history and cultures, I found the magazine boring, even though I sensed its value for others. Other more kid-friendly publications that feed a right-brained child's cultural interest are *National Geographic World®*, *Moo Cow Fan Club®*, and *Kids Discover®*.

Again I noticed that an enjoyable creative outlet can connect a right-brained child either to an intense learning opportunity or a potential future career. My artist son's love of video games led to a desire to know about Japan and its history. He spent many hours researching the people and drawing what he learned. Eventually, my artist son developed a goal to live in Japan for a season. He began teaching himself Japanese during his teen years and found an adult friend from church willing to tutor him. When she discovered his desire to live in Japan, he was invited to join her family on one of their biennial trips to see her family. She even went so far as to find two friends of her family willing to share hosting him for the summer. My artist son fulfilled that goal the summer after he turned 18. While in Japan, he lived in a townhouse in a small city and in a family home in the outlying country on the island of Shikoku. He experienced the day-to-day cultural aspects of Japan, like being responsible for cutting the wood for the outdoor bath and lighting it on a daily basis for one of his families. He visited many ancient historical monuments, museums, and locations. This visit and hands-on experience continued to inspire him to pursue a career related to the Japanese culture.

Many right-brained teens have a particular fascination with the Japanese culture. (Image[4])

Mythology

Once they start dabbling in ancient histories, it won't take long for right-brained children to discover ancient beliefs in the otherworldly. Superstition breeds imaginative ideas that attempt to solve the puzzles of mankind. With its fantastical and imaginative structure, it's no wonder that mythology fascinates a young, right-brained, creative child. One might think that more ancient peoples were right-brained to succeed in an environment with a stronger need for astronomical navigation, knowledge of nature for medicine and sustenance, and the need to use one's hands to subsist. With those imaginative minds, it must have been easier to come up with the diverse gods and fantastical creatures like unicorns and dragons, all traced to Greek origin, to explain the ancient historical thinking process. Then there's Egyptian mythology surrounding religious rituals and gods. All of these treasures for creative expression were unearthed through ancient histories and cultures when my children studied them. The knowledge that otherworld entities can be brought to life inspired many drawings and stories.

Children of both genders love dragons and unicorns in the early years. My artist son's six year birthday party theme was dragons. We wrote a dragon-themed invitation and played dragon-themed games, created and handmade by my son. With my husband's help and son's direction, dragon masks were designed for coloring by each attendee in place of traditional birthday party hats. All of this creative-enriched fun initiated by my right-brained son was unfortunately not reciprocated by his left-brained mother—only a plain chocolate cake was served.

Dragonology was popularized by the book by the same name *Dragonology: The Complete Book of Dragons.*[5] My writer daughter's imagination took off with this. She learned and wrote in dragon language, created a blog where others could study dragons with her, and awarded dragon certificates to participants. My writer daughter also collected unicorn-themed books and unicorn figurines, and enjoyed unicorn-themed clothing, coloring books, and toys. Though girls tend to favor unicorns and boys favor dragons, both are often attractions for the right-brained child's imagination.

Dragon script as used in my daughter's journal writing.

Animals

Is there a connection between the imaginative creatures of mythology and the exotic animals found all around us? How many times do we get to see these wild animals up close and personal? Not often except when we go to the zoo, and then it's only the smallest percentage of animals. This is why visiting zoos was one of our top priorities. My children loved the excitement of seeing new creatures. We have a book called *The Animal Atlas*[6] that was one of the only books that fell apart from sheer overuse. The book featured large colorful depictions of animals from various parts of the world. The upper left corner of each two-page layout shows the world with the featured area colored red so a reader can get a holistic view of where those particular animals live. *The Animal Atlas* is organized by location and topography. Through his strong interest in animals, my son learned all of the various topographies of countries and continents.

Atlases are great visual learning tools for the early years. One of ours was used so much, it fell apart. (Image[7])

I particularly remember my artist son's interests in whales, sharks, and penguins. He was especially interested in the size comparisons of whales, as well as the locations where they live. I believe he knew every kind of whale before this interest was saturated. During one of my bookstore runs I found a book containing stats for each kind of whale. I thought he might like it because of his interest in size stats. I observed how he used the size comparisons on his own. He meticulously drew a smaller-than-normal sized ruler that worked on the scale in which he likes to draw. He cut out this small ruler and began to draw comparative-sized whales as measured with this small-to-scale ruler, based on the stats from the book. He did this for hours and for weeks before he grew bored of it. He then moved on to sharks, and learned most of the types and locations for those.

The Pebble and the Penguin[8] movie sparked his penguin interest. As he learned and researched this animal category, I was surprised to know there are so many types. My artist son shared details with me as I showed interest in listening, and he created many pictures and stories during this time frame. I mentioned my son's interest to a friend, and discovered her husband, a geologist, had been to Antarctica some years before. While there he filmed the penguins he'd seen, and later agreed to share his film and knowledge. My artist son eagerly viewed the film, sitting on the edge of his seat as the images appeared. Before the Ph.D. scientist could share his knowledge, my artist son identified each penguin and blurted out the information he knew about each. Our scientist friend was impressed with our then 8-year-old son. We have to remember our right-brained children can impress us with knowledge of early subjects they love instead of worrying about the left-brained skill sets of reading and math fact drilling. Both are valuable and can be attained at the right time for each brain processing preference.

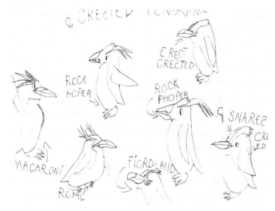

Animal or geography studies can be as impressive as knowing arithmetic.

My children didn't seem interested in having their own pets until the 8 to 10 year range. I wonder if the worldwide animals' imaginative qualities outweighed the nitty-gritty reality of taking care of a real pet. As potential evidence of this, my daughter accumulated multiple electronic pets during this time frame. These pets were attached to her 24/7 as she attended to their every "beeped" need. Her favorite toys were Littlest Pet Shop™ animals and stuffed animals. Eventually, she gathered a large collection of Ty Beanie Babies®. Thanks to my children's appreciation of the animal kingdom, they took good care of them when pets did come into our home.

316

Nature

Each of my children seems to have reverence for God's creation. For instance, the movie *Fern Gully*[9] shared a theme that left my sensitive children rallying for the preservation of nature's gifts. My writer daughter was and is what I call a nature girl. This aligns with the idea of the seven intelligences theory developed by Howard Gardner.[10] He later added two new intelligences: existential intelligence and nature intelligence. As noted in Chapter Two, I believe both of these intelligences are often strengths of a right-brained person. My sixth child (my theater son) is also attuned to nature with a heavy interest in plants, flowers, and the Native American culture. Both spent as much time outdoors as possible communing with nature.

A nature person may have an interest in Native American cultures.

One season when my writer daughter was around 6 to 7 years old, we discovered a type of worm growing under bushes around our house. Each worm was growing in a tight cocoon, wiggling inside. My daughter spent a lot of time watching these worms transform. Other times, she collected bucketsful just to see them moving as a whole unit. Throughout this same summer, she and her father visited a different park each week, identifying trees and collecting leaves.

When she was 8 to 9 years old, we lived on top of a mountain in a log house. She spent that entire summer watching an ant colony build and maintain their home life. I saw a lot of experimenting as she created problems for the ants with a stick. On the other hand, she also often protected the colony when a new puppy tried to lie on their premises.

From about 11 to 15 years old, my writer daughter delved into learning about animal behavior, starting with weekly horse riding lessons and a strong interest in our two dogs. More importantly, she had the strong desire to explore with her dogs a stretch of woods between our subdivision and Kyle Petty's 100+ acre farm. I gave her safety rules, took a deep breath, and let her go every week for some years. She knew every square inch of the area she named Mye Creek. When she completed her season of exploring, my writer daughter meticulously journaled and documented her area and the places therein for posterity. I believe she copied and buried it at the location. Maybe someday she'll take her children to find it.

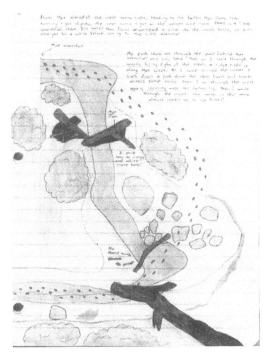

One of my nature daughter's maps of her special exploring spot.

My writer daughter kept a menagerie of animals from about 14 to 18 years old. She always made sure they had a clean cage, sufficient food and water, and interacted with them in an animal-friendly way. Eventually she collected four birds from owners who didn't want them, some gerbils, and a hermit crab. And she had her prized gray tree frog, raised from an egg.

During one of her explorations in the horse field that abuts our home, she found a puddle of frog eggs and tried to

318

rescue them. On her way home after the rescue attempt, she noticed a lone egg clinging to her jacket. She decided to see if she could raise it. She was successful and it grew into a full-sized tree frog. Each night she found the frog's preferred food of crickets, worms, moths, pill bugs or any other small creeping thing, and hand-fed it. It was quite tame and sat near her as she wrote novels on her computer.

The nature intelligence seems to come easily to some of our right-brained children. It appears when they're young in the most innocent ways, such as collecting worm pupa or watching ants. Even those right-brained children who don't have a propensity for nature often reveal a strong reverence for the creation of the world, possibly due to understanding their place in the grand scheme of things. My young, creative, sensitive children had an appreciation of and wonder about the beauty and grandeur of all that we have dominion over, and each took that responsibility seriously.

Science

Associated with nature and animals is the common early childhood boy interest in dinosaurs. My oldest artist son was no exception. I don't know whether to classify this study as science or animals, but it's usually listed under science. My artist son scoured the library bookshelves to find every dinosaur book they had, especially non-fiction books. We amassed our own quality dinosaur books, too. By the time he was 5 years old, he knew at least 50 dinosaurs, what period they were from, and additional facts about each. During his kindergarten year, I created a unit study for him and another young friend. We played games, created a huge chart of all the different dinosaurs, and made a life-sized paper image of one of the well-known dinosaurs. He wanted to be a paleontologist for the longest time.

	Characteristics	Time	Plant/Meat	Legs?	W/S/Fly
Ankylosaurus		Cretaceous			W
Pteranodon		Cretaceous			F
Stegosaurus		Jurassic			W
Compsognathus		Jurassic			W
Pachycephalosaurus		Cretaceous		2	W
Lambeosaurus		Cretaceous			W
Plesiosaurus		Jurassic			2
Dimorphodon		Jurassic		2	7
Quetzalcoatlus		Cretaceous		2	7
Elasmosaurus		Cretaceous			

Dinosaurs are a common interest for right-brained boys.

Because my artist son is a verbal- and visual-oriented learner, he enjoyed print and video science resources. We discovered the *Eyewitness Books* and videos[11] when they first came out and began a collection immediately. My children watched the movies over and over again. Each of my successive children continued to enjoy the format of these tapes. My oldest had these books out constantly as he grew; I'd say the *Eyewitness Books* were his core science curriculum. He took a standardized test at 14 with a science section and scored in the 99th percentile, so I'd also say they were effective.

During my daughter's early years, my husband offered a year-long opportunity to do science experiments with him that he playfully named, "Science Time with Mad Dad." The oldest two enjoyed the hands-on approach and social interaction as the time was modeled after the *Bill Nye the Science Guy* television program[12] my older children enjoyed.

My builder son especially loved science experiments. A builder is a hands-on kinesthetic learner and science experiments require those skills. Using several great visual science experiment books we owned, my builder son liked to puzzle out things for himself using the pictures since he was a pre-reader. My builder son ended up going through an entire traditional science curriculum in high school. He and his two older siblings also enjoyed watching *Mythbusters*[13] during their teen years as well. For right-brained learners, the experiment process takes advantage of their strengths.

Scouting® is another avenue to pursue nature and science activities. (Image[14])

I've found that the right-brained child's early subject strengths often become a fond side interest in his life, or an element of his career choice. One was a huge history buff in his early years who built on that over the years and today incorporates that knowledge into his career of manga artist. Another was a nature person in her early years and beyond. Today, she chooses to live in the country and surround herself with God's creations. The other child who was interested in science experiments at an early age today is pursuing a career as a math and science geek. My next two children have an intellectual disability that prevented their full interest in the natural early subjects. The last two children also have a knack for the early subjects. The sixth is another nature person and I have no doubt he will enter a career related to nature and the outdoors. (He insists he'll live on an Indian reservation someday.) The last child, a kinesthetic learner, leans toward science and the outdoors (his form of nature). My hubby is still a huge history buff who is discovering late his love of nature.

These early subject strength interests of history, mythology, cultures and geography, animals, nature, and science pursued by right-brained children are as valid as the reading acquisition, math facts, spelling, and story writing that are pursued by left-brained children in the early years of 5 to 7. Because our society values the left-brained time frame for learning subjects, sometimes we forget the subjects that are early favorites for right-brained children. But these subjects should be a foundation for right-brained children in their early, 5 to 7 year learning lives. Each is a subject that draws upon the natural creative and imaginative core that is a strength of their brain processing preference.

References and Notes

[1] About half of the *American Girl* series books were written by Valerie Tripp. Each girl has a set of six books. There are currently eleven girls: Addy, Felicity & Elizabeth, Josefina, Julie & Ivy, Kaya, Kirsten, Kit & Ruthie, Marie-Grace & Cecile, Molly & Emily, Rebecca, and Samantha & Nellie.

[2] There are various authors for the *Dear America* series. They were originally published by Scholastic from 1996-2004 and there were 36 titles in the original series. This series has been re-launched in 2010 with 17 titles so far, with many new titles.

[3] Kindersley, Barnabas & Anabel. *Children Just Like Me.* Dorling Kindersley, 1995.

[4] My artist son is standing in front of the Itsukushima Shrine on the Japanese island of Miyajima in 2005.

[5] Drake, Ernest and Dugald Steer. *Dragonology: The Complete Book of Dragons (Ologies).* Candlewick, 2003.

[6] Lilly, Kenneth. *The Animal Atlas.* Knopf Books for Young Readers, 1992.

[7] Ibid.

[8] Bluth, Don and Goldman, Gary. *The Pebble and the Penguin.* Metro-Goldwyn-Mayer, 1995.

[9] Kroyer, Bill. *Fern Gully: The Last Rainforest.* 20th Century Fox, 1992.

[10] Gardner, Howard. *Frames of Mind: The Theory of Multiple Intelligences.* Basic Books, 1983.

[11] *Eyewitness Books,* published and ©2012 DK Publishing, 375 Hudson St. New York, NY 10014. There are currently over 100 titles in the series. Time Life Video® put out the documentaries on video with 39 titles and 1 special.

[12] Created by Bill Nye, PBS ran this educational children's show from 1993 to 1998. There were 100 episodes over 5 seasons.

[13] Created by Peter Rees, Discovery Channel began running *Mythbusters* in 2003 and still is in production. So far, there have been over 200 episodes over 10 seasons.

[14] The uniform in the picture is the official uniform of the Cub Scout™ program and are all registered trademarks of the Boy Scouts of America®.

323

Section Four

Common Labels

What We Believe.

If my child can't focus, has lots of energy, or acts without thinking, he has a problem or a disability.

Shifting Perspective.

We all have different levels of attention, energy, and the ability to self-regulate. One type of attention level can work well in one setting or with one activity and not another. Maturity and skill-building can help each child use the attributes that make up who they are to benefit their gifts.

Chapter Seventeen highlights the factors that contribute to differing focus, energy, and impulsivity features. Examples of skills and strategies that strengthen the nature of a right-brained learner in these areas are shared.

What We Believe.

There is a genetic predisposition to having dyslexia, dysgraphia, and dyscalculia because my child's relative has it, too.

Shifting Perspective.

Being right-brained and left-brained is genetically based. Schools are structured to support left-brained learners. Understanding the right way and the right time that right-brained children learn is crucial. The mismatched learning environment found in school set up our right-brained learners to fail, including contributing to the proliferation of learning disability labels like dyslexia, dysgraphia, and dyscalculia.

Chapter Eighteen makes the direct connection between how right-brained children learn naturally and the signs and symptoms of all the "dys-"abilities. This chapter shows how to support right-brained children on their natural learning path to reading, math, and handwriting that maximizes success for these learners.

What We Believe.

If your child is weak in processing auditory information, isn't that a disadvantage to learning, so shouldn't we fix it?

Shifting Perspective.

Schools *do* use auditory teaching tools extensively. This *is* a disadvantage for those who don't prefer the auditory input modality. That doesn't mean the child needs "fixing," though. Many people use a variety of input modalities and schools should reflect that.

Chapter Nineteen explains how input modalities work and describes the three most commonly used senses for learning: auditory, visual, and touch (kinesthetic). Skills and strategies are shared to better support the brain processing preferences and different temperaments utilizing input modalities. Understanding the developmental connection between hearing and learning, and the brain connection between vision and processing information is discussed.

Kinesthetic learners need full body experiences to learn best.

What We Believe.

If you're highly intelligent, you learn everything faster than everyone else.

328

Shifting Perspective.

This is a partial truth, but it doesn't share the whole picture. The gifted *sometimes* learn subjects earlier and *sometimes* learn more easily. Brain processing dominance and individual temperament still impact a child, even with high intelligence.

Chapter Twenty outlines how giftedness and being right-brained dominant can both be supported without negatively labeling the differences. Each major gifted factor is discussed and the right-brained element is acknowledged. Examples of how *both* traits play out in the learning and social realms are addressed.

What We Believe.

Children with autism learn in a completely different way than their peers.

Shifting Perspective.

There are more commonalities between the learning development of those with autism and right-brained dominant learners than we initially notice. Children with autism have *more* intensity in many realms, so we may not pay attention to the underlying similarities.

Chapter Twenty-One sifts out the intensity factor contributed by autism to help parents and educators recognize the right-brained patterns of learning. When we recognize the connection, it can help us provide support to children with autism educationally, socially, and behaviorally that steers them along their natural developmental path.

What We Believe.

There's nothing a person can do to change the tide of the labeling epidemic in our large schooling system.

Shifting Perspective.

One person *can* create a small change, but *many* empowered parents and dedicated professionals can create a full-blown grassroots movement. Historical evidence proves the power of the common person in making huge impacts in the world.

Chapter Twenty-Two gives examples of empowered people making a difference in our society. It shares ideas of the types of changes that could improve education for right-brained children. This chapter also shows individual and collective ways to become involved ourselves and celebrates examples of those doing so.

Chapter Seventeen

Paying Attention
to the Connection

Shift Begins with Me

At 10 years old, my builder son wanted to memorize some statements of faith that were part of a program for our children's group at church. Standard memorization strategies just weren't working for him. Try as he might, the statements wouldn't stick in his brain. I knew he'd been teaching himself the piano for the past year, and I also knew these statements of faith had been put to music. I told him this and suggested he give that a try to see if it helped. My builder son eagerly plucked out the music to get the rhythm enough to learn the words. He noticed it was beginning to work! He did some troubleshooting and discovered it worked best if he learned the music piece on the piano first, before learning the words. In this way, the rhythm was established in his brain, and the words flowed more easily into place. After a while, he could state the words without the music. Within a month, he memorized all thirteen statements of faith and recited them in front of the children's group at church to earn his reward.

Fast forward to age 14 when my builder son began attending an early morning scripture study class at our church. Each of the four high school years, the youth studied a different book of scripture. Each year, there were 25 scriptures to be memorized, passing them off in front of the class or the instructor. My builder son's goal was to memorize all 100 over the four-year period. As he set out to memorize each, he discovered that his visualization skills had developed well enough to use and easily memorize the scripture passage in a seemingly typical manner. Did he have a memory disability at 10? Apparently not. But if he'd been in school, would he have been labeled because of his lack of ability to memorize "in a typical manner" the first time around?

There are certain skill sets that tend to develop over time for some children. Memory skills are one of those sets. My builder son needed more time to develop his visualization skills to utilize them as a most effective memory tool. Because a right-brained learner tends to prefer using long-term memory versus short-term memory (see Chapter Seven), it may take longer and it may take more pre-skills for that child to learn to access the less preferred process. As noted in my charts in Chapter Four, the beginning stage of efficient collaboration between the hemispheric specialties is 8 to 10 years old. Proficiency is usually reached between 11 and 13 years old. The memory story above seems to validate that time frame.

Another area where development is similar is attention. One of the most common labels for a right-brained learner is attention deficit disorder/attention deficit hyperactivity disorder (ADD/ADHD). Do some children need more time to develop certain skills to be proficient based on their preferred processing system? As noted in Chapter Three, there's considerable overlap of traits between those diagnosed with ADD/ADHD and the right-brained processing preference. This same builder son who needed more time to become proficient with memory tools also needed more time to become proficient with attention skills. His best attention development occurred in the 11 to 13 year time frame. He still exhibited outstanding learning capabilities, especially those with regard to the gifts of the right-brained learner, as he developed his pre-skills while awaiting the appropriate developmental shift required for better attention capabilities during non-preferred activities.

Inattention

Many of the inattention symptoms for ADD/ADHD correlate with the high level of creativity and imagination that are at the foundation of a right-brained learner. One of the common myths of ADD/ADHD mentions that children with ADD/ADHD can often concentrate on tasks they enjoy and desire, but if a task is considered boring or repetitive, they often lose the ability to pay attention.[1] Worksheets, listening to a lecture, and **performing tedious symbolic work** have little to no creative and imaginative aspect to them. With these it's no wonder the right-brained child:[2]

- ❖ Doesn't pay attention to details
- ❖ Makes careless mistakes
- ❖ Has trouble staying focused; is easily distracted
- ❖ Appears not to listen when spoken to
- ❖ Has difficulty remembering things and following instructions

❖ Has trouble staying organized, planning ahead, and finishing projects
❖ Gets bored with a task before it's completed
❖ Frequently loses or misplaces homework, books, toys, or other items

When this same right-brained child values and enjoys **creative and imaginative activities**, you will see a higher level of:[3]

✓ Pays attention to details
✓ Makes careful work
✓ Stays focused; stays on task
✓ Listens intently when spoken to
✓ Remembers detailed pieces of information and follows instructions
✓ Comes up with unique ways to approach the task
✓ Stays with a task indefinitely
✓ Utilizes a variety of books, toys, or other items and keeps them in a stack

Matched Learning Environment

What did I do to promote more of the latter traits listed above and less of the former if a right-brained child is prone to attention differences when approaching repetitive tasks he doesn't consider interesting? I required less boring and repetitive tasks from my child! More importantly, I applied all the lessons about how children learn that I've shared throughout this book with my children and discovered the good information about right-brained learning I'm sharing now. In his book, *The Power of Neurodiversity*, Thomas Armstrong clarifies the attention question: "Children (and adults) labeled ADHD are actually *very good at paying attention.* [T]hey are actually *good* at two different forms of attention [a "homing" attention and a "roaming" attention] and have problems primarily with one other form ["central-task" attention"]." Armstrong describes the roaming attention as the ability to quickly notice details in a setting, the homing attention as the ability to stay focused on something of interest for long periods of time, and central-task attention as being able to work on routine activities often created by others to perform. [4] I created a strengths-based learning environment that fits the gifts of the right-brained child.

When it's a creative project, detail and focus are not a problem. (Image[5])

I didn't find school boring or repetitious. What I was taught in school, and the way in which it was taught, matched my learning style and I enjoyed it immensely. I expected this same love of learning in my children. If it wasn't happening, I assumed I needed to change the learning environment, not the child. As I observed what attracted my children in the learning and attention realms, and as I added to that foundation similar activities and subjects, each child developed a love of learning. That's what happens when the learning style and time frame match the learner.

335

Listening Strategies

I noticed my children with competent auditory input facilities (see Chapter Nineteen for those without) created their own attention strategies when they wanted to listen to something or someone but found their attention easily wandering. During our read-aloud times, my artist son drew and my writer daughter colored as they listened (see Chapter Nine). Their chosen creative activities helped turn on the right side of the brain without distracting them from listening and comprehending the read-aloud. During an activity requiring concentration, some of my children found that listening to music helps them focus. Even now as adults, I noticed they continue to utilize similar strategies, such as listening to their iPod while doing chores. Doodling while taking lecture notes is another listening strategy utilizing a creative outlet—in this case, drawing. A study published in *Applied Cognitive Psychology* by University of Plymouth professor of psychology, Jackie Andrade, validates the benefits of doodling on focus.[6]

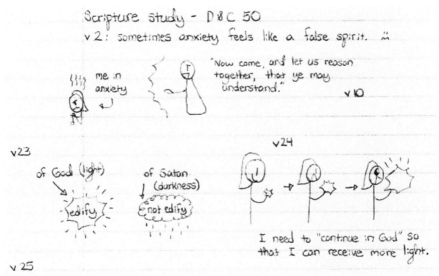

My writer daughter doodles as she takes notes during a sermon to better pay attention.

Gender Differences

Does this mean attention issues don't exist? Not to the prolific level we see in our schools today. In the *New York Times* bestseller, *Raising Cain: Protecting the Emotional Life of Boys.* by Dan Kindlon, Ph.D. and Michael Thompson, Ph.D., the authors state, "In our experience it is evident that most of what is being called ADD today would not have been called ADD fifteen or twenty years ago and that much of it falls within the normal range of boy behavior."[7] As I mentioned in Chapter Two, I don't view the right-brained learning information in a bubble. There are a myriad of contributing factors to consider. One of those factors is gender. It does appear that more boys than girls represent as right-brained and are labeled ADD. That's because the boy gene tends to have the strengths aligned with the traits of a right-brained person: big picture thinking, spatial-oriented, non-verbal prone, and intuitive. In the self-help psychology book *Be Your Own Therapist*, the author claims "the evidence is clear that women hang out more in their left brains, whereas men tend to hang out more in their right brains."[8] Again, nothing is said in a bubble. We know there are right-brained women and left-brained men. This is simply more information to consider and make part of our overall view of how children learn.

Co-Morbidity Situations

In my experience, those instances where attention may be a problem mostly show up as co-morbidity to something bigger. For instance, I have a child who eventually was diagnosed with bipolar. One of the early symptoms was lack of concentration, even in his areas of strong interest, like drawing. The inability to concentrate on his interests didn't emerge, though, until the bipolar symptoms became visible in his mid-teen years. A significant change in the ability to appreciate and pay attention to something normally enjoyed is a red flag signifying something is wrong.

Another of my children has an intellectual disability which impacts his language competency. He's always had a difficult time even listening to a person as they speak to him. But is the difficulty related to his inability to understand, so he uses a "tuning out" strategy to not look stupid for not getting what's being said? Quite possibly, since he can sit and listen to a movie or spend hours at a reenactment, pursuing his Indian interest, or searching for gems at a gem mine.

If focus in desired activities can be achieved, ADD needs to be questioned.

Focus Strategies

While my two inattentive children were growing up, I accommodated their lack of ability. Instead of giving a two- or three-step direction, I started with one-step. Until each son could complete a direction right in front of me, I didn't send them to another room. ("Please get your shoes right there.") As each son successfully and consistently followed one level of instruction, I moved to the next level. Don't get me wrong. As a multi-tasking woman with strong focus skills, I was dumbfounded in my weak moments with how a simple instruction right in front of them couldn't be accomplished. Luckily, the majority of the time I accepted our differences without judgment and gave value to who they are and what their strengths and weaknesses bring to the table of humanity.

At the developmentally appropriate time (starting between 11 and 13 years when the brain shift occurs), we collaborated more efficiently in implementing new skills and strategies. My builder son stated he had trouble staying focused on activities heavily-laden with language. The imaginative world inside his head, or the interesting project awaiting him and contemplated in the recesses of his visual mind, is difficult to resist in those circumstances. My builder son brainstormed ways to use visual note-taking to help him focus during group activities centered in language. He also developed better attending skills when speaking with another person.

Although my son is aware of the medication route so many take, he declined it for himself at this time.

Practicing focus skills with trusted mentors is beneficial.

I do believe we are over-medicating a trait that has useful attributes. The seeming inattentive nature of my builder son on language-based tasks (central-task attention skills) may assist him in his equally beneficial strength of focusing for long periods of time on a project of interest (homing attention skills). There's a running joke around my home that my children can tell I'm in heavy concentration mode on the computer when they ask me something and I respond both vocally and visually in a spacey mode. Can this spaciness to outside distractions be a good thing that leads to full concentration and achieving flow in a preferred project (see Chapter Nine)? Each of us has strengths and weaknesses that develop who we are; let's celebrate that instead of fearing it.

Hyperactivity

A child can be diagnosed with ADD/ADHD inattentive type as discussed above, or he can be defined as ADD/ADHD

with hyperactivity. I only have one child who falls into this category. He's also my son that has other contributing attributes that none of my other sons have in combination. The most obvious is he's my only extrovert. Other attributes worth noting are that he's "all boy" and he especially loves to be outdoors playing sports and working in the yard.

Extra energy usually means more need to be outside and active.

He's what I call the dynamo right-brained child (as described in the book *Dreamers, Discoverers & Dynamos*[9]). Do the signs and symptoms of hyperactivity actually shape this high risk, high energy child into the person he's meant to be?[10]

- ❖ Constantly fidgets and squirms
- ❖ Often leaves his or her seat in situations where sitting quietly is expected
- ❖ Moves around constantly, often runs or climbs inappropriately
- ❖ Talks excessively
- ❖ Has difficulty playing quietly or relaxing
- ❖ Is always "on the go," as if driven by a motor
- ❖ May have a quick temper or a "short fuse"

Extroversion Factor

Let's talk about the extrovert factor. This is a temperament trait typically considered genetic. How many of the symptoms of hyperactivity can be explained by the traits of an extrovert? In the book *Nurture by Nature*, by Paul D.

Tieger and Barbara Barron-Tieger, they say "most of the behavior problems extroverted children have in school are the direct result of being confined to a chair, and required to work for an extended period of time on a paper-and-pencil activity in a room where silence must be maintained." [11] Doesn't that explain at least five of the criteria? This quality in my risk-taking son is what I noticed first when we began his learning activities. He always wanted to be with someone, he needed constant engagement with people, and playing alone or having quiet time wasn't an option. He gained energy from people and it was noticeable. As an insatiable learner, people were part of the equation for the best environment for him. It's no wonder this little dynamo spent a lot of time with his father outside with lawn tools expending his energy while meeting his extrovert needs.

Working outside with his dad meets both his extrovert and energy needs.

Gender Factor

We need to factor in the boy aspect of high energy that comes with a hyperactivity diagnosis. Our culture often views active boys as acting like animals. Plato defined boys as being "of all wild beasts, the most difficult to manage." And yet, we constantly ignore the strengths of the trait. My high-risk son isn't afraid to put himself out there and figure it out as he goes. He's the first to challenge himself to enter the adult world of work (especially outdoor machine type), play (mine keeps up with the big boys both physically and with problem-solving in airsoft matches), and relaxation (watching outdoor channel and sports). In *Raising Cain*, Kindlon and Thompson share some strengths: "Their energy is contagious, especially among other boys, and that physical energy can translate into a kind of psychological boldness."[12]

Active problem-solving ability often accompanies high energy. Let's practice fishing in the pool!

Emotional Regulation Factor

Finally, let's discuss the quick temper issue. It's common for a younger right-brained child to have emotional regulation difficulty. Because right-brained children are less verbal-oriented in the developing years between 5 and 10 years old, it's highly beneficial for them to have mentors that help with the development of emotional intelligence.

The emotional and creative worlds of right-brained children are hugely significant in their healthy development. These children feel deeply which contributes positively to creative expression. However, while the emotional regulation is underdeveloped in the early years, learning how to understand and manage these strong emotions is essential. Maybe that's another reason why academic instruction is best delayed. Developing the emotional intelligence of my right-brained boys was at the top of my priority list when they were between the ages of 5 and 10 years old.

Too many right-brained children are shamed for the very traits that define who they are. Understanding the benefit of various traits while recognizing the difficult parts can help us as parents and educators mentor these children in developing skills and balance. The Hebrew sage Hillel, over two thousand years ago, warned, "A person too anxious about being shamed cannot learn." If the very traits and temperaments that create a person are valued, especially in the important childhood years, everything is possible.

Maturity Factor

I explain in this book that a right-brained child is developing his foundational traits that rest in the creative outlets. I find the dynamo/extrovert child is developing the risk-taking attributes as well. These are the traits that will serve him well in the particular career fields that may be pursued. As mentioned in Chapter Four, a parent or educator will notice a shift that begins in the 8 to 10 year time frame. I noticed this about my high energy son. After having the space to grow into himself, I found that at around 8 to 9 years old, he was better able to sit at a desk from time to time and start exercising his mental capacities now that his physical needs were well satiated. Further, at around 10 years old, I began to notice his growing emotional maturity. He may also become focused in his active needs, such as organized sports, and take more notice of other focused creative outlets, such as developing a musical talent. My active son progressed in this way starting near the 8 year side of the time frame with soccer, swim team, karate, and basketball. He initiated learning music and a foreign language at the 10 year end of the time frame. The right-brained time frame differences are even more important to understand when a child shows these types of differences, such as having more energy, to create his optimal learning environment.

Sports are a great outlet for high energy children.

These high-energy children flourished during the era when children enjoyed more free time, outdoor time, and physical interaction activities, so that's what I gave my children. In fact, we moved to the country to facilitate this, providing activities such as wading in the creek catching crawdads, stacking wood after working with dad with the chainsaw, and building forts and climbing trees in the woods. Kindlon and Thompson said it best: "It would be a diminished world if everyone skated in precisely the same way around the circle [of a skating rink] or if the only deviation allowed were to skate graceful, skillful turns in the center of the ring. On the ice, in our schools, and in our lives, there is a need for the bold energy of a sprint of the spirit. [It's] life-affirming. If you never had that, you'd miss it."[13]

Impulsivity

The last attribute of an attention difference is impulsivity. The signs and symptoms for impulsivity are:[14]

❖ Acts without thinking
❖ Blurts out answers in class without waiting to be called on or hear the whole question
❖ Can't wait for his or her turn in line or in games

❖ Says the wrong thing at the wrong time
❖ Often interrupts others
❖ Intrudes on other people's conversations or games
❖ Inability to keep powerful emotions in check, resulting in angry outbursts or temper tantrums
❖ Guesses, rather than taking time to solve a problem

As we began our short-teaching moments during the 8 to 10 year time frame (when I believe boys in particular are finally ready for some short seat work), my risk-taking son constantly wiggled and even sang. He talked out loud as he worked. Interrupting others is common for him throughout the day. Tieger and Tieger from the book *Nurture by Nature* continue to explain the extrovert connection: "Extroverted children frequently interrupt others, unable to hold onto any thought or idea for any length of time without expressing it. When you interrupt an extroverted child's words, you interfere with her thinking...extroverted children do tend to think out loud, and they may simply say things to see how they sound."[15] Auditory input is a viable way to learn (see Chapter Nineteen). In fact, we seem to value it as a primary mode of instruction in classroom settings, and yet, when a child is young and uses his own voice to utilize that input modality, he's criticized and told to be quiet. As noted in the inattention section of this chapter, some skills and strategies take time to develop. Processing out loud as thoughts come into mind is a viable learning method, yet adults don't support or have the patience required for the skill to reach its peak efficiency.

Lack of Self-Regulation

I always viewed my risk-taking son and his incessant talking, and constant interrupting, and limited patience as an energy *attribute,* as noted in the hyperactivity section. It's my theater son who strongly represents what I would classify as impulsive. Impulsivity is about having no stops, or a lack of emotional self-regulation. Right-brained people are highly emotive people and it takes a young person some time and practice to learn to manage and balance the intense emotions felt. To the young right-brained person with underdeveloped emotional self-regulation, right and wrong seem less important than accomplishing the creative expression being sought.

As a strong right-brained child with a highly developed imaginative life, most of my theater son's impulsive actions are directly related to achieving a particular goal within his "otherworld life." For instance, I've had countless pieces of clothing or towels or toys destroyed in the name of making just the right costume. I've had countless dangerous objects taken or actions completed in the name of legitimizing an imagined scenario. Speaking or acting out of turn can be about an idea triggered within his mind and it's full throttle ahead. The good news is that the passage of time and maturity bring self-control for our right-brained children when coupled with the introduction of emotional intelligence skills. My right-brained children moved toward competence with emotional self-regulation during the 8 to 10 year time frame, and grew more competent during the 11 to 13 year time frame.

A soccer jersey has been "altered" so that Teddy matches my theater son.

Coexisting Behaviors

Coexisting behaviors may appear with an impulsive right-brained personality. I've dealt with compulsive lying and food binging, hording, or stealing, that may include pica, the act of eating non-edible objects.

346

Telling Stories or Compulsive Lying? Young children go through a developmental stage during which they like to tell tall tales or fish stories, sometimes as early as preschool age. The foundational trait of a right-brained child is imagination. Embellishing a story is simply a creative way to make something small and irrelevant more exciting and interesting. If pressed, children in this natural stage will usually let you know they understand the difference between the reality and the story told. With my impulsive theater son, though, I noticed a different reaction when I tried to get him to acknowledge the true story. He had an almost panicked need to have no stops to his version of the story. This red flag showed me that he needed support to be able to release his impulsive need and desire to utilize imaginative expression in this manner.

I employed several strategies to help him stop impulsively embellishing stories. The first important thing I did was carefully choose my labels. I feel that people live up or down to the labels we place upon them; I wasn't going to call him a "liar." If I chose to do that, it would take the act of creative expression and turn it dark. Shame tends to hurt, not help, the sensitive soul of a right-brained child.

Second, I removed his need to defend his position. I didn't ask him, "Are you telling me a story?" This question simply gave him space to entrench in his impulsive choice. Instead, I labeled what I was hearing: "Oh, I hear you adding fun things to the real story." Third, I gave him permission to exercise creativity while clearly differentiating between it and reality. So, I would continue by saying, "It's okay to tell stories about real things. That makes it more exciting and interesting." Finally, I would end by giving him permission to tell me the real story. "I enjoyed your story part, so now tell me the real story." Often I would begin with my version of the real story. "You *did* see some deer on the drive home, it just wasn't fifteen with a buck with ten points. What was it, three doe?" This basic strategy seemed to lessen the hold of the impulsive creative process over him.

When we started working on this, he seemed to go a few weeks at a time before letting go of the habit. Now that he's in the 11 to 13 year stage, he may fall back into the behavior once a year for a few days at a time before dropping the old habits again. Controlling my reactions to his adamant stance on a story's truth by recognizing the creative process involved in the habit—and the strong hold the impulsive trait played—was an important shift for me. Understanding this helped me give my theater son the support and skills he needed to release the impulsive attribute connection.

Food Focus: Pica or Stress Relief? Impulsivity extends to food for my theater son as well. I noticed early on that he was always on the hunt for food. At first, I reacted to his higher need to seek out food by controlling his food intake. My desire to control only fueled his drive and encouraged food stealing. I knew I had to work with his natural urge, and learn to understand the function of his higher need to eat, rather than try to stop it. I observed the types of food he most craved, and then worked to provide an appropriate choice in that food genre. I brought in the fruits and raw vegetables I knew he liked. Finally, I set up an area where he had free access, any time, without asking. This relieved his need to defend and battle.

Over time I shared information to help him pace his impulsiveness toward food and help him understand the sensory and anxiety-releasing needs the food filled. Chewing is a stress reliever. We collaborated to find other ways to get the same effect, such as chewing gum or recognizing boredom.

Most of his pica choices were paper. Since paper is easily accessible in our home wherever you are, such as magazines, drawing paper, and our choice to use paper plates for meal times, it was the readily available choice to chew on paper to alleviate his anxiety nature. I helped him recognize why he was using paper, and steered him toward the food choices and other alternative choices we discussed. Most of all, we patiently waited out the maturation process while at the same time solidifying skills and strategies.

348

Chewing is a stress reliever, and food can be a choice to fill that need.

Kindlon and Thompson reveal, "All boys fit somewhere on a spectrum of distractability, impulsivity, and hyperactivity. The fact that they are more physically restless and impulsive than girls makes many more boys than girls 'look' ADHD."[16] Two to four times more boys than girls are diagnosed with ADD/ADHD. Boys are much more right-brained oriented than girls. Attention-based differences often indicate the need for a more creative and interest-based environment. The solution is adapting the environment and style of learning to the needs of the students, including the need for activity, hands-on experiences, and developmental appropriateness. It's about accepting and embracing differences instead of fixing and medicating differences away. Instead of spotlighting what we consider to be negative consequences to attention differences, we need to recognize what attention differences are telling us about existing education processes.

Our right-brained children are shouting out through the ADD/ADHD epidemic that we need more creativity in the classroom, more movement during the day, and more hands-on experiences in the curriculum. The success of our right-brained children during the early years of school is the measuring stick to true educational reform. As parents and educators, we must say no to remediation and drugs, and say yes to appropriate developmental processes and policies that suit our right-brained children.

References and Notes

[1] At the Helpguide.org website, under Mental Health, is listed ADD/ADHD. This takes you to the ADD/ADHD Help Center where you can press a link labeled ADD/ADHD in Children. This is where the site lists its "Signs and Symptoms of Attention Deficit Disorder in Children." This is a direct link: http://helpguide.org/mental/ adhd_add_signs_symptoms.htm.

[2] This list of signs and symptoms for ADD/ADHD in Children is taken from the Helpguide.org website under the subheading "Inattentive Signs and Symptoms of ADD/ADHD." A direct link is: http://helpguide.org/mental/adhd_add_signs_symptoms.htm.

[3] Ibid. This is a reverse list of symptoms I created from the list taken from the previous endnote.

[4] Armstrong, Thomas. *The Power of Neurodiversity: Unleashing the Advantages of Your Differently Wired Brain.* Da Capo Press, 2010.

[5] The pictures drawn in this image are characters from the Nintendo® game Super Smash Bros.® Melee called Marth and Mr. Game & Watch®. Use of these images were for personal use and were not intended to challenge any copyright but was the innocent enjoyment of a creative person.

[6] Andrade, Jackie, School of Psychology, University of Plymouth, Drake Circus, Plymouth, PL4 8AA, Devon, UK. E-mail: j.andrade@ plymouth.ac.uk. Copyright ©2009 John Wiley & Sons, Ltd. http://www.lamalla.cat/media/000000000002415/000000001207002.pdf.

[7] Kindlon, Dan and Michael Thompson. *Raising Cain: Protecting the Emotional Life of Boys.* New York: Random House Inc., 2000.

[8] White, Thayer. *Be Your Own Therapist—Whoever You Hire Is Just Your Assistant.* Purple Paradox Press, 1995. http://www.psychologyhelp.com/gend134.htm.

[9] Palladino, Lucy J. *Dreamers, Discoverers & Dynamos: How to Help the Child Who Is Bright, Bored, and Having Problems in School.* New York: Ballantine Books, 1999.

---

[10] This list of signs and symptoms for ADD/ADHD in Children is taken from the Helpguide.org website under the subheading "Hyperactive Signs and Symptoms of ADD/ADHD." A direct link is: http://helpguide.org/mental/adhd_add_signs_symptoms.htm.

[11] Tieger, Paul D. & Barbara Barron-Tieger. *Nurture by Nature: How to Raise Happy, Healthy, Responsible Children Through the Insights of Personality Type.* Little, Brown and Company, 1997.

[12] Kindlon, Dan and Michael Thompson. *Raising Cain.*

[13] Ibid.

[14] This list of signs and symptoms for ADD/ADHD in Children is taken from the Helpguide.org website under the subheading "Impulsive Signs and Symptoms of ADD/ADHD." A direct link is: http://helpguide.org/mental/adhd_add_signs_symptoms.htm.

[15] Tieger, Paul D. Tieger & Barbara Barron-Tieger. *Nurture by Nature.*

[16] Kindlon, Dan and Michael Thompson. *Raising Cain.*

Chapter Eighteen

Dissing the "Dys-" Phenomenon

Shift Begins with Me

My new unschooling friend was at our house with her teenage daughter and we shared learning stories from our past. She enthusiastically pronounced a particular reading program as the best around. She emphatically credited the program with helping her daughter learn how to read, despite her dyslexia. I asked the mom to explain the backdrop.

When her daughter was about 6 years old, my friend noticed that she struggled with learning to read. Mom grew concerned and discovered her daughter could be labeled dyslexic. Someone recommended a program to help break down the reading process using a multi-sensory foundation. Mom committed to the financial output required and began teaching her daughter each set of rules using each of the senses, as outlined in the teacher guide. This continued for two to three years. At around 9 years old, her daughter began reading.

As I got to know her daughter over the years, I discovered that she considered herself "not good at reading." She had remained a slow and laborious reader and felt too self-conscious to read aloud at all. This lack of confidence about reading led to self-esteem issues in other areas. She often considered herself "not smart," and in no way considered herself college material at any level. Her goal became to find a good husband so she could embrace the mother niche she knew she was good at.

Research that tracks the development of children throughout their school careers concludes that the learning patterns established by third grade heavily influence the remaining years in school. This was certainly true for this young lady. In *Raising Cain*, the author found himself lamenting with a colleague about the difficulty in creating psychiatric evaluation reports with any substance. Though his response was cloaked in cynicism, the author's colleague spoke truthfully: "We probably shouldn't waste the time because the reports really all say the same thing: 'Kid has trouble learning to read in first grade; starts to hate school; his self-esteem goes to hell; and when he's a teenager, he's pissed off or taking drugs.'" The author admitted that he had seen this same story repeatedly play out in the lives of children hundreds of times.[1] It breaks my heart. When we know better, we should do better. It starts with better information.

There's an epidemic of learning disabilities being diagnosed today that I feel has more to do with, first and foremost, need for a different learning time frame and style of learning. The other factor is the focus on a generalized education that pathologizes any variation in a child's learning instead of using a strength/weakness based thinking model.

The three most common learning disability labels that I feel can be directly linked to the right-brained processing preference are dyslexia, dysgraphia, and dyscalculia. As noted in Chapter Three, the idea that there's considerable overlap in criteria for various learning disabilities should raise a red flag about their validity. It's a huge eye-opener when it's also understood that so many of the symptoms of these disabilities have a direct correlation to how a right-brained learner comes to information based on the way the right side of the brain processes information. Is this even a disability? Or is it another way of learning that's misunderstood and not supported properly as Brock L. Eide, M.D., M.A. and Fernette F. Eide, M.D., have concluded in their book, *The Dyslexic Advantage*?[2]

Dyslexia

Our society puts a high premium on print and literacy; the sooner a person can independently access these resources, the more independent the person functions in his learning life. However, just because there's great benefit to having the skill doesn't mean pushing it sooner is better.

Right-brained children typically learn to read "later" than schools prescribe. It's not that a right-brained child isn't learning to read because he doesn't see the value. Instead, the reason a right-brained child isn't learning to read is because he isn't developmentally ready to do so based on his brain processing preference. In the meantime, he's building other important skills (see Chapter Eleven and the picture at the beginning of the chapter).

It's common to introduce reading to all children, including right-brained learners, by the age of 5. Unfortunately, by not understanding the ideal time frame for a right-brained child to begin to learn to read, and by not understanding the ideal strategy to use so that a right-brained child *can* learn to read, misperceptions occur.

Comparing Dyslexia Symptoms
to Right-Brained Traits

Many of the signs and symptoms for dyslexia correlate to the information found in this book about how a right-brained learner processes information. Throughout this section is a list of typical signs and symptoms for dyslexia for the ages of 5-10 years of age.[3] Most of the reasons I give for why a right-brained child exhibits these traits have been explained in earlier chapters, so here I briefly recap the relevant details and provide chapter references for your convenience.

- ❖ Delayed learning of tasks such as tying shoe laces or telling time on a watch or clock
- ❖ These children start talking very late as compared to children of their age group

These two signs and symptoms relate to acquisition of skills based on a left-brained-centered time frame. A delay in learning to tell time is described in Chapter Nine. Right-brained people tend to be better with space concepts than time concepts. Time concepts *are* learned but within a later time frame. Like late learning to tell time, I'll admit every one of my children took longer to learn to tie their shoes, too. None of them were interested in learning the task. They all find shoes restricting so it might fall under the sensory category. Thus, a lack of interest often leads to a lack of ability, at least on a timely basis.

Each of my children felt wearing shoes was restricting. Each of my children learned to tie shoes later. Is there a connection?

It's well known that boys are prone to later speech development because of a natural visual and movement focus, and still others are prone to an additional high energy need. Since boys tend to speak later, and boys favor the right side of the brain (see Chapter Seventeen), then *some* right-brained dominant children may develop speech later. A right-brained child is also focused on the image versus the word in his early development which could also contribute to delayed speech.

- ❖ They have a confusion of their right and left side or are confused with arithmetical signs
- ❖ It's difficult for them to spell in a phonetic manner
- ❖ They have difficulty with reading and spelling

I explained the reason for later development in certain subjects, like reading, math, and spelling, in Chapter Seven. To recap, a right-brained child is more focused on the *image* of math before age 8 to 10 and a left-brained person more easily integrates symbols, such as math signs, before that age. Difficulty with learning to read before age 8 to 10 is explained in Chapter Eleven. Words are symbols just as math signs are symbols. For the right-brained child, symbol development comes after a solid foundation of image development is built. Spelling ability comes after reading fluency because right-brained people are whole-to-part processors; reading is considered the whole and spelling the parts. Similarly, sight word reading or spelling uses more of a whole focus, while any phonetic application is learned later because it's a part focus.

The words right and left are symbolic word labels for places in space. Most of my children didn't pick up the functional use of these labels until 8 to 10 years of age. This is when a right-brained person is beginning to integrate left-brained strengths more fully. Right-brained children simply have a different time frame for certain subjects because of a focus on imagery instead of words and symbols before the age of 8 to 10.

❖ They may face difficulty in letter reversal, such as 'D' or 'B'

❖ They may not recognize 'Inversions' such as 'd' and 'b,' 'm' and 'w,' or 'u' and 'n'

In Chapter Five I explain the right-brained learner's universal gift of three-dimensional pictorial thinking. Three-dimensional pictorial thinking means that an image or symbol can be viewed at any angle—up, down, left, or right—all done visually inside of the mind. When we notice letter reversals or inversions, we're seeing that these letters can be viewed from any angle. When two letter symbols are similar but facing different directions, the three-dimensional view leaves this child unable to remember which way it should go. In fact, as shown in Chapter Fifteen, other letters can be reversed just as easily. To a right-brained person, every symbol or object has many possible positions. During the appropriate time frame of 8 to 10 years old, we can help these young people understand that letters are meant to be written one way in order to correct this trait. This phenomenon common in right-brained children can be attributed to their equally phenomenal three-dimensional asset.

Even though my artist son reversed letters, I didn't miss the big picture: fantastic storytelling skills!

❖ They may also have problems with transposition of words, such as 'house' and 'home,' 'come' and 'go,' or 'give' and 'take'

Transposing words is also related to a right-brained person's focus on pictorial imagery. In Chapter Five, I explain how every symbol, every word, and every number are translated to an image. While learning spelling or reading, the word may be placed under the picture in the mind. When the word is seen on the page and translated to a picture, another word that means the same thing may have been filed under the picture, so when it's time to say the word out loud, sometimes the similar word is said instead. (This trait is explained in Chapter Eleven as well.)

As an example, the first time "give" is seen and read, it's translated as a picture of a person giving an object to another person taking the object, and the word "give" is placed under the mental picture created. During another reading time, "take" comes up and it's also translated to a person taking an object from another person giving the object. It's the same image in reverse. When the word previously placed under the mental picture is viewed, it comes up as "give" because of the original translation. It's really quite fascinating!

❖ They may not be able to recognize similar or closely related words, such as 'Town' and "Down,' or 'Mine' and 'Dime'
❖ They may take a lot of time in learning vocabulary

Right-brained children often learn to read by using context clues (see Chapter Eleven) because of the whole-to-part preference to learning. A right-brained person tends to read in chunks and whole words, so when they are just beginning to learn how to read, and they see a partial chunk that's recognized such as "ouse," they often ineffectively try context clues. Is it "mouse" or "house" or "louse" in the context of the story? Sometimes, especially when phonics are over-utilized in the beginning, a right-brained child will see a letter such as a "c" and start guessing based on context. Time tends to smooth out the rough edges of strategy used by a right-brained early reader. This is why getting books that *encourage* context reading can be a successful way to minimize failure while applying a perfectly legitimate strategy.

Utilizing context may be why some right-brained learners take a longer time learning new vocabulary words. Often, new vocabulary is taught totally out of context of a story. This makes it difficult for a right-brained child to create a lasting image to help him remember in a way that works.

❖ May not be able to recollect or remember facts

To help children remember facts, schools often employ the memorization strategy, a short-term memory tool. As outlined in Chapter Seven, right-brained people like to use long-term memory utilizing the strategy of association. Learning by association works best if a great visual or interactive (kinesthetic) activity can be linked to another sensory pathway, such as a good auditory story or a memorable and detailed picture or video. A visual or kinesthetic "hook" (see Chapter Nineteen) helps solidify the details and facts more easily through an imagery format, stored in long-term memory, for later recall. Thus, recollection of facts occurs when the strategy is used that takes advantage of the natural strengths of the right side of the brain.

❖ They may face difficulty in organizational, planning, and time management skills
❖ They might even have poor fine motor coordination or struggle to perform sequential motor tasks, such as tying or untying shoe laces

In Chapter Seven, the attributes of being a global or sequential thinker were discussed. A right-brained person likes to think whole-to-part or globally. The ability to organize, plan, and manage time is all about sequencing. Sequencing strengths lie with part-to-whole thinking. And part-to-whole thinking is the strength of a left-brained person. This would also include any sequencing activity, whether it's planning out tying shoes or long division. A right-brained person can get lost or distracted along the path to the end.

This isn't to say that a right-brained person can't be organized or plan; it just needs to be done in a way that plays to the strengths of that brain processing preference. For instance, stacking items in a pile is often a strategy used by right-brained people because if it's out of sight, it's out of mind. Right-brained people are highly visual, so using a to-do list is not effective. Mind mapping was created with the right-brained person in mind. Because they think globally, and often see entire images, many thoughts can flow out at once. Creating a spider webbed organization process while it all pours out, also called brain dumps by my friend, can be helpful in getting it all out. By creating multiple links to one idea in a spider web is an attempt to somewhat connect the overall initial associations.

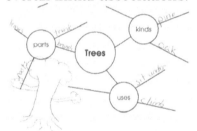

Mind mapping is an organizational tool for right-brained global thinkers. (Image[4])

The Right-Brained Reading Path Is Valid

I have at least three children who would fit these criteria if I had followed the left-brained scope and sequence to learning to read. Instead I honored a different time frame to work through their particular processes and wasn't afraid to embrace other ways of learning. Each of these children has a positive relationship with print and reads fluidly. Each child was in the ballpark of right-brained time frame stages to learning as I've outlined throughout this book. Each worked out the differences as presented in these descriptions for dyslexia on his own and in his own time. There's a valid path to learning to read for the right-brained child, just as there is for the left-brained child. Getting information that helps us understand these differences is the first step to eliminating these kinds of dys-abilities from being attached to and believed by our sensitive, creative children. There's nothing wrong with their process!

Straighten Up Your Attitude

I've found that the second most important strategy to help a creative child learn to read joyfully is the attitude of the adults in the equation. Often I hear parents lament that their child has labeled himself stupid because the child wants to learn to read like many of his peers and is not able. Where does the desire to learn to read at a specified time come from? I believe our societally conditioned attitudes that we project greatly contribute to a child's belief that he's deficient in some way.

How often do we spotlight the reading idea? You may have whispered conversations about your fears that your child isn't reading, make big deals about younger siblings or relatives or friends' children reading, constantly ask your child if he wants to learn to read, compare or measure your child against norms, have your child sit next to you to sound out words or finish sentences, or try to get your child excited that "you get to learn to read in first grade!" All of these interactions occur in households everywhere.

What happens if you don't engage in these behaviors? (After all, we don't behave like this about history!) A child doesn't know to self-label. None of my children (from two genetic pools) felt conspicuous about not being able to read until they were older. I consciously monitored *my* attitudes and behaviors regarding reading to achieve the best possible relationships with reading for my children. Somehow I knew how they felt about themselves as they approached learning the subject would be highly important.

Does Dyslexia Exist?

I have one child that I'm not sure will learn to read. He's currently 12.5 years old and not even close. Is it dyslexia? I believe it's a lot more than that. He has an intellectual disability made more profound because of memory issues, both possibly stemming from his premature birth. He's very weak in auditory processing which can make learning to read more difficult. Yet, I have a son with autism, with an IQ in the mentally retarded range, who has strong weaknesses in auditory processing and easily learned to read at 4 years old (though he was limited in how far he could go based on his comprehension). My son with autism had a strength with patterns and memory to hook into to build his reading skills.

I'm still looking for that hook of strength for my 12-year-old.

Patterns were a learning strength "hook" for my son with autism to learn to read at 4 years old. (Image[5])

Do I understand difficulties with learning to read *can* occur? Sure. Do I think it goes beyond the criteria that define dyslexia? Yes. I think most of the signs and symptoms associated with dyslexia are right-brained traits. Knowledge and understanding of the time frame involved in acquiring skills for right-brained children could eliminate the ability to diagnose most children. I believe children who have significant difficulty learning to read have a co-morbid attribute, such as a diagnosis of Down Syndrome, mental retardation, or premature birth that creates multiple weak areas. If the right-brained time frame and process is

362

understood and honored, I believe dyslexia as a stand-alone diagnosis is questionable.

Dysgraphia

The last sign and symptom for dyslexia of "gripping their pencil in an awkward fashion" leads me to dysgraphia since it pertains to pencil grip. Let's look at how many of the signs and symptoms of dysgraphia[6] can be correlated to the right-brained information.

* ❖ Students may exhibit strong verbal but particularly poor writing skills
* ❖ Random (or non-existent) punctuation, spelling errors (sometimes same word spelled differently), reversals, phonic approximations, syllable omissions, errors in common suffixes, clumsiness and disordering of syntax, an impression of illiteracy, misinterpretation of questions and questionnaire items, disordered numbering and written number reversals
* ❖ Generally illegible writing (despite appropriate time and attention given the task)
* ❖ Inconsistencies (mixtures of print and cursive, upper and lower case, or irregular sizes, shapes, or slant of letters)
* ❖ Unfinished words or letters, omitted words
* ❖ Inconsistent position on page with respect to lines and margins and inconsistent spaces between words and letters
* ❖ Cramped or unusual grip, especially holding the writing instrument very close to the paper, or holding thumb over two fingers and writing from the wrist
* ❖ Talking to self while writing, or carefully watching the hand that's writing
* ❖ Slow or labored copying or writing - even if it's neat and legible

Let's start with the first two signs and symptoms because they both relate to a skill in which a right-brained child typically develops later. As noted in Chapter Thirteen, ability to express one's ideas with words on paper often doesn't develop until 11 to 13 years old, after fluency in reading is established. This is because right-brained learners are whole-to-part learners. Fluency with reading words, which requires translation into imagery, is the whole. The ability to reverse the process of seeing a visual in one's mind to translate that into words requires the ability to break the whole image down into the parts of word choice order, spelling, and grammar (see Chapter Seven). Thus, reading fluency comes first (the whole) at 8 to 10 years old, followed by spelling and grammar (the parts) at around 11 to 13 years old. When I see a set of signs and symptoms for a disorder involving subject-related skills that naturally develop later for a right-brained child, it's frustrating to realize how misunderstood the learning time frame is for this processing preference.

The attributes of reversals, word omissions, disordering of words/numbers, mixtures and inconsistencies on a page can be traced to the three-dimensional imagery that a right-brained child is developing especially during the early years. Three-dimensional objects can be viewed from multiple angles and positions, and right-brained learners naturally process three-dimensionally. When performing a two-dimensional task during the stage of primary development of three-dimensionality (up to 8 to 10 years old), reversals, disordering, and inconsistencies of placement can occur. Word omissions may happen when the word isn't relevant to the imagery created by the content written. The word "an" may be more likely omitted accidentally by a right-brained child than the word "house" because it bears less relevance to the meaning (see Chapter Eleven). (Notice how many times these "dys-" ability criteria overlap—are we describing the same learner from a different angle? Yes!)

Let's skip down to the signs and symptoms that focus on talking to oneself while writing and slow or labored copying or writing. These may be associated with left- and right-brain dominance and preferred modality input. Let's start with the explanation of brain dominance. Drawing, calligraphy, and cursive all stem from the right side of the brain because of the creative aspect of these ways of writing. Print stems from the left side. Thus, sometimes in order to succeed at printing, a right-brained child will actually *draw* the letters being written in print to continue using the dominant processing side that's most effective. Obviously, this can come across as slow and labored because the child is literally creating art instead of printing words. Along this same line, a child who is strong with auditory processing may speak out loud to "talk himself through" the process of printing words.

Print as an art form is common with right-brained children.

The final dysgraphia difficulty addresses the grip of the pencil or awkward use of it as indicated in the dyslexia signs and symptoms (another overlap of criteria). This could be a low muscle tone issue, a sensory difference, or a readiness problem. Each of my children with this difficulty has low muscle tone, sensory differences, and other developmental delays. The other of my children who didn't have a problem with pencil grip, yet had developmental delays, didn't have low muscle tone and had milder sensory differences. Could there be a connection in this area?

I shared examples in Chapter Fifteen about how my fifth child, who has an ineffective grip that falls in this category, developed his handwriting ability. While he was young, we did a lot of sensory hand-strengthening activities. He practiced handwriting enough to understand how to write letters in his childhood years. But we didn't focus on it extensively until the 11 to 13 year time frame when he was old enough to put some focused effort into improvement because of higher awareness of himself in the world. There was good improvement.

I don't believe handwriting can be normalized strictly from sheer repetition. There are too many components linked to various body functions that must come together to create the performance of handwriting, such as sensory differences, motor planning, and muscle strength, to name a few. If we can focus on what level of ability is actually necessary (many believe handwriting is obsolete because of technology), and time frames can be extended to incorporate maturity, then a more positive relationship with handwriting can develop for these children. Maybe competency can even be achieved.

Dyscalculia

The last common learning disability associated with a right-brained learner pertains to a subject that our society currently heavily values: math. I believe it's a subject in which only some will excel, though most should be competent at the basic level. Because math is so highly valued, it's prioritized at a young age as a subject for which all children should show proficiency. Understanding how a right-brained child learns math is crucial to knowing how their process reflects the criteria for the disability called dyscalculia. Here are those signs and symptoms:[7]

- ❖ Shows difficulty understanding concepts of place value, and quantity, number lines, positive and negative value, carrying and borrowing
- ❖ Has difficulty understanding and doing word problems
- ❖ Has difficulty sequencing information or events
- ❖ Exhibits difficulty using steps involved in math operations
- ❖ Shows difficulty understanding fractions
- ❖ Is challenged making change and handling money

❖ Displays difficulty recognizing patterns when adding, subtracting, multiplying, or dividing
❖ Has difficulty putting language to math processes
❖ Has difficulty understanding concepts related to time such as days, weeks, months, seasons, quarters, etc.
❖ Exhibits difficulty organizing problems on the page, keeping numbers lined up, following through on long division problems

One of the foundational traits for a left-brained child is learning in sequential order. The other is thinking in words. Notice how many of the criteria listed above depend on these two traits. A right-brained learner incorporates these two traits later, beginning between the ages of 8 and 10. Sequencing information or events, using steps in math, recognizing patterns with adding and multiplying, putting language to math and organizing problems on the page or following through on long division problems are all attributes of a young left-brained learner. A right-brained math person needs to pursue the subject in a different manner (see Chapter Twelve). If these math tasks are introduced in a manner and time frame that work for a right-brained child, fewer problems will arise.

The strength of a right-brained learner during the early years of developing math knowledge is concepts through visualization or hands-on manipulation. If math is taught through symbolization and word notation before 8 to 10 years old, it can be a problem. For example, if a child is shown how borrowing numbers is written out in symbol form on a paper, it could be confusing. But if a right-brained child visualizes having 23 marbles and the need to give his friend 16 of them, the answer may be intuitively evident (see Chapter Seven). This same child may not be able to make sense writing it out symbolically at the given time. The same could be said for word problems or making change and handling money. If a right-brained child has a desire to buy something from the store and is given opportunity to earn money and manipulate it, competency may be achieved.

Right-brained children often need a compelling reason *to them* before competency can be developed. Most of my children had no desire to earn and spend money for items at the store. Thus, money knowledge and handling didn't occur until much later, usually in the 11 to 13 year time frame. As mentioned in Chapter Nine, most of my children were also uninterested in days, weeks, or months. Each of my children definitely aligned with the knowledge that right-brained people are more space-based than time-centered. Once they reached the 11 to 13 year time frame, I told them they would learn to read an analog clock, know their months and holidays related to those months, birthdays, and manipulating money. Even though the compelling reason wasn't there, each child picked up the skills because maturity *was* in place to capitalize on; both sides of the brain were working more effectively together.

My builder son dabbled in understanding time in his young years. As evidence of the right-brained stage, it's pictorial.

One website that lists signs and symptoms for dyscalculia shares a disclaimer that a potential diagnosis needs to be compared against the idea that a child just isn't interested in math. [8] Take my daughter and math as an example. She decided to learn up to algebra, and then declared it was sufficient. With her English/writing focus, math wasn't relevant to her getting accepted into the university for which she applied. Her ACT score proved that she had sufficient competency in math to not interfere with her college goals. Weaknesses don't have to mean "difficulty learning based on a deficiency." I'm not keen on history and would have to work hard to do well in it in a school setting. I don't have a natural inclination toward it. I don't have a history disability; my lack of interest in it means I wouldn't learn it easily.

Each of my children had subjects to which they never gravitated in some way by the time they reached the 11 to 13 year old stage because they were "not that interested in it." For my oldest, it was math, and some formal grammar. For my daughter, history and math. For my third child, spelling and writing. It wasn't that they *couldn't* learn these things; they just didn't hold enough meaning to pursue. Each child did improve in these areas, learning enough of a skill set to better learn the subjects at the appropriate developmental time frame. My daughter's lack of early proficiency in math didn't mean she was "disabled in math." She just wouldn't be choosing a career in math, nor did she choose a university that required a lot of math.

The same is true for my son and writing. Over time, he became proficient enough that writing didn't impede progress with his math and computer talents. In other words, each child collaborated effectively with me to learn less interesting or non-gift areas at the developmental time frame appropriate for right-brained learners. By that stage, each child knew enough about how they learn that we could work together finding appropriate learning resources and processes.

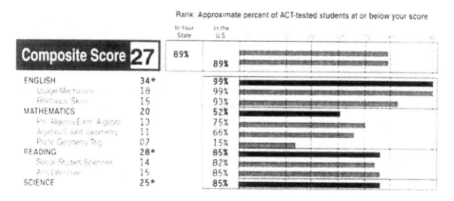

My writer daughter's strengths outweigh her weaknesses to get her accepted into her first choice university.

If my children had been in school measured with the left-brained time frame, there *would* have been labels. How many children in school right now are being labeled with learning disabilities when, in reality, they are misunderstood right-brained learners?

Why are right-brained learners misunderstood and overlabeled? Because the academic measuring stick used in school aligns with the process and time frame of left-brained learners. Our society looks to place every child in that developmental box. Right-brained learners have a different process and time frame than what's valued in our schools.

If parents and teachers recognize the gifts and patterns of their right-brained children, then schools will need to make room to educate according to the natural development of the right-brained learner. If schools shift and expand to include the scope and sequence of the right-brained learner, then society will begin to value the right-brained learning style. If the right-brained learning style is accepted and valued in our society, more research will emerge to validate and support our right-brained children. Let's begin the domino effect by advocating for the right side of normal!

References and Notes

[1] Kindlon, Dan and Michael Thompson. *Raising Cain: Protecting the Emotional Life of Boys*. New York: Random House Inc., 2000.

[2] Eide, Brock L. and Fernette F. Eide. *The Dyslexic Advantage: Unlocking the Hidden Potential of the Dyslexic Brain*. Hudson Street Press, 2011.

[3] Dyslexia Symptoms, "Signs and Symptoms of Dyslexia among Kindergarten to 4th Grade Children," *Signs and Symptoms of Dyslexia in Children, 2011*. http://www.dyslexiasymptoms.net/children/symptoms-of-dyslexia-in-children.html.

[4] American Education Publishing. *Comprehensive Curriculum, Grade 3*. Columbus: McGraw-Hill Children's Publishing, 2003, p. 107.

[5] Tucker, Sian. *A Is for Astronaut (My First Lift-the-Flap ABC)*. Little Simon, 1995. Bill Martin, Jr. *Brown Bear, Brown Bear, What Do You See?* Henry Holt & Co., 2008.

[6] West Virginia University, Eberly College of Arts and Sciences, Inclusion in Science Education for Students with Disabilities, *Dysgraphia,* May 31, 2007. http://www.as.wvu.edu/~scidis/ dysgraphia.html.

[7] From the LDA of California and UC Davis M.I.N.D. Institute "Q.U.I.L.T.S." Calendar 2001-2002, *Dyscalculia,* http://www.ldanatl.org/aboutld/parents/ld_ basics/dyscalculia.asp.

[8] Rajeev, Loveleena. *Dyscalculia Symptoms,* 9-23-2011. http://www.buzzle.com/ articles/dyscalculia-symptoms.html.

Chapter Nineteen

Input Modalities

Shift Begins with Me

I was in fifth grade when I thought it would be a good idea to gain a bit of attention by purposely flunking the school's vision test. I recalled from previous screenings that the test consisted of determining the direction of an "e." Little did I realize that my memory wouldn't serve me well. I remembered that the letter was an "e," but I didn't remember it was an uppercase "E."

I smugly sat down to begin my screening. I remember my panic as I realized that I couldn't see the "e!" Did I really need glasses? Did someone, somehow, know I was going to purposely flunk and turned the tables on me? These thoughts and more raced through my mind in that moment. I desperately searched for a lowercase "e," but it wasn't there. All I saw was a blurry blob as I scrutinized the image and stabbed in the dark at the hopefully correct answer: up? left? About two-thirds of the way into the screening, I cleared my mind enough to realize it was an uppercase "E" this whole time. Suddenly, I could clearly see! From that moment forward, I finished the screening confidently with all the correct answers.

What had just happened to me? I was young and didn't quite understand. What seemed to have just occurred was that since my mind had been sure it was a lowercase "e" I'd be seeking, that's exactly what my mind was looking for. I was literally "blinded" because my brain had controlled the visual interpretation of what I was seeing. I filed away the scary and unusual experience for later recall in case anything matched up to explain this phenomenon.

In Chapter Two, Linda Kreger Silverman chose to categorize a left-brained learner as auditory-sequential and a right-brained learner as visual-spatial, based on attributes prevalent in the respective learning styles.[1] I don't like that differentiation. It implies right-brained people can't be auditory learners or left-brained people can't be visual learners. These are input modalities, the sensory pathways by which information is received. In our instructional world, we're most familiar with using three of the five senses: auditory, visual, and kinesthetic (touch). Smell and taste certainly come into play in such professions as cooking and general environmental assessments. As I became more familiar with input modalities through my research, and as I observed how each sensory channel worked for those in my family, I came to discover some interesting connections between input modalities and brain processing preferences.

In our instructional world, we are most familiar with using three of the five senses: auditory, visual, and kinesthetic (touch).

Auditory

I have seven right-brained children and one right-brained husband. Four of them do well with auditory input. Three of them do quite poorly. My daughter has the capacity to listen as long as she can use an attention tool. I'm a strong left-brained learner. According to Silverman, I should be strong aurally. I thought I was, but then something happened that changed my understanding of auditory input.

The Word Hook—The Left-Brained Way

A few years ago, my builder son read something aloud to me from the computer. I'm sure this type of thing happened many times before, but I never made a connection until this time. I couldn't for the life of me process that auditory information without getting up to look at the words! It appears that I also don't process information aurally very well; I need to see the words.

I started thinking about how schools are set up. They're lecture-based with note taking. This fits how a left-brained person could process auditory information effectively. If they can write or see words (many times notes were put on the board or on overheads or in outlines as the lectures were given) as they receive the auditory input, they can effectively and efficiently process that information. Because our society favors the left-brained processing structure, I didn't need to

374

figure out creative ways to accomplish auditory information processing. Now I know why I had considered myself auditory, but in actuality, I needed the word writing hook to actually process the information.

The Visual or Kinesthetic Hook—
The Right-Brained Way

A right-brained person's natural gift isn't words, but pictures. Often, a right-brained child can't take notes and listen at the same time. That's because the hook is the words for note-taking, and that isn't their strength. My builder son, who's natural at math, easily follows a lecture in his math class because inevitably the instructor is working out math problems as she explains. Thus, a visual that makes sense to my son is hooked to the auditory, it makes sense to him, and he can process it effectively. If this son goes to a class at church and the teacher brings in pictures (visual) or hands-on activities (kinesthetic), he processes the auditory information fine. If the teacher doesn't, he struggles to pay attention and process the auditory input.

My artist son, who processes auditory input easily, prefers to hook auditory information with the visuals in his mind. For this reason, he prefers to sit and listen to lectures without taking notes, which would be too distracting. My husband was one of those people in high school who hardly took any notes and still aced the tests. These are right-brained auditory learners who easily hook auditory information to mind visuals and store it in long-term memory. By college, however, both my artist son and my husband had to learn a system of note-taking that worked for them because of sheer volume and content difficulty level in order to be successful.

2. think respiration

always opt air into blood

drop off passengers pick up passengers

inside cell chemical activity (nutrition)

Cellular respiration

Inhale/inspiration = in
Exhale/expiration = out

Very mechanical process

Often, a right-brained child can't take notes and listen at the same time. My artist son "practicing" taking notes from a science video.

My builder son prefers to process visually and kinesthetically, two of the three common input modalities. He can process with the third one, auditory input, when it's paired with one of the other two. He's been able to use the input modality knowledge and apply it to various settings and situations to achieve successful outcomes.

Classroom work. My builder son knew he needed to process information aurally while in college. He worked out creative ways to accomplish this by choosing learning environments that favored how he best processed information in that subject matter. On-line classes were a great option for him with liberal arts lecture-based classes. Everything was written, so he could take his time reading and processing the information at a pace that worked for him. Yes, he had the option of getting a disability plan to tape record his lecture classes, but why? My builder son subconsciously resented the idea that he needed a "disability plan" when he felt quite capable of learning the information if it was presented in a way that worked for him. So, isn't it the learning environment that's "disabled?" It works for certain people, but not for others; yet, if it were structured differently, bringing in all three common input modalities, most people would have fewer problems. My builder son easily received a high A for his psychology class online. He enjoyed the material and talked about what he was learning all the time. Wouldn't it be a shame to miss enjoying a subject or learning something interesting simply because the way it's presented doesn't work for you?

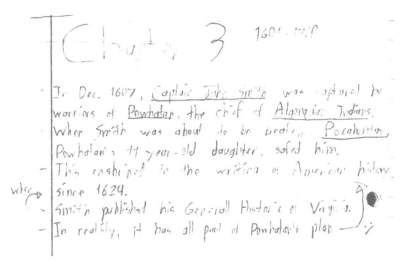

My builder son could take notes from his textbook for an on-line class instead of struggling to take notes from a lecture.

Conversations. What about processing auditory information from a conversation or from someone explaining something to you? My builder son has a common problem for right-brained visual people. He needs to look away from someone speaking to him to retrieve a visual from his mind to help him process the conversation. The problem is he can't look at the person because the face isn't a visual hook to the conversation, so it can be distracting; yet it's considered rude not to look at someone while they're speaking. It's common to look up and away when retrieving a visual in one's mind (go ahead, try it), yet he then risks being distracted by other visuals and not hearing at all. I asked my builder son how he processes our conversations.

He said he trained himself to concentrate on the mouth and the words coming out of it. If it's a topic of high interest and background knowledge he's already accumulated, he can hook the auditory conversation to the ready visuals in his mind more easily while maintaining eye contact. If it's entirely new information being discussed, he's found that looking at the person allows him to concentrate on what's being said. It's less distracting than looking away and he's able to

377

do this for short periods of time. He's also learned to be confident enough to ask for information to be repeated, as necessary. In his day-to-day life as an introverted computer geek, he isn't confronted with an excessive amount of weakness-based conversations. I don't foresee this being a future problem, either, because the area of work he'll go into will be one based on his strengths, and the friends he'll associate with will be those who have commonalities.

Broken Child Paradigm

Compare my builder son's auditory skill development with a similar story of a young person, a public school student, who worked for me one summer shadowing my theater son at a day camp. It was apparent the first time I gave this young man instruction that he was unable to process the auditory information while looking at me. At first when he looked away when I spoke to him, I could tell he was listening, but it wasn't long before I lost him when something else caught his eye. When I asked him to repeat my directions, he didn't remember half of what I said to him (this is often translated as ADD). I told the young man he needed to come up with some strategies to help himself, but he had no tools to pull from, and he had just graduated high school with high grades! Shortly after, I bumped into his mother. When I explained what happened, she was concerned that he had relied upon the attention medication he takes to learn. She had performed a few "placebo experiments" with her son, and found that he's reliant upon the medication to focus. This is the typical paradigm seen in school: a difference is seen in a child, he's referred to a doctor for diagnosis, and then he's medicated. No understanding of what's going on, no skills or strategies developed, and no adjusting to use preferred learning methods. It's the broken child paradigm.

Strengths/Weakness Paradigm

Because of our family's unschooling environment, I based my builder son's learning on his strengths and his preferred input modalities while he was young to create a strengths-based, gift-centered learning environment. When his brain shifted between 11 and 13 years old, as explained in Chapters Four and Seven, he could process more abstract information. This includes the ability to determine what's working and not working in one's life. I found my children are more willing and able to partner with me as a more knowledgeable person during this stage of development so they can create tools and strategies to improve weaknesses.

For instance, I watched my builder son learn to program computers from adult level print resources starting between 13 and 14 years old. I asked how he could learn from such deep language texts since that's a weakness of his due to living with autism. He shared with me his instinctual gift-centered solution. Most computer programming resources share samples of programming. My builder son would input the programming, play around with it spatially and mechanically, and figure out what it did and why. Then he went back and read the text as confirmation. He used his universal gifts first to give him the step up to navigate the left-brained elements more easily. This is a valid strategy for learning and shows once again how a right-brained learner needs strategies that are opposite from the needs of their left-brained counterparts. Luckily, right-brained learners tend to be those writing computer programming books, as well as the precursor building creative outlet instructions such as LEGO® booklets.

I'm more than pleased at how my builder son is finding his place in our society, whether it's based on his strengths or his weaknesses. We live at a time when there are many options, and he takes advantage of them. When he chooses an alternative, he doesn't see it as a deficit, but as a smart choice that allows him to enjoy the experience because it's based on his areas of strength. In other words, he knows how he learns, and he's not afraid to use that knowledge!

My builder son successfully serving a mission in California despite his language and auditory weaknesses.

My builder son has learned his weak areas and how to compensate for them so well, he's chosen to pursue a life experience that involves most of his weak areas. He's serving a full-time mission for our church where he has to speak and communicate and process auditory information on a constant basis. He shares with me that it's been difficult, but he's learning to use his strengths (noticing patterns) to try to get more efficient with language, while relying on his often more capable companion. On the other hand, he brings his own strengths to the experience that others appreciate and value.

Auditory Processing Disorder

Would engaging in various therapies be helpful to someone with auditory processing difficulties? I witnessed an interesting experience with my builder son that matched the information I would uncover about the right-brained learning process. Once again, the answer lies in the natural learning time frame for the right-brained learner, and using well-matched resources.

It was obvious in his early years that my builder son had difficulty processing auditory information. As mentioned in the Chapter Seventeen story, he also had memory differences. Because he was a non-reader until 10 years old (see Chapter

Ten), and had received a diagnosis of autism and weak language skills, a computer software program called *Earobics®²* was recommended to help with his memory and auditory processing skill development. Since it was a more affordable program than its predecessor *Fast ForWord®* ³ (requiring implementation by a licensed speech-language pathologist), I decided it was worth trying.

There are six skill-building activities. My builder son worked through most of them over time. Because of his love of trains, he really wanted to beat the train game, a game that developed auditory phoneme awareness. As hard as he strived, he just couldn't get far in the game and skill development. Because of his intensity in trying to win, I instinctively helped him release his need to beat the game. He was around 8 years old at the time.

The software Earobics® can be fun practice for building auditory and memory skills if there's no pressure. (Image⁴)

From time to time he revisited the train game, but to no avail. As mentioned in Chapter Ten, at 10 years old and using *Bob Books®*, reading suddenly made sense to him and he took off in his reading ability.⁵ (Notice this therapy didn't help him read sooner or memorize better—see Chapter Seventeen.) That's when an interesting thing happened that I didn't understand until I researched right-brained learning traits: my builder son got back on that train game and easily completed it. What just happened? No hours and months and years of practice. Just all at once, ability meets task.

Let me explain. Here are the attributes we have discussed in this book about how right-brained children develop from picture-based thinking to include word-based thinking:

- ✓ Translates spoken words to pictures between 5 and 7 years old
- ✓ Translates written words to pictures between 8 and 10 years old
- ✓ Starts with easily visualized words first, such as nouns and verbs
- ✓ Last to translate are less easily visualized words, such as Dolch words[6]

Those right-brained children who don't prefer the auditory input modality, or had chronic ear infections as young children that inhibited the effective development of this input modality, may find these time frames shift one stage later. This is what happened to my builder son who had chronic ear infections from 1 to 2 years old. (But remember, as described in Chapter Ten, builder types tend to develop each skill at the later age norm for right-brained learners, anyway, because they are less exposed to words.) For my builder son, translating the spoken word to images occurred in the 8 to 10 year time frame. He started with the easily visualized words at the beginning of that stage and ended with the less easily visualized words at the latter part. Separated phoneme sound practice falls under the more difficult to remember because these words can't be easily visualized. So, the first "ability" he needed was translating the spoken word; it just came later for him. No amount of extra practice was going to allow him to skip a developmental stage.

School professionals and specialists support the left-brained developmental stage of decoding words between ages 5 and 7. They commonly want to drill and kill the decoding skills with those children they identify as having "problems," or engage them in specialized programs, such as *Earobics®*. Though my builder son was exposed to the *Earobics®* program, I never insisted upon a daily dose of intervention. It was offered, and he played it when he wanted to. Basically, he went through those games that challenged him but could be completed, and abandoned those that were near impossible for him to "beat." Coincidentally, he tried on several occasions to revisit the once-impossible activities just to confirm he still wasn't able.

Instead of *Earobics®*, when my builder son was 9 years old, we played a lot of word association games specifically so he could build up his word comprehension with visualization practice. We did that for six months. Within six months of this, he started his learning to read process.

And then, *after reading began,* which means the shift to being able to translate the written word had to have occurred, voila! My builder son *easily* completed each of the games that before had been impossible. I've heard other similar stories of a child not being able to do a task at one time but can at another (such as in Chapter Ten about the inability of a pre-reader to gain reading skills from one resource, only to be able to do so a year later). Is there a connection between certain abilities and specific stages of brain development? We all know it's common for young children to mishear a word in a song or a phrase that gives us a chuckle. And yet, there comes a time when this is less likely to occur. I believe there's an optimal time when ability meets task, and my builder son accidentally gave some experiential evidence to support that idea.

Reading readiness for my builder son coincided with the ability to process vowel sounds.

383

If I had insisted that my builder son work on this intervention daily from 8 until 10 years old, would it have worked sooner? It hasn't been my experience that it would have. What it would have accomplished is a poor self-image and often even poor task ability (see the Chapter Eighteen story). Do I think programs like *Earobics®* are harmful in and of themselves? Probably not. Learning skills in a short, fun way, like speech therapy, could give "practice." Traditional games can strengthen and give "practice" in this area, too, like Simon Says, the telephone game, tongue twisters, word association, and rhyming games. But as seen in my builder son's life, and now repeated in my theater son's life, success is about understanding how a person learns, finding a way to honor that, and developing skills and strategies to support that child's individual developmental time frame for learning.

Visual

There's misunderstanding among many people that visual information is anything that can be seen. To them, seeing your pet dog, seeing a picture of a chair, or seeing words on a blackboard would all be considered visual input. That's not true. Visual input is anything in image form—pictures, that is—not words or symbols. Since right-brained people see pictures in their minds, it makes sense to conclude that the visual input modality would be highly preferred. What might not be obvious, though, is how vision affects learning. This section sheds light on the vision connection with right-brained learners.

The Eye-Brain Connection

I may have found my answer to what happened to me during that vision screening while I worked to understand the right-brained learner. There's a connection between what the eyes see and how the brain processes it. The eyes are simply the mirror through which we view objects. Making sense of those objects and how they are viewed is the job of the brain. Since my brain had already determined it was looking for a lower case "e," it didn't matter that the eye was mirroring an uppercase "E." The brain interpreted the image the way I had predetermined it would look. This is evidence of the eye-brain connection.

My brain didn't "see" this altered position uppercase letter because it was looking for a lowercase letter.

Right-brained people convert all that they see into an image. They process things three-dimensionally during the foundational years of ages 5 to 7. As a young right-brained child receives an image from the eye to the brain, the brain wants to process it through the right side and file and document it three-dimensionally, since that's the specialty of the right side of the brain. When a right-brained child views a two-dimensional item, the right side of the brain wants to file it as a three-dimensional item, but it can't. The right side of the brain needs to work with the left side to accomplish translating two-dimensional items, but the brain of a *young* right-brained child isn't effectively accessing left brain skills to accomplish this task yet, so he's not quite ready to convert two-dimensional items. Instead, the brain may simply reject the two-dimensional item and produce a blur (like my eye exam), or try to convert it, well or poorly. The brain is trying to do its job: process information primarily through the dominant side of the brain during the 5 to 7 year time frame. In the case of the right side of the brain, that's three-dimensional processing.

The Brain-Modality Connection

During the foundational years of age 5 to 7, children should be primarily instructed in their most direct input modality associated with the universal gifts of their brain processing preference. For left-brained children, that's words; for right-brained children, it's pictures. Schools are currently structured to be word-focused during the 5 to 7 year time frame. That's fine for left-brained children, but what happens to right-brained children when their picture-focus needs aren't honored?

Picture books are perfect for both word and picture focuses in the 5 to 7 year range.

Physical manifestations may occur when right-brained children are expected to engage in left-brained preferred learning systems like phonics, math worksheets, or spelling during the foundational years of 5 to 7 years old. At this stage, right-brained children take in word- and symbol-based information, but the dominant picture-focused right side of the brain can't make sense of it. Does the brain send a message to the eye to physically adjust itself to see if it can bring something different back? Could this cause moving words, double vision, or blurring? Is it possible the more the brain can't process something, the more it tries to adjust the physical body to retrieve what it wants? Could this cause a need for glasses, or create headaches or other vision-related difficulties? These are questions worth asking.

In *Better Late than Early*, the Moores mention that "the tissues of young children's eyes ... are softer or more plastic than older eyes," and that the outer covering of the eyeball "can be drawn out of normal shape by undue strain." Dr. Moore recommends holding off on close work, like learning to read, until the eyes stabilize around 8 to 9 years old.[7] I noticed when right-brained children are allowed to process images (three-dimensional things) in the foundational years of 5 to 7 years as I have shared here, the eye and brain work together seamlessly since images are what the right side of the brain seeks to make sense.

The Eye-Time Frame Connection

The Moores share an eye study by Henry Hilgartner, an ophthalmologist from Austin, Texas, and his eye specialist father, that kept track of the 8- to 12-year-olds who came to their practice over a 50 year period. They discovered a noteworthy trend. In the early 1900s, there were 7 to 8 far-sighted cases to every near-sighted child. Far-sighted is considered the norm for young children in this age range. When their state of Texas lowered the compulsory school attendance age down from age 8 to 7, the Hilgartners discovered the ratio also reduced to two far-sighted children to every one near-sighted child, a significant shift! Does this provide proof in favor of the 8 to 10 year time frame for formal, close-work studies? When Texas again dropped the compulsory attendance laws to age 6, another shift was noted, now a ratio of one to one. Finally, with the advent of television, another significant drop occurred: one normal far-sighted child to five near-sighted. (Another eye specialist noted similar findings during that time period.)[8] What does this have to do with right-brained learners? The two significant *negative* eye functioning shifts occurred when formal or close work started before age 8.

Everywhere we look, evidence supports the right-brained time frame for reading acquisition of between 8 and 10 years old. The eye-brain connection, the boy gender connection, and the right-brained connection all shout for current learning time frames to be scrutinized. Even experiential evidences abound, such as young readers of between 5 and 7 years old who often use their finger or a ruler to keep track as they read, indicating the eye's unreliable tracking at this early age. Yet, by 8 to 10 years old, use of this tool declines. When will we demand better time frames for our right-brained children's learning? (See Chapter Twenty-Two for ideas on how parents and educators can affect change.)

The Time Frame-Resource Connection

Can we cause vision or reading problems with early reading instruction programs that are not conducive to a right-brained child using his strengths? Can the brain be trained to function in a different way than it naturally does? Yes, research has shown the brain to be quite malleable, for good or bad. When a brain is trained out of its natural functioning, such as through years of early phonics training, it doesn't operate as efficiently or effectively as when it's trained with sight words at the right time. Often times, those right-brained dyslexic children heavily trained in phonics and dyslexic programs are slow and laborious readers. Yes, they are reading, but certainly not joyfully or confidently.

A homemade picture book featuring a child's interests is more likely to create a positive relationship with books than extensive phonics training in the 5 to 7 year range.

Are there ways to rectify a malfunctioning brain processing pattern? It can be difficult after a certain age, but I don't think it's impossible. (See the story in Chapter

Eleven about the woman who took a speed reading class in college.)

Does Vision Therapy Help?

The latest therapy fad for reading difficulties involves developmental optometry. It's said that a child who's having trouble reading in the school time frame may have eyes that don't work "properly." A regular optometry visit won't note any vision problems; it's a developmental optometrist who studies how the eyes function together, track, focus, coordinate, and perceive. The first problem I have is that most every child who ends up at a developmental optometrist and is diagnosed as needing vision therapy is right-brained. As soon as it's primarily one kind of learner with the same or similar "problem," I ask questions. Since a right-brained child's brain is seeking three-dimensionality, does it signal the eyes to look at objects a certain way? And if this happens, does that mean the right-brained child's eyes function differently than those of left-brained children, whose brains seek two-dimensionality?

I've heard stories of a right-brained child diagnosed with vision "problems," the parents decided *not* to do the exercises, and later the child no longer had vision problems. I've also noticed that no matter when the vision exercises begin, improvement doesn't occur until the child reaches his developmental shift some time between 8 to 10 years old. Does this mean that when the brain shift occurs between 8 and 10 years old, the eye function shifts with it? Again, these are all important questions researchers need to investigate.

Let's say my theory is right: the eyes of right-brained dominant children function differently since they focus on three-dimensionality before 8 to 10 years old. When the brain shift happens between 8 and 10 years old, and two-dimensionality and symbolization are incorporated, the eye function shifts along with it. That would explain why some children appeared to have eye problems in the 5 to 7 year range, but the problems "self-corrected" during the 8 and 10 year range. How much do we know about how the eyes function based on brain processing preference?

If a mother brought her 9 month old baby to the doctor with concerns about the baby not walking, using the acceptable common time frame of walking acquisition, the doctor would assure the mother that waiting will result in her baby walking. As with the continuum of acceptable time frames for learning to walk or talk, the research community needs to take an interest in developing a similar continuum of acceptable time frames for eye functioning for right-brained children. Is there a common time frame of eye function difference that shifts in correlation with the 8 to 10 year old brain shift for right-brained children? When this question is properly answered, professionals will stop using vision therapy to "jump start" the natural shift that occurs between 8 to 10 years old for the right-brained child. Instead, if a mother came into a developmental optometrist with her 6-year-old right-brained child concerned about eye differences, the developmental optometrist could assure the mother that waiting will result in her child's eyes functioning in the way they were designed as a right-brained dominant learner.

15 months.   10 months.
Just as there's an acceptable window for learning to walk, there should be a larger acceptable window for learning to read.

I mentioned that because of the brain's malleability, if a right-brained child receives extensive phonics training for two to three years before the age of 8 to 10, it's possible that the brain can be "trained out" of its natural path of learning. This usually results in what appears to be permanent and persistent "disability," such as slow and laborious reading skills. In their new book, *The Dyslexic Advantage,* Drs. Brock and Fernette Eide share, "Individuals with dyslexia who are trained sufficiently to produce the kind of right-to-left shift in their reading circuit...usually don't become indistinguishable from fully 'normal' readers but instead become their own unique variety of highly skilled 'dyslexic readers.'"[9] Perhaps after changing the brain functioning in this manner, which simultaneously may change the eye functioning, vision therapy can help put how the eyes function back on track. Of course, instead of fixing what *we* broke, it would be better to understand and honor how right-brained children learn and not *cause* issues with mismatched teaching methods and resources.

It's also possible that a right-brained child doesn't experience the eye shift by the end of the 8 to 10 year range to begin better incorporating two-dimensional activities. It may be useful to consider vision exercises to assist in the switch between the ages of 11 and 13. But we should first honor the natural time frame for right-brained children that involve integrating the left side of the brain that coincides with vision changes, including any expected delays due to individual circumstances. Of course, most vision therapy specialists have no understanding about this information regarding right-brained learners. The natural learning process for a right-brained learner needs to be better understood by everyone, both parents and professionals, before recommending programs or exercises that change eye function.

We as parents and educators have to learn to trust the natural process of right-brained learners as it pertains to how the right brain prefers to process information. There's a time for everything if we can be patient and have faith. Our fear of our children "falling behind" and our reliance on the latest research that simply shows what today's limited understanding looks like does a grave disservice to many children. To restate what the Eides shared in their book *The Mislabeled Child*, "Too often we try to teach children using only a narrow range of options. This narrow approach actually aggravates—and in some cases even causes—many of the learning difficulties children encounter."[10] Is our narrow understanding of how our brain functions causing learning difficulties? I believe greater trust in the natural rhythm of timing and appropriate resources would alleviate many problems.

Kinesthetic (Touch)

The last of the three common input modalities is hands-on, kinesthetic activities. A kinesthetic activity is a body experience, such as manipulating something, acting out something, or creating something. Early education, such as preschool, commonly offers diverse activities of exploration, experimentation, and discovery through kinesthetic, hands-on manipulation. Pegboards, blocks, community helper dress-up, musical instruments, and puzzles are common tools found in preschools everywhere. Even the first couple of elementary school grades offer kinesthetic opportunities, such as counting objects for math, craft-making time, or building a solar system for science. Unfortunately, it seems the older a child gets, the less hands-on activities are offered. Somewhere along the line, we've equated hands-on learning with immaturity and less intelligence.

Memorizing math facts is viewed as superior to the quick manipulation of an abacus to find answers. Giving an oral report on the dinosaur time periods is considered more competent than a diorama depicting each of the same time periods. Showing pictures or videos of the pyramids is rated more educational than building a pyramid out of building blocks. And yet, maturity and intelligence are exhibited in professions such as engineering, architecture, mechanics, medicine, and sewing, all requiring a strong kinesthetic quality to succeed.

Kinesthetic activities are common in the early grades, like preschool. The kinesthetic input modality should be valued in later grades as well.

Right-brained builder types and high energy children especially thrive with kinesthetic learning. My two children who benefited from kinesthetic learning are showcased in Chapter Six (dabbling in hands-on creative outlets such as building, music, and puzzles), Chapter Twelve (developing math ability through manipulatives, computer programming, and patterns), and Chapter Eighteen (contributing with yard work, sports skills, and animal care). Providing kinesthetic learning opportunities in school requires an experimentation-oriented learning model. Such a model would include a mentor-based teaching structure with a demonstration testing assessment.

Kinesthetic learning promotes innovation, creativity, and initiative. Yet, we demoralize hands-on learners. Do we remember looking down on those students who chose home economics and wood shop class in middle school? These young people may have gone on to become our home builders and sous chefs, both kinesthetic-based professions. Kinesthetic learning needs to be infused in all levels of education to benefit all students, especially right-brained hands-on learners.

Sensory Differences

Right-brained children are often sensory sensitive. Both heightened senses and heightened emotions mean a right-brained child has the capacity to feel deeply, which translates positively to the creative outlets in which they excel. But day-to-day living with these differences can be challenging. This is where the label sensory processing disorder (SPD) may arise.

Right-brained children with heightened sensory needs require consistent exposure to kinesthetic, sensory experiences so they may achieve balance, especially in their young years. Natural activities such as bouncing on trampolines, swinging on swing sets, participating in a variety of physical sports, spinning on merry-go-rounds, and general roughhousing among boys have all declined over recent years outside of scheduled opportunities. Similarly, finger painting, playing in the sandbox, getting messy, working with Play-Doh™ or clay, and creating and executing an obstacle course seem to have been replaced with structured, adult-directed

activities. Have the changes to a kinesthetic-rich childhood filled with these unstructured, messy, and outdoor physical play activities led to more sensory-deprived children?

A consistent, easily accessible sensory diet was important for my sensory-seeking children, at least through 8 to 10 years old.

Because our homeschooling environment allowed the freedom to access sensory-stimulating activities throughout the day, my sensory-seeking children filled that need. I observed the need was especially great between the ages of 5 and 7 and that the 8 to 10 year shift resulted in a calmer balance. (See Chapter Twenty-Two for my school setting recommendations that address this in the 5 to 7 year stage.) Those children who are extreme sensory averse—often on the autism spectrum—especially in the eating or pottying realms, benefit from professional expertise or specialized techniques.

Energy Differences

The attention deficit hyperactivity disorder (ADHD) label tends to emphasize the high energy needs versus the idea that these children are almost always strong kinesthetic learners (see Chapter Seventeen). School tends to focus on the passive learning elements instead of the hands-on, active engagement these children crave. ADHD and sensory-seeking types are made to feel they are a behavior problem for having higher sensory and kinesthetic needs. Kinesthetic learning enhances certain sets of skills and knowledge, visual learning enhances another set of skills and knowledge, and auditory provides yet another avenue to certain sets of skills and knowledge. Each input modality should be valued and honored for the children who learn best with each.

I believe we need to exercise the power of observation more so that we may learn to truly individualize education for our children. A child-centered approach with a strengths-based model would reveal the thousands of ways of learning that should be available to every person. We need to assume that a child can and will learn when placed in a learning environment conducive to and supportive of that child's particular way of learning, utilizing both brain processing traits and input modality preferences.

Beginning with a strengths-based foundation is crucial. Meeting each child's developmental readiness throughout a broad range of topics while understanding there are many valid time frames to acquiring the different subjects is critical. The key is learners engaged with subject matter as they develop positive relationships with those subjects. Right-brained children will flourish like their left-brained peers when the learning environment right for them is offered utilizing their particular strengths, optimal subject timing, and more kinesthetic, visual activities. By doing so, schools will acknowledge and honor the right side of normal.

References and Notes

[1] Silverman, Linda Kreger. *Upside-Down Brilliance: The Visual-Spatial Learner.* Denver: DeLeon Publishing, Inc., 2002.

[2] *Earobics® Step 1 Home Version: Sound Foundations for Reading and Spelling™*, CD ROM, Houghton Mifflin, 1997. *Earobics® Step2 Home Version: Sound Foundations for Reading and Spelling™*, CD ROM, Houghton Mifflin, 1997.

[3] Fast ForWord is ©2012 Scientific Learning Corporation.

[4] Image found in the software *Earobics® Step 1 Home Version: Sound Foundations for Reading and Spelling™*, CD ROM, Houghton Mifflin, 1997.

[5] Maslen, Bobby Lynn. *Bob Books*. Scholastic, 2006. There are currently Sets 1-5, plus additional specialty resources.

[6] Dolch words are the top 220 high frequency sight words that can't be learned by pictures or phonics.

[7] Moore, Raymond S. and Dorothy N. Moore. *Better Late than Early: A New Approach to your Child's Education*. Reader's Digest Association, 1989..

[8] Ibid.

[9] Eide, Brock L. and Fernette F. Eide. *The Dyslexic Advantage: Unlocking the Hidden Potential of the Dyslexic Brain*. Hudson Street Press, 2011.

[10] Eide, Brock and Fernette Eide. *The Mislabeled Child*. New York: Hyperion, 2006.

Chapter Twenty

Giftedness—Twice as Nice?

Shift Begins with Me

When my oldest artist son was 3 years old, we visited my family's home in Michigan for Thanksgiving. We'd just arrived for the festivities, and as he entered the home and smelled the good food cooking, he exclaimed, "What's that lovely aroma I smell?" It surprised me as much as the next person, but I saw my sister's eyes enlarge as she asked, "Did he just say what I think he said?"

This same child was sitting with my husband and me at the dining room table when he was 5 years old. For some reason, my husband and I were discussing camels. The question arose if camels only have one hump. I mentioned that I believed that to be true. My artist son quipped with his usual preemptory statement, "Well actually, Mom, there are two kinds of camels. The dromedary camel has one hump and the Bactrian camel has two." He continued eating. My husband and I looked at each other as I said, "We're in trouble if our kindergarten child is already correcting us."

My oldest artist son's obvious high intelligence and desire to learn subjects like science, ancient history, geography, cultures, mythology, and animals were the initial reason we considered homeschooling. He was always engaged in actively learning something and feeding that interest was working for him, so we simply decided to continue. This insatiable appetite for learning is one of the two commonly recognized attributes of a gifted child (a person with an IQ higher than 130). The other common attribute associated with a high intelligence factor are those children who are very early and fluent readers and enjoy learning using the print resource. In fact, these gifted children come to many subjects early and easily and read voraciously to obtain that information. When being labeled gifted means early acquisition of skills, the label is clear. However, being gifted doesn't always mean learning subjects early, and that's when the mislabeling begins. My artist son's experience tells this story well.

Intelligence Mislabeled

High intelligence...check. Precocious vocabulary...check. Insatiable appetite for learning...check. Unusually high interest in books at a young age...check. Learned to read at age 9...whoa, wait a minute. Developed his writing skills at age 11...uh-oh. Reversed letters until age 10...Houston, we have a problem! Because school personnel and other professionals don't understand the right-brained connection with later subject development, my artist son would be classified with "asynchronous development," at best, "twice exceptional," at worse.

Asynchronous Development and Twice Exceptional

Asynchronous development means that a child isn't learning "evenly." If you can learn all these early subject strengths for right-brained children (see Chapter Sixteen), like history, science, and geography at such a high level so young, then reading, spelling, and math should come as early and easily, especially if you test as highly intelligent. Right? Twice exceptional means not only did the gifted child *not* learn certain subjects early, he struggled to learn the subjects when taught *at the standard time in school.* You mean a gifted child reverses letters, doesn't spell well, and can't memorize Dolch words? He must be dyslexic *and* gifted. Right?

For my son, it wasn't asynchronous development or a twice exceptional problem! After all my other research about right-brained learning, I found that these gifted children are simply right-brained learners who require the right time frame to learn certain subjects. *The attributes of being right-brained and being gifted don't negate each other.* Both need to be understood so that this unnecessary confusion by professionals doesn't result in a gifted child being mislabeled.

My young gifted artist had an insatiable appetite for learning (gifted aspect). He still preferred highly visual material (right-brained aspect).

When a child is gifted *and* right-brained, I noticed that once he reaches the appropriate right-brained learning stage, he often picks up skills easily and painlessly. For instance, when the right-brained reading time frame of 8 to 10 years occurred, my artist son easily took in the information. After learning to read, he jumped straight to reading an adult novel with his newly acquired skill. On the flip side, he also settled back into typical right-brained resource material of comic books, manga, and high interest magazines. In other words, sometimes he chose high level reading material because of his gifted nature, and sometimes he chose highly visual, entertaining reading material because of his right-brained nature. Both sides of the coin can co-exist without discounting one for the other.

My artist son easily developed writing skills once he entered the appropriate right-brained time frame between 11 and 13 years old. Gifted children often start with a "big splash," as my artist son did. He started with a novel and a full-length script. Compare that to my writer daughter and builder (computer programming) son who began with "little splashes" in their gift area when they were between 11 and 13 years old (writing short stories and learning to write a short program, respectively), and then made "big splashes" between 14 and 16 years old (starting a novel and writing more complex programs, respectively). I noticed this difference with the early right-brained subject strengths between 5 and 7 years old, too. My artist son engaged in these subjects at a higher level and intensity at that stage than did his siblings who wouldn't be classified as gifted.

Asperger's Syndrome

Four years after we officially began homeschooling our children, the autism diagnosis hit our home (see Chapter Twenty-One). I wondered if my artist son's high intelligence and social awkwardness were related to Asperger's Syndrome, two traits commonly associated with this diagnosis. In the book, *Misdiagnosis and Dual Diagnoses of Gifted Children and Adults,* the authors recognize this misunderstanding between giftedness and Asperger's Syndrome, even with diagnosticians. But, they clearly state that Asperger's Disorder "is not an appropriate label for those who are simply awkward, eccentric, or uncomfortable in social settings."[1] What we did observe in our gifted, right-brained child was a need for appropriate support in both the learning and social realms.

High intelligence doesn't always mean early acquisition of all skills or always using adult-level resources. My gifted son enjoying a comic book after learning to read at age 9.

A gifted person's traits are often an asset to the learning aspect of that child's life, but those same traits can cause complications in the social arena. In this chapter I will share some of these gifted traits, and explain how you can sift out the right-brained component from the gifted arena. I'll also share examples of how each trait presents itself in the learning realm versus the social context.

May I Have Your Attention Span

It's said that those who are gifted often enjoy cerebral activities and possess a long attention span at a young age that helps them learn. As a result, many gifted children spend time alone thinking things through. It takes a longer time to satiate their appetite for learning because their peers often can't keep up with them. My artist son clearly had a longer attention span with regard to his interests in the learning realm, and he played in a much more detailed way than his peers or siblings in the social realm.

Learning

I vividly remember two instances that caught my attention, even as a new mother, that I felt reflected my artist son's focus as unusual for such a young child. Now I understand the gifted and right-brained traits that combine

401

to create each situation. The first example is when my artist son was as young as one year old, he spent hours with books. He not only listened to books read and movies played, he remembered everything in detail. Attraction to highly visual materials—such as pictorial books—is a common right-brained trait. The extraordinary visualization skill found in right-brained people allows them to remember details. My artist son's voracious appetite for learning, beginning at such a young age, could be attributed to his gifted side.

As the second example, my artist son spent a lot of time delving deeply into the early right-brained subject strengths (see Chapter Sixteen) and his particular creative outlets (see Chapter Six). Creative projects on topics such as dinosaurs, animals, ancient history, meat-eating plants, and snakes that lasted hours, days, and weeks were common for my gifted artist son. He spent hours by himself, introspective time that included deep engagement, creative pursuits, and lots of percolating. I understood the value of his thinking mind; a right-brained child often does just as much internal work using his highly visual and pictorial mind as he does with concrete experiential activities. On the other hand, learning that reaches the high school level while kindergarten age is definitely a gifted trait.

Because of high intelligence, a gifted child can take his learning interests to deeper levels than his peers. This, of course, takes more time, so a longer attention span results. A right-brained child can have a long attention span for creative interests, too. Both gifted and right-brained children can lose attention quickly like any other child, though, with non-interest activities or with subjects that typically develop later for right-brained children.

Social

My gifted son also used his preference for cerebral activities, coupled with a long attention span, in the play arena. He liked to play with girls up until about 4 years old because they naturally engage in higher level play for longer periods of time. This might concern some parents, but I noticed it was a result of the gifted trait in him for more in-depth social interaction. At 4 years old, he also found some value in playing with boys. He naturally liked boy themes and knew boys would be the playmates that would want to pursue these. But he was also attracted to male playmates who were more willing to follow, yet also possessed the intellectual or play ability to act out the scenarios he created for the length of time and to the depth he desired to take the play activity. This desire for followers could be attributed to his right-brained side. He could visualize the creative ideas for play and really wanted to see those ideas come to life with willing participants.

Most of my gifted son's best friends before the age of 4 were girls.

The depth and length of play was another reason my gifted artist son often chose playing alone versus including others. I understood that he enjoyed the complex, lengthy forms of play scenarios, so he sometimes preferred them over the shallower, quick-hitting forms of play of his current peers. Since my artist son is a social introvert, however, I now realize why he often sought out his sister's companionship as he played, created, or learned alone without being alone. Even as an adult today, he's challenged to find the balance between his need for deep, solitary engagement in a project and his need for social companionship.

403

Deep Thinkers

Typically, children are concrete thinkers in their childhood years of 5 to 11. After the brain shift between 11 and 13, typical children can think more abstractly. Gifted children are capable of abstract thinking at a younger age. This is a result of asking a lot of questions because a gifted child wants to know the why and how of acquired knowledge. The ability to think deeply in this way leads to gifted children "getting it" quickly. I noticed this trait in my son's learning and social life.

Learning

I remember teaching my artist son about maps when he was around 5 years old. I figured he could make a map of our neighborhood, since that's what one starts with at this age, right? As usual, he asked more questions about the task and discovered that his neighborhood was in a city. On our city map, we looked up the location of our neighborhood. He wanted to go farther. Out came the state map on which we found our city. We looked at the map of the United States, then North America. (Oh, how he would have loved Google Earth™ if it had existed!). As he let this information percolate, a few hours later he stated, "So, if I was standing on the map of our city, I would be this big." He held up his fingers to a small entity. He continued, "And if I was standing on a state map, I would be this big." He shortened the height. "And if I was standing on a country map, I would be a tiny dot. And if I was standing on the continent map, I would be so little, you would need a microscope to see me. And if I was standing on the map of the solar system, I would be smaller than a germ." Wow! That was deep, I thought. It all began with introducing the idea of maps using our neighborhood, like any other kindergarten curriculum. The interest in and understanding of maps is a right-brained strength as it utilizes the ability to visualize, yet the depth of thought may stem from the gifted aspect.

Social

I noticed these same traits of gaining information through questions and answers affected the parent-child discipline arena. When my son was very young, I could explain about right and wrong, and he easily understood, almost instantly changing his behavior to align with what was right. For example, it might be as simple as explaining to him that I needed him to hold the hand of a younger sibling because I didn't want the sibling to stop paying attention and wander off. Or I explained I wanted him to grab hold of the cart at the grocery store because we could shop faster when I knew where he was. If he accepted my rationalization, he simply did it the first time and thereafter. Giving him good information and explaining why things operated a certain way were the only ingredients he needed to make an informed choice.

Heightened sensitivities translated to kindness to babies for my son.

He continues to have a deep sense of right and wrong; it goes against his nature and sensitivities to choose something harmful to self or others. The core of this attribute is being highly sensitive, a trait of a right-brained learner as well as a gifted trait. If a trait is "doubled," it will probably be heightened. In some instances, like the examples above, this made parenting extremely easy! However, remember the two-sided coin analogy? Parenting heightened, highly sensitive children can also be tricky.

405

I had to be especially careful regarding safety-oriented discussions. Because he and my other children were highly sensitive due to being right-brained, they have a natural affinity to be safe. With my artist son's heightened sensitivity because of the added gifted element, too much information or fear-based reasons could easily scare him. The goal was for my children to have a balanced awareness, not to live in fear that danger lurks around every corner. My sister-in-law told me that she had lain awake in bed every night wondering when she would be kidnapped while she slept. I didn't want that for my children. High sensitivity is a right-brained *and* a gifted trait, heightening its impact, and being able to process information easily is a gifted trait.

Because gifted children easily assimilate good information, watch out if your reasoning is faulty. Gifted children easily spot inconsistencies. They are often perceptive, have stored a large quantity of information for easy recall, and might not be inhibited by authority figures. This means they're not afraid to voice their disagreement with anyone if they feel you don't present a valid reason for your actions or requests. This can be perceived as the gifted child always negotiating everything. It's not easy for them to give in because they have such a breadth of knowledge and awareness at their disposal. I think many of us parents predict a lawyer in the making.

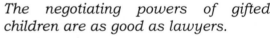

The negotiating powers of gifted children are as good as lawyers.

Since a strong sense of fairness is another trait for a right-brained person as well as a gifted person, I created a family adage that states, "Fairness doesn't mean equal; it means getting one's needs met." That helped a lot. Another strategy that worked well during the times I had to make "best choice" decisions that

406

worked for most family members, but not all, was for me to state my decision, let my artist son know I understood that it wasn't fair or logical, but that I made the decision anyway, and then proceed to walk away. Because I admitted it wasn't fair or logical, he had no defense to use. I didn't need to do this often. Having a child like my artist son helped me live more mindfully by thinking through my decisions and actions, and taking more time to problem solve to find win-win solutions. In the end, it can be a positive thing!

Adult Understanding

Another common trait for a gifted child is an attraction to adult-level resources and interactions. It's important to remember, though, possessing the intelligence to keep up with adults doesn't equate to having an *emotional* intelligence that can keep up. They may speak like adults, but they're still children.

Learning

On the learning side, it's nice to see your young child head to the adult non-fiction section at the library. My artist son wanted real depictions of real things to learn about and from so he often rejected the cartoon-based material in the children's section. He was attracted to meaty information in magazines like *National Geographic®* and *Scientific American™,* and in magazines that value child intellect, such as *Ranger Rick®, Kids Discover®,* and *Zoobooks®*.[2] These are all highly visual materials, though, versus largely text-driven. The latter magazines were chosen by his pictorial right-brained side. He sought information from adults because he knew they had the depth of knowledge that he craved. That meant the adults in his life were always impressed with his intelligence and maturity. However, that didn't always translate to his peers.

Social

The social aspect of attraction to adult-level interactions was split for my artist son. During childhood, he managed to find peers, with my support, that fit his personality style. Because of the creative intelligence that often accompanies being both right-brained and gifted, these children can appear "bossy" if placed with peers who don't match up well to the needs of this playmate. My artist son seemed to find followers, or those who filled complementary roles. I've mentioned several times in this book that for a good period of his growing up years, he had two friends who complemented his strength of creative producer. When he was younger, he tended to avoid other creative leaders, but as he got older, he learned how to share the creative stage. His teen peers admired his creative prowess and even sought out his contributions in this area.

The teen years are an entity unto itself, a creation mainly caused by the organization of school. Our culture uses school attendance as a sort of holding tank for young people between the ages of 12 and 18. Typically, unschooled children are ready to understand adulthood starting between ages 11 and 13. Our gifted children are even more ready to head in that direction. I do believe the teen culture is the most difficult stage for our gifted children. This teen culture has an almost dumbed down component to it because when children can't progress naturally into the adulthood stage, there's a form of digression.

My artist son first noticed the shift for teens when the usual topics of conversation with some of his childhood friends were no longer acceptable. A particular incident triggered his perceptiveness. He'd been discussing Pokémon® with one of his friends as usual when another older teen walked by. His friend momentarily stopped talking, looked self-conscious, and then resumed speaking after the teen peer passed. My artist son asked me about the phenomenon. I explained that there's a shift in priorities during the teen years from an interest-based focus to a teen-based focus on girls, sports, clothing, and other such "cool" elements. He tried to combat the shift for about a year, but with a strong awareness of others and their perception, he did want to find his place, so he acquiesced to the teen scene as best he could.

For my gifted artist son, an interest-based focus came more naturally than a socially-based focus. (Image[3])

There's no hiding intelligence at the level of the gifted, though, no matter how much you want to blend in with the teen scene. Initially, my artist son proclaimed, "There's *no* way I'm going to talk like a teen!" But he realized that "if in Rome," he must be willing to accept and adapt to the culture to some extent. Being a guy has some benefit; girls have an even harder time. Guys tend to accept all kinds within their circle, although one still has to actively desire to be part of the group to be invited on group outings. My artist son found a group of boys who accepted his idiosyncrasies without requiring him to give up too much of his intellectual gifts. He shared with me that when the boys didn't understand words he used, they would shout, "Translation, Gaddis!" He'd find simpler words to replace them. I remember one time he lamented, "I had to simplify one phrase three times!" Although the social standing wasn't exactly what he had hoped for, particularly with the girls, he knew it was probably the best he could do in that stage of life without giving up the core of who he was. As it was, depression came into play constantly during this time because he couldn't totally bridge the gap.

Laughter Is the Best Medicine

Humor is a healing trait for any of us to incorporate into our lives, so it was interesting to discover that humor is well developed in gifted persons. It's a trait often found in right-brained people, too. My artist son is no exception.

Learning

My son often used humor to keep his concentration during the formal stage of his education. I enjoyed going through his notebooks just to discover the humorous treasures he always smattered throughout his schoolwork. I'd laugh out loud. Because it interested him the least, my artist son used humor with math the most. Chapter Ten features a picture of him creating with art his own playmates for a dice game. During that same period, he made his own "rating system" for math lessons to amuse himself with what he saw as a boring activity. It was all hilarious and quite clever! This was definitely a right-brained strategy used to minimize the boredom of the left-brained task.

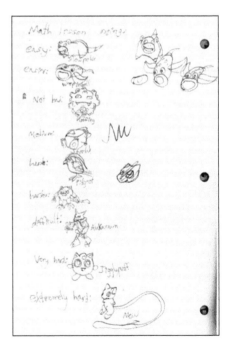

My gifted son created his own "rating system" to amuse himself during math. (Image⁴)

Social

I've often encouraged my artist son to consider stand-up comedy. He rejects my cajoling by stating that he does best spur-of-the-moment rather than rehearsed. When he was 13 years old and we moved to a new area, he was trying to find his place in the group of teens at our local church. They happened to have a talent show as a small group activity and my artist son chose to go up on stage and perform a comedic rendition of a Brack song.[5] He allowed his creative license complete freedom, and everyone who witnessed it admitted that such courage and sheer talent was to be commended, especially as they'd never dare expose themselves that way during the fragile teen stage.

Caution: Road Block Ahead

It's interesting how people view being gifted. At the obvious level, most people feel that having high intelligence is a great thing, even a preferred thing. Don't we all strive to help our children excel in school? Isn't that what we stress over as homeschooling parents, questioning whether we're providing enough intellectual stimulation to maximize our children's mental growth? When we think of gifted, we usually only think about the intelligence factor; the idea of being "smart." But there are other attributes of being gifted that can counter the benefits of high intelligence if they aren't acknowledged and addressed. I noted four attributes that fall under this category:

➢ Self-Awareness
➢ Perfectionism
➢ Spiritual Attunement
➢ Attitudes Toward Success

Magic Mirror on the Wall: Being Highly Self-Aware

A gifted child realizes how different he is from his peers. A gifted child realizes that others don't think as deeply as he does. A gifted child realizes the great insignificance or

411

significance everything has. A gifted child recognizes the discrepancy between what she knows and what she's capable of doing in this world. Couple this with a highly sensitive nature, and the result can be a constantly troubled heart. On the flip side, a right-brained child has a strong attachment to childhood because of its imaginative wonders. This means that the right-brained side of a gifted child often operates in a sort of oblivion. But then there's the self-awareness trait of the gifted child, constantly creating blasts of stark reality causing guilt, fear, and anxiety. A gifted child struggles with awareness of his place in the world at an age without matching authority of power, or personal emotional intelligence to deal with it. On the other hand, the oblivious imaginative aspect that the right-brained component brings to a gifted child's life can soften the harsh effects of the gifted side.

Peer Awareness. My artist son's self-awareness benefited him as he used this knowledge to accommodate his peers. A gifted child, as well as a right-brained child, often has a stronger intensity and longer duration of interest in various subjects. When I realized this was a difference between my son, then 9 years old, and his peers, I asked if he knew about that. He'd noticed that his peers' interest in the same topic lasted up to about three months. He knew his interest lasted six months plus. He told me that he already adjusted his expectations of play with his friends because of self-awareness of the trait. He further shared that he could tell when the peers grew bored listening to his commentary on any given interest. He'd already learned to judge the length of time to allow himself this pleasurable pastime, based on his self-awareness.

My gifted son knew his interests were more intense and lasted longer than his friends' so he adjusted accordingly. (Image[6])

Misinterpretation of How Others View Him. Sometimes my artist son misinterpreted how others viewed him. In fact, I would say this happened often. A common instance during childhood was my gifted son's reaction to anyone telling him "no." His interpretation of this response was that the person thought he was a bad person for having asked. As an example, he always wanted his friends to come over to his house to ask him to play. Sometimes he'd ask me to call his friend for him. When I asked why he didn't go over himself when he was 8 years old, he said that he was afraid his friend's mother or father would answer the door. He admitted that he thought his friend's parents would react negatively to his play request.

To help, we play acted scenarios of one of the parents answering the door. I started with humorous scenes, like the mother opening the door and quickly declaring, "What do *you* want?" in a sneering voice. My son laughed at the prospect, knowing that the mother was a kind-hearted person who would never do that. Through the play acting, he realized he thought such a response was possible without having mindfully questioned it. I eventually enacted more realistic scenarios, explained the possible reasons for various responses from the parents, and provided opportunities to rehearse some responses. I emotionally supported him when, one day, he went next door, and I waited for his return and report. In this way, he received immediate feedback, either sharing that the situation occurred as we had predicted, or troubleshooting any new circumstances that arose. I had to constantly support my son in this manner for this particular representation of his high awareness abilities.

Picture Perfect

Perfectionism is another common trait among the gifted that can counter the high intelligence factor if it isn't adequately addressed. And it makes sense! When possessing highly perceptive awareness of self and others (gifted), the ability to visualize well (right-brained), and the diverse knowledge at a young age that comes with high intelligence all get married together, it might be difficult to deal with a discrepancy between ability and product. I shared some perfectionism stories about my gifted son in Chapter Eight that highlight this. In that chapter, I also talk about the need for parents and educators to become effective mistake coaches to minimize the frustration perfectionism can create.

As always noted, every trait has a good and a difficult side. Perfectionism's good side is that it can provide motivation to produce excellence. However, it can also act as brakes that stop progress for fear that the creation will never be good enough. To minimize the negative aspect, my artist son continually reminded himself that art isn't a science. Science has procedures and tests that can be completed. Art, on the other hand, has an inherent aspect of incompleteness because more can always be added or changed based on individual perspective. It was a process for my artist son to allow his work to be seen as complete, even as his perfectionism triggered his artist eye to do more to make it better. Perfectionism requires balance.

Why Do I Exist?

Right-brained people are naturally spiritual people because of their highly sensitive natures and their intuitive trait. Right-brained people also gravitate to big picture concepts such as integrity, faith, and compassion. The gifted component of deep thinking and perfectionism can be combined for both *good* and difficult situations.

414

Man's Search for Happiness. Who are we? Why are we here? Where are we going? Most people ask these questions about their own existence at some time in their life. Gifted children may ask these things at an unusually young age, even as young as 5 to 7 years old. If death occurs to a loved one or a pet, deep questions may arise. Though gifted children ask these adult questions, they still often have the emotional maturity of a child. Answers have to be tailored accordingly so as not to scare them, but still address their need to know. If a parent has spiritual beliefs, gifted children can grasp deep concepts at this time.

If a parent doesn't have spiritual beliefs, these questions from their children can prompt the parent to seek answers with him. I know of a gifted woman who was tormented with these very questions of wondering about her existence at the age of about 5. Her fear gave way to a longing toward spirituality. Raised in a non-religious home, she nevertheless constantly begged her mother to bring her to a church. Finally relenting, her mother dropped her and her little sister off at a local church—on their own! Even though her desire was strong, this gifted little girl felt insecure trying to figure out her spiritual promptings on her own, without an advocate. (Remember, even though young gifted children have big ideas, this doesn't change the fact they're still children and need support.) She decided that she would just have to wait until she was older to fulfill this need. At 17 years old, she did just that. Today, she considers her mother's lack of support at that time yet another testament to not being understood or supported in her unique needs. Every parent without their own religious or spiritual bent will need to decide for themselves how to support the individuality of their gifted child in this area.

Obedience. Most religions have an element of obedience to God's commandments as part of its practice. Many religions prescribe to the idea of "strict obedience" to parents for children as their practice to this principle. This type of "blind obedience" can create resentment later in gifted, right-brained children and can be a catalyst for the departure from

415

organized religion (even though many still have deeply held spirituality). That's because these children need to know why. Gifted and/or right-brained children are capable of *choosing* to obey for themselves because it makes sense and have developed a meaningful relationship with God.

Each of my children initiated wearing a tie or carrying their scriptures.

I remember hearing parents talk about creating spiritual habits with their children such as prayer and scripture study. Upon reflection, that seems like a left-brained strategy. Somehow, I decided I trusted that my spiritually-minded, sensitive children would choose and establish these habits and spiritual traits for themselves because they were meaningful to them. Each has done so. Nurturing spirituality through the love of Christ versus the fear of God is much more conducive to spiritual development in gifted, right-brained children.

Perfection and Sin. Faith without works is dead and most religions require "walking the walk" through making good choices. The flip side of this is when we sin, or make a bad choice. This has been the trickiest area for perfectionist, right-brained children who are highly sensitive. A gifted child who is prone to misinterpreting how others view him, even God, can create within himself a constant source of guilt, shame, and inadequacy even in an upright and good life. Self-preservation from the consistent reminder of these self-inflicted feelings is yet another reason a gifted, right-brained person may steer away from organized religion. Gifted, right-brained children need a gentle, loving view of God or they may not benefit from their spiritual nature.

Much of this stems from the gifted side that is highly aware of the discrepancy between where they are (an imperfect mortal) and where they're supposed to be (perfected in Christ). One of my mantras is: this world is a place to learn from imperfection, not perfection. We can't achieve perfection in this life on our own. The perfectionism trait can cause more angst in this way or it can make us believe that our achievement alone brings us worth in the sight of God and others. Neither is healthy or true. If we can help our gifted and/or right-brained children in these ways, an authentic, fulfilling spiritual life can result.

You Either Got It or You Don't

Although this isn't a trait, but more a perspective, this last attitude common to gifted people that counters the positive effects of high intelligence is their view on how success is achieved. Studies have found that those with the attitude that success is the result of natural intellectual capacity for learning are less successful than those with the attitude that hard work can overcome natural ability. The latter understands that even if he doesn't naturally know something or can't easily learn it, if he works hard at it, he can learn it and do well with the knowledge. My builder son is a lot like this. The former people, with the attitude of natural intellectual capacity, have a harder time progressing. I speculate that many gifted people might fall into this category. My gifted artist son is a lot like this.

The problem is that gifted people are between a rock and a hard spot. Learning comes easily to them at a young age. This intellectual capacity can't be changed, so it's not often that natural opportunities arise that help these children learn that hard work has its merit. A parent or educator would have to specifically create many opportunities to develop this attribute in the gifted. This attitude of natural intellect as foremost in the lives of these children can be detrimental to them when it comes to achieving their goals for success.

417

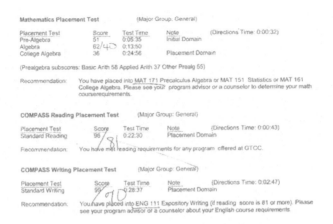

I thought my gifted son would "learn a lesson" about not putting in effort when he refused to study for his community college placement test. Nope, he passed everything, even math, into college level at age 16.

In conclusion, as noted in Chapter Three, there are a lot of cross-over traits of a gifted child *and* a right-brained child. Certainly there are traits of a gifted child that go above and beyond the right-brained realm. The sheer intelligence factor and deep-thinking process stand out as gifted. On the other hand, a right-brained child has his own intelligence level expressed especially through multiple creative endeavors. And because of his global, big-picture thinking, a right-brained child can say astounding things that make an adult ponder. Most importantly, though, don't consider a gifted child to have problems or disabilities simply because he may follow the typical right-brained learning time frame for various subjects. One must look beyond the timing of skill acquisition. Gifted intelligence is deeper than that. Many of the strategies that support a right-brained learner can also apply to the gifted. Typically, the gifted need additional support, particularly in the realm of social interaction with peers. The gifted also need guidance from adults who can help them recognize attributes that could cause them to stumble on their path to their goals. Understanding the right-brained traits as found in this book for a gifted, right-brained child should provide ideas on effective supports and strategies for this learner.

References and Notes

[1] Webb, James T., Ph.D., Edward R. Amend, Psy.D., Nadia E. Webb, Psy.D., Jean Goerss, M.D, M.P.H., Paul Beljan, Psy.D., F. Richard Olenchak, Ph.D. *Misdiagnosis and Dual Diagnoses of Gifted Children and Adults.* Scottsdale: Great Potential Press, Inc., 2005.

[2] The resources listed in this sentence are as follows: For *National Geographic®* magazine, visit their website at http://ngm.nationalgeographic.com/. For *Scientific American™* magazine, visit their website at http://www.scientificamerican.com/. For *Ranger Rick®* magazine, visit their website at http://www.nwf.org/Kids/Ranger-Rick.aspx. For *Kids Discover®* magazine, visit their website at http://www.kidsdiscover.com/. For *Zoobooks®,* visit their website at http://www.zoobooks.com/.

[3] The characters, Saturos, Menardi, and Alex, depicted in this drawing by my artist son can be found in the GameBoy Advance® video game, Golden Sun™, published by Nintendo® in 2001. Use of these images were for personal use and were not intended to challenge any copyright but was the innocent enjoyment of a creative person.

[4] The images drawn by my artist son were characters from the Pokémon fad. Pokémon and its many characters are registered trademarks and ©Nintendo. Use of these images were for personal use and were not intended to challenge any copyright but was the innocent enjoyment of a creative person.

[5] Brak was one of the cartoon character co-hosts of the variety show, Cartoon Planet™, created by Keith Crofford and Mike Lazzo, shown mostly on Cartoon Network, from 1995-2000.

[6] The game that my artist son is playing with in an extended version imaginative play is *Forbidden Bridge,* published by Milton-Bradley in 1992.

Chapter Twenty-One

Sifting Autism Spectrum Disorder from Right-Brained Learning

Shift Begins with Me

When my fifth child was 10 years old, he constantly said he wanted to go to school. I probed to figure out the reason he wanted to attend. He asked if schools had ceiling fans and I told him that most schools don't. I wondered if his interest in ceiling fans was the catalyst for his interest in school, but knowing school didn't have ceiling fans didn't deter his continued requests. I arranged for my electronics son to visit a school. He asked the teacher conducting our tour of the school if the school had any ceiling fans. She thought for a moment and said, "No, we don't have any ceiling fans at school."

As we approached the cafeteria, my son's eyes lit up and he declared, "Ceiling fans!" Sure enough, six ceiling fans hung throughout the cafeteria. He was in hog heaven. As my electronics son was allowed to turn the fans off and on as some of the regular students in the cafeteria looked on in surprise and envy, the teacher embarrassingly commented, "I can't believe after working here seven years and visiting the cafeteria every day that I didn't realize it had ceiling fans." A couple other school personnel who were with the group consoled her as they admitted that they hadn't realized either.

During the rest of the tour, before entering any room, I witnessed the entire group look up first thing to see if there were any ceiling fans. What have I learned from this son's interest? I notice the little things more now. That day he helped every person in that group realize that what's important to notice is all in the eye of the beholder, based on each person's unique perspective and perceptions.

My electronics son was diagnosed with autism in February, 1997, when he was just over two years old. Today, at seventeen, he would be classified high functioning. Many children diagnosed with high functioning autism or Asperger's Syndrome are right-brained, creative learners. There are delays in learning certain things and unique traits in those with autism. There are delays in learning certain things and unique traits in right-brained dominant children. How do you know which is which?

Two years after the first diagnosis of autism, our family was preparing to move to another state. I gathered together all the support people who had helped two of my children flourish and progress to a thank you/going away party. My electronics son was right in the middle of everything, being very social even though he was limited in ability. My fourth son, diagnosed with autism at three years old and age 5 at the time of the party, was off away from the party, hanging out on the stairs, watching from afar. I remarked to a friend and mentor that "it's funny how their autism is so different; this one is in the middle of everything and that one doesn't like to be where there's too much action." My friend reflected on what I said for a moment and then responded, "I don't see it as autism. I see your electronics son as being social and outgoing like his sister and I see your forever son as being introverted and liking his own space like his father." It was a light bulb moment for me. Because autism was such a huge change of perspective for me, everything became colored by it. At that moment I understood I had to learn to sift out autism from the holistic child who still had likes and dislikes, strengths and weaknesses, temperament and personality.

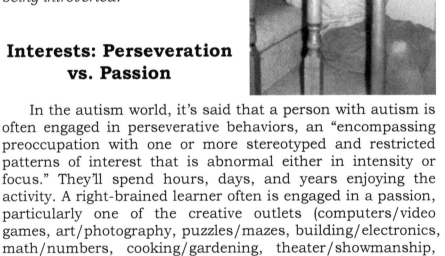

When a right-brained child with autism sits off by himself, is it "being in his own world" or part of being introverted?

Interests: Perseveration vs. Passion

In the autism world, it's said that a person with autism is often engaged in perseverative behaviors, an "encompassing preoccupation with one or more stereotyped and restricted patterns of interest that is abnormal either in intensity or focus." They'll spend hours, days, and years enjoying the activity. A right-brained learner often is engaged in a passion, particularly one of the creative outlets (computers/video games, art/photography, puzzles/mazes, building/electronics, math/numbers, cooking/gardening, theater/showmanship, music/dance, and fashion/sewing). They'll spend hours, days, and years in pursuit of excellence. Is there a connection between the two? Most of the "perseverative" interests of those with high functioning autism or Asperger's Syndrome fall under the category of a creative outlet. Because the autistic mind can sometimes focus on either the sensory aspect of the interest or some of the smaller details of the interest, they may need a bit more direction to shape the interest to provide meaningful benefit. If done successfully, the "perseverative" interest can be a catalyst for engagement in a full life and an eventual creative outlet career choice.

Let me share how my electronics son's long-standing interest in ceiling fans led to opportunities for building family connections, expansion into career skills, social interaction, fine motor skill development, and a potential career path.

Family Connections (Age 6)

I hear my electronics son's loud, but rhythmic humming sound with periodic giggling emanating from the bedroom he shares with his older builder brother.

"Hey, what's going on in here?" I happily ask as I open the door. I see the boys' blankets tucked into the top bunk and draping softly as they surround the bottom bunk. A flashlight moves underneath. Strewn on the floor is a large collection of LEGO® with my builder son plopped in the middle, head bent over, periodically sifting through the piles, looking for the next piece as he concentrates on some project.

My electronics son peeks out of the blankets. "Come see what he made me!" he says excitedly, quickly reverting to his hum and finger rubbing.

I bend over to look as he directs the beam of light to the "ceiling" of his bunkbed house, which is the wood pallet of the top bunk. Taped throughout are the LEGO® ceiling fans that his builder brother made for his pleasure. They're both immersed in what they love, intertwined as brothers through their momentary complementary interests.

Interest Expansion (Age 7)

"May I look at the house plan books?"

"Of course!" I set my son up in front of the small book and magazine rack at our local supermarket and continue grocery shopping. After each aisle, I check back with him to see if he has found "the one."

When I'm about three aisles away, I hear a familiar voice, "Mom, Mom, where are you?"

I peek around an aisle and reply, "Here I am." My electronics son clutches a magazine to his chest while he skips over to me.

"Can we buy it?" he asks hopefully.

"We'll have to see at the checkout."

He tags along beside me with his magazine flopped open. Whenever I stop and tarry, my son plops down on the floor to be more comfortable. He gets up and continues once I turn the corner. My job is to direct him back to the cart if he wanders too far lest he bump into something or someone as he flips the pages. Finally, it's checkout time. It appears the budget will allow for a house plan book this trip.

"Well, can you buy me this house plan book?"

I see the checkout counter woman's eyebrows rise in surprise, wondering if she heard correctly.

My son continues his plea, "It's a good one, Mom. See?" My son eagerly shows me the glossy photos of a ceiling fan decorating featured rooms. This one also has house plans that depict ceiling fan placements in typical rooms within the black and white plan dimensions.

The store clerk slightly shakes her head in disbelief that a 7-year-old would want a house plan book.

Not only do I buy the house plan book that day, I subsequently buy a whole shelf full to promote his connection to house building and ceiling fans. My husband also often took my electronics son to new construction sites and let him "tour" the buildings. My electronics son was always excited when it came time for the ceiling fans to be installed. At 17 today, one of the primary outlets for his ceiling fan interest is creating house design and construction on software.

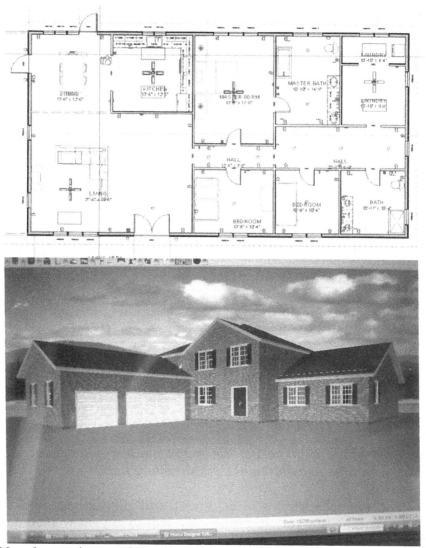

My electronics son's ceiling fan interest led to an interest in architecture. (Image[1])

Socialization (Age 8)

"Does she have ceiling fans in her house?" my electronics son asks me of a new caseworker, who's visiting our house for the first time.

"Why don't you ask her?" I prod.

"But I'm shy," he whispers as he glances at the caseworker.

"I'll be right here. You can do it," I insist gently.

My son haltingly looks at the caseworker, and breathily says quickly, "Do you have any ceiling fans in your house?"

"Well, let's see," the caseworker contemplates, "I think I have three ceiling fans."

My son's eyes light up and he continues the conversation boldly now, without reservation. "What rooms are they in?"

The litany of questions continues in the general format my son uses to gather the first pieces of critical information that take a person from stranger to acquaintance to friend. Age, occupation, location of residence, children...boring. Number of ceiling fan blades, color of blades and motor, light options, length of down pipe, room locations...fascinating...to my electronics son.

My electronics son's ceiling fan parts: blades, downspout, and light, which he uses to build custom ceiling fans.

As my electronics son grew and flourished socially through his interest, it eventually led to my now teenaged electronics son finding like-minded peers at ceiling fan forums online. He met another local fan lover who volunteered at the Habitat for Humanity® ReStore repairing ceiling fans. My electronics son also attended a ceiling fan symposium in a nearby state, chaperoned by his father, hosted by an acquaintance from the online fan forum. Inspired by both of these acquaintances, he learned to navigate software to competently display pictures and videos at online sharing sites. He's also created and maintains a blog about his diverse interests. Starting with simple conversations about his interests has led to many social opportunities and computer skill-building.

Fine Motor Development (Age 9)

"Whatcha doin?" I ask as I look over my electronics son's shoulder as he concentrates on our computer monitor.

"I'm going to look at ceiling fans. Adrienne showed me how. Watch me, Mom. It's really cool." I do watch as my son hunts and pecks for the words "ceiling" and "fans," entering them into our server's search engine and hits enter. A number of options pop up. There are installation videos; always great to get visuals and movement, which is the best part about ceiling fans for my son. There are product sites with many interesting and unique ceiling fans from which to choose. My son zeroes in on his favorite site.[2]

"Look, Mom, I can build my own!" Sure enough, the site provides different choices of motors, blades, lights, and downspouts to explore in any type of combination.

"What kind do you want, Mom?" I give him my choices, and he asks me to explain why I would like each item.

Once the fan is completed, I muse, "Hhhmmm. I think that would be a good one for the family room."

"I'll show you my favorite." And he assembles his preferred choices.

Having piqued his curiosity, he asks, "Where do you think my fan should go?"

"Hhhhmmm. I don't know. What do you think?"

"I think it should go in the foyer." I laugh to myself because I know how exciting it is for him to contemplate less typical locations for fans. Unique locations for my unique son.

He prints out his favorite ceiling fan creation onto stiff paper. Although improving scissor skills isn't high on his priority list, he painstakingly cuts out the fan to enhance its reality and so he can tape it alongside a growing collection of prints on his bedroom walls and ceiling.

Career Development (Age 12)

It's almost midnight when I hear shuffling around in the hallway at the toolbox near my bedroom. It's my electronics son, newly turned 12 years old.

"Hey, isn't it time for bed?" I encourage.

"I just want to change out the old multi-colored ceiling fan bracket for the new one," he explains.

Can't you do it tomorrow?"

"No! It won't take long," my son insists.

"Can't the same bracket that's there be used for the new ceiling fan?" I probe.

"Yes, but the new one's white, and the old one's black. I want the white one now. Can you help me? The screw is stuck tight."

I consider rejecting assistance, but I know that once he has it in his mind to do something, he's going to do it.

"Alright, I'll try."

The first ceiling fan in my electronics son's collection.

We proceed to his room with the correct tools. I lie on his bottom bunk bed and begin to loosen the problematic screw attached to one of the top bunk support rails. A few Christmases ago, with the only thing on my electronics son's wish list being a multi-colored ceiling fan, we got the great idea—as an added surprise—to attach it to one of these supports so he could have a "ceiling fan in his room." (Placing one in the actual ceiling wasn't possible due to it being a drop ceiling.) He was thrilled and more than happy to make room for his fan (minus the electricity) as he slept.

After loosening the screw, my son disassembled the old bracket and replaced it with the new one in preparation for this latest fan that he would finish assembling in the morning. I see the power drill with bits awaiting fast installation of screws, as well as various tools at the ready, all eagerly mastered in response to his ceiling fan interest.

His focus on assembling and disassembling ceiling fans evolved into learning about electricity and circuitry to wire his fans. Over time, he gained an interest in retro and vintage fans, inspiring him to earn enough money to buy, sell, and trade fans in second-hand stores and at diverse online swap locations. He's since had mentors who are a mechanic and a car restoration guy. He'd like to become an electrician as a career choice.

A highly developed interest can inspire development in weak areas, like drawing.

For my son to accomplish all of this, I needed to differentiate between what were the categories and difficulties pertaining to autism, and what could be viewed and steered through the lens of natural right-brained traits. Sometimes, the interests of those with high functioning autism are more "typical," such as trains, dinosaurs, and LEGO®. It's easy to see how we can expand these interests as we would for a typical right-brained learner. Other times, the interests are "unusual," such as ceiling fans, garage door openers, or The Beatles™. If we look past the initial oddity of the interests, we can see how expanding them *can* occur, as noted with my electronics son's ceiling fan interest. Interests can also be used as fodder, such as when my electronics son decided he should learn to create his own comic book stories and short stories, which often involved ceiling fans. He also learned to draw ceiling fans, even when holding and using pencils is a common difficulty in those with autism (see Chapter Fifteen). So, do I view my electronics son's ceiling fans as perseverative interests as viewed in the autism world, or as a passion like most right-brained people pursue? It may have begun as a perseverative interest, but it's most certainly a passion today.

Sensory: Self-Stimulatory Behaviors vs. Sensitivities

All my right-brained children are sensory sensitive (see Chapter Nineteen). Most of them have acute hearing and can hear the softest whisper, especially if it's about something of interest. On the flip side, they become overwhelmed with too much auditory stimulus, especially in group settings where people or children are all talking or shouting. None of my birth children liked baths, and most of my children are not cuddlers, even though they are all loving. Many of my children were particular about the type of clothing they wore, especially in their young years. They resisted changing clothes, brushing teeth, and wearing shoes, all for sensory reasons. I respected these sensory differences as part of who they are without putting a judgment call on them. Each child became more tolerant of sensory stimulation with maturity, emotional regulation, and alternative skills developed to comply with social acceptance to the level they desired.

On the other hand, aren't most of the creative outlets filled with high sensory experiences? Playing an instrument, working with paints or clay, video game playing, gardening, and cooking all enhance the auditory, visual, kinesthetic, olfactory, and taste senses. Does the high level of sensory sensitivity elevate creative expression? My right-brained children taught me to look beyond the physical expression of sensory sensitivities to understand that complex needs on one side of the coin mean equally beneficial attributes exist on the other.

Halo, by Beyoncé[3]
My writer daughter has an entire sensory experience when listening to music. These are the colors (oranges and yellows) and patterns she sees when hearing this song. How amazing!

One of the common traits seen in people with autism is their self-stimulatory behaviors or activities. These are stereotyped body movements (such as flapping hands, rubbing fingers together, or walking on toes), or a preoccupation with parts or sensory qualities of objects (such as opening and shutting windows, being in tight spots, or an aversion to feeling wet). My fourth child, age 19, diagnosed with autism (moderately to severely affected), flips coins into a pile over and over again. He loves how they feel on his fingers, how they sound as they rhythmically clink, and how they look as they float into an arc and onto the pile created. My electronics son makes a particular noise while tensing up his body and rubbing his fingers together as a way to express his sensory satisfaction.

I think the categorization of "self-stimulatory behavior" is viewed as a negative attribute in the autism world and one to be expunged from the child's repertoire of acceptable behaviors. But like my right-brained children taught me, how did I know if the function of this seemingly "unnecessary" trait didn't have benefit? My electronics son's ceiling fan passion started as a self-stimulatory behavior. As a 2- to 3-year-old with limited cognition, he enjoyed watching the blades spin around and around and got a kick out of the

431

sensation he received from watching it from certain angles. Over time and with some guided opportunities, my electronics son realized there were more benefits to ceiling fans than just the thrill of viewing them. Even though he's expanded his understanding and enjoyment of ceiling fans as noted previously, my electronics son still constantly "stims" (autism shorthand for self-stimulatory behavior) on watching ceiling fans spin. *The sensory enjoyment of his ceiling fan interest motivates him to also delve into the passion of learning.*

Although my electronics son assembles, wires, and collects vintage fans, his love of the sensory experience motivates his continued passion.

Another example is my builder son, age 21, diagnosed with high functioning autism at 5 years old. Beginning at the age of 1.5 years old, he spent hours with trains. He would lie down, meticulously linking the metal cast die trains together, close one eye, and pull the train toward and then past himself as he watched his creation from various angles (see Chapter Five). Most professionals and parents in the autism community would label this as "fixating on parts," but there may be another explanation. Because so many individuals with autism are right-brained learners, they may be exploring their three-dimensionality gifts by bringing parts up close and personal for a season while they are young.

Particularly in the early stages of development, when young people with autism are still trying to figure out our "culture" of cognitive understanding, they may be more interested in things sensory in nature because their sensory system is so attuned to their surroundings. It's important that we assist young children with autism by adding more interactive benefits to their interests beyond the sensory nature, or we risk the interest becoming obsessive because they don't know where else to take it. I find that as we expand a child with autism's understanding of their place in the world, and how the development of their interest fits into our world, the interest becomes a healthy passion just like anyone else enjoys.

Obsession: Obsessive-Compulsive vs. Emotional Regulation

Our culture debates the obsessive effects and addictive qualities of today's technology, such as video games, television, and computers. Since these are creative outlets for right-brained children, it's important to help our children understand how to develop talents using screen activities in a healthy way. In the autism world, a comorbid trait of obsessive-compulsive is common. To understand or recognize these effects or qualities, I needed to define each for myself with regard to autism and regular child-rearing needs. These are the definitions I came up with:

- ❖ Obsession is when an interest takes over a life *devoid of other enjoyable activities* and *there's no longer joy* associated with the interest.
- ❖ Compulsion in autism is when there's a patterned impulse *requiring* engagement in an activity *devoid of mental control* because of cognition differences.

❖ Addiction is when a child has a *physical response to an internal impulse* requiring engagement in an interest *devoid of mental control.*

Each of these attributes has occurred as I raised my children. Each time, I needed to figure out how to help my child shift the obsession or addiction back to passion or enjoyment, and how to keep compulsions in balance and enjoyed as a satisfactory activity. The secret is cognitive development and emotional regulation. Cognitive skill development is a common need for those with autism, and mentoring in emotional regulation is a common need for young right-brained children.

Compulsion

The first example is my fourth son who likes to flip coins. I noticed when he hasn't had any cognitive stimulation going on in his life (someone helping him with academics, going out in the community with him, or developing language with him), his mind starts doing what it does best: creating patterns within his mind that he links to the coin flipping. Within a short time period, this patterning begins to cycle into a compulsive nature. For instance, he might begin by associating every flip with spelling a word, but since there's no end to the flipping, or if he doesn't get the spelling just right, he restarts. He becomes noticeably agitated while flipping, his actions become spasmodic, and the sounds he makes grow intense. He's no longer enjoying the experience, and often has a difficult time completing whatever cycle he's created that has taken over the process. So, instead of using his coin flipping as a sensory outlet and a calming, enjoyable action, it becomes compulsive in nature. Daily cognitive stimulation is the key ingredient needed. Since this doesn't come naturally to him, someone has to commit to being part of his life to keep him in balance. As a young adult now, he's learning to independently pursue a schedule I helped him create to meet his cognitive needs.

My fourth son's coin flipping can turn compulsive without consistent cognitive stimulation. (Image⁴)

Addiction

The next example takes us back to my electronics son and his ceiling fan interest. He started this interest as a self-stimulatory sensory activity, but at about 3 to 4 years old, his sensory interest in fans shifted into addiction. Suddenly, it was as if the joy of watching no longer existed, and was replaced with a *need* to frantically turn the fan on and off. He didn't want to do *anything* else, in any way, shape or form. We saw the act as addiction when he took no pleasure in it, and he couldn't seem to stop his need to do it all day long. Being so young without age appropriate cognition or the ability to self-regulate his emotional and sensory needs, he was at the mercy of his autistic pull to sensory satisfaction. We tried to teach him some skills, but because of his age and autism limitations, we were forced to remove him from the unhealthy activity. We "broke" all the fans in the house by

435

turning off the power at the source, and that helped him "snap out of it" after a few months. We could then "fix" the fans so he could go back to enjoy watching them again at a balanced sensory level appropriate for a child with autism at his developmental stage.

Obsession

A last example is my oldest right-brained artist son who *loved* playing video games starting at 5 years old. At around 8 to 9 years old, he went through a stage that appeared to be obsessive. In actuality, it had shifted into that realm (just like self-stimulatory can warp to passion, so can passion deteriorate into obsession) because he didn't have self-regulation skills. Video games weren't fun anymore, and he acted out in frustration, refusing to stop playing because he had to make it to the next level. His actions became spastic and his attitude ugly. While my 3- to 4-year-old needed a break from ceiling fans to escape from the addictive nature he was in because of lack of cognition and self-regulation, I could give my 9-year-old good information about what he was experiencing, how to manage it effectively, and explain what had happened to something that was of high interest to him. After a year's time of discussion, collaboration, and knowledge sharing, he was able to self-regulate and maintain balance to place his video game interest back into passion mode without needing a break from it.

Shifting Perspective on Balance

Spending long hours in the pursuit of something doesn't make it an obsession. We're so focused on being a little good at everything that we forget what it takes to specialize in and excel at something. To develop a passion to excellence, one must dedicate many hours. This is what a strengths-based, gift-centered learning environment looks like.

Spending a lot of time on an interest doesn't have to indicate a "problem."

I noticed in our family that everyone has their own balance in life. Being "in balance" is different for various children because of temperament and learning traits. Some are introverts and need less interaction time than those who are extroverts. Some cerebral types of children need less physical activity than those who are active and high energy. "In balance" also looks different at various stages of development, not to mention extenuating circumstances, like being diagnosed with autism. A young child with autism with less cognitive ability and awareness will engage in more sensory activities than an older child with autism who has been able to develop more cognition. A child with high functioning autism in the 8 to 10 year time frame may desire less social interaction as he engages in his passion areas than an 11 to 13 year old of the same functioning level.

The beginning stages of a passion, particularly with people with autism, may seem "out of balance" at a certain stage. Focusing on one interest could be confused with obsession, or with not being connected to the world. When my builder son was 1.5 to 4 years old, he spent hours creating train tracks and playing trains. Then, from 4 to 12 years old, he spent an equal amount of time with LEGO®. During this time frame, he had no interest in friends, although he had consistent interactions in formal settings to which I brought him. He had many odd ways of interacting and difficulty communicating effectively, yet my builder son was gaining much pleasure from his interest. He was competent in diverse ways, he continued to learn and grow from his interests, and he appeared in balance for the stage of autism he was at during that time.

Label Stereotypes

Regardless of observing that he appeared "in balance" for the developmental stage he was in, I worried that he wasn't doing certain things like everyone else. I reacted to the common concern in the autism world that a child may focus on a particular interest to the exclusion of "more important" things, such as social interaction or physical activity. In other words, I used the label "high functioning autism" to justify worry that he needed social support. I actively looked for a playmate who was a good match for him to develop some social skills. I noticed another homeschooled girl who seemed to be "odd" like him, and I wondered how they might get along. Little did I suspect I would soon learn something about my son from this friendship.

To facilitate the initiation of diverse activities, I created an idea board of things in the house they could play with, and each could take turns making a choice. It was interesting to observe what they chose as their first three activities one day. First, they picked a puzzle with many pieces; I think it was 100 or so. They both bent over the activity, deep in concentration as they constructed this puzzle. Next, they chose a fun board game that took luck and playful interaction. Last, they created their own interest by each cutting a long piece of yarn from a skein and attaching it to the back ends of their waistbands. They found a circular path in our home and following that path, let the yarn drag behind hoping it was long enough to see the end of it when they rounded the corner. Spying the end of their own yarn, each child would leap forward to try to grab it...a *strange*, yet delightful to them, escapade.

Suddenly, I saw why my builder son had a difficult time finding friends! He went from a highly cerebral activity, to a traditional (normal) activity, to an odd activity. Normally, he would lose a playmate in the transition, as so many children would enjoy one, the other, or the last, but not all three. His diversity of interest created a division in peer match-ups. His lack of friends didn't have to be about autism at all, but viewed as part of his unique personality traits that made it difficult to find good matches. He proved himself capable with the right playmate. Instead of acting on stereotypes from a label, I should have honored my original observations of my builder son's temperament, strengths, and interests as I factored in what constituted balance for him at his developmental stage.

My builder son enjoyed cerebral and odd activities as much as a typical one.

Add an Asterisk—Plus More

I have observed that children with high functioning autism have all the temperament traits of a right-brained person, with an asterisk next to it interpreted as "plus more." What I mean by this is many right-brained people have a hard time trying new things because they like to visualize things first, so their first reaction is to avoid the thing that can't be visualized. A high functioning person with autism has a *really* hard time trying new things. A right-brained person has a strong sense of fairness. A high functioning person with autism has a *really* strong sense of fairness. A right-brained person is often an introvert. A high functioning person with autism is often *really* introverted. The same can be said for being sensory sensitive, reactive to change, or anxious. In other words, many of the temperament traits that make it difficult to co-exist with a typical right-brained person are even *more* difficult to live with and balance with those diagnosed with Asperger's Syndrome or high functioning autism.

Academics: Delayed Learning or Delayed Time Frame

It's easy to wonder if, for instance, late reading, spelling, or writing occurs because of a language delay, or other co-existing problems associated with the foundational diagnosis of autism. However, just like I realized each child still has his own social style, each also still has his learning time frame based on brain processing preference. What part of autism might affect his academic performance? I found the key to be language development. My child's desire to have a positive relationship with books could be impacted if he doesn't understand what he's hearing in read-alouds. In fact, one of my children with autism never sat in on read-alouds due to a poor auditory input modality and language comprehension difficulties. Yet, he did learn to read, strengthen spelling, and develop writing in a typical time frame for a right-brained learner. I focused less on *academic* acquisition and more on *language* acquisition as a need above and beyond that of a typical child due to autism. With language acquisition came the pre-skills for academics. When language was developed enough, other academic skills still occurred on a typical right-brained time frame.

Sifting out autism issues was needed in relation to other skills, too. Difficulty with graphomotor skills (using a pen or pencil) is common for children with autism because of low muscle tone and poor motor planning (your brain's ability to tell your muscles how to move in a sequence). Yet, right-brained children tend to develop graphomotor skills on a later time frame, too, because printing and words are a left-brained function that tends to develop between 8 and 10 years old for right-brained children. Lack of play skills is common for children with autism because of a lack of imitation skills. Yet, right-brained children tend to be introverts and often like solitary or one-on-one play interactions, which can be viewed negatively by society. The secret to sifting out autism needs while honoring right-brained processing preferences is to understand each child's current developmental stage, and to use each child's learning style and temperament to help him learn.

For instance, because right-brained children usually aren't ready for handwriting practice until between 5 and 7 years, I wouldn't help my son develop better motor planning by having him write letters during this stage. Instead, I might help my son with autism string beads in a pattern, yarn sew cardboard animals, or gather diverse, interesting objects that my child could pick up with a clothespin. These activities are far less frustrating for a right-brained child with autism at the 5 to 7 year stage, but still develop better motor planning and strengthen muscle tone in the hands. At the same time, I assessed my child's nature and where his inclination lay. My electronics son showed great social interest, but didn't have the ability because he was missing imitation skills due to autism. I helped him learn these skills using one-on-one play activities with me that incorporated his preferred interests, two common play attributes for a young right-brained child. I could then coach him during one-on-one play dates with peers, and finally generalize the skills in small group opportunities. I helped him gain enough skills so he could show me how far he wanted to go socially so that he could achieve it. I didn't want autism to choose for him. I didn't do that for his next older brother because he showed me his nature was to be less socially-inclined. I remember when my builder son approached me in his early teen years and said, "I would like help being more social, but not *too* social." Everyone has their own temperaments and social style to consider.

My electronics son learning to play with others.

It's typical for right-brained children to do best with "delayed academics," according to the current time frame for subject acquisition found in school. Of course, this book declares that it's not *delayed* academics at all, but exactly the time frame during which a right-brained child is meant to learn optimally. Although rote identification of letters and numbers came extremely early for all of my children with autism (1 to 2 years old) without any effort on my part (this is fairly common in autism), my high functioning children learned most of their academic subjects during the typical right-brained time frame outlined in this book. Early intervention in language development, play skills, and imitation skills is an important prerequisite for later learning, just as these skills are important prerequisites for typical children (see Chapter Four). Waiting out the appropriate brain processing preference learning time frame is just as important to those with autism as typical children (see Chapter Ten). A child with autism deserves a strengths-based learning focus in his foundational years just as much as his typical peers.

The Right-Brained/Left-Brained Continuum

There's one noteworthy element regarding autism and the right-brained/left-brained continuum. My builder son, classified with high functioning autism, can often appear more left-brained in his thinking. This is because people with autism are often gifted at noticing patterns. They also like predictability. Thus, my builder son can be quite organized and systematic in his approach to many things. These are both strong left-brained gifts. They can also be female gene traits, so right-brained women can sometimes exhibit these left-brained traits as well. However, as a whole and as a foundation of processing preference, I find my builder son strongly represented as right-brained, as depicted in this book. Teasing out these attributes as stemming from autism helps to see that more clearly.

left	*whole*		*right*
schizophrenia—			
"word salad"	(most teachers)	ADD dyslexia	autism
<——>			

Jeffrey Freed's theory taken from Right-Brained Children in a Left-Brained World. (Image[5])

Because I've had several children on the autism spectrum, and I've studied the attributes of a right-brained learner, I've noticed many crossovers that make me consider the idea Jeffrey Freed outlined in the beginning of his book *Right-Brained Children in a Left-Brained World:* autism may be a far-right point location on the right-brained/left-brained continuum.[6] Why do there seem to be more right-brained boys than girls? Girls are more prone to being word-based while boys are more object-based. Why do more boys have autism than girls? Recent speculation suggests that autism results from a double male gene. It's always interesting to consider the possibilities, but the bottom line is to always view our children holistically.

It can be fruitful to bring into closer view certain parts from time to time as long as we always span back out for the big picture, lest we lose understanding of how all aspects work together. I was careful about the labels I placed on my children's actions and behaviors because they influenced my view of their place in life and in the world. The autism label helps me be aware that my electronics son may need more coaching to expand his interests beyond the sensory experience. But if autism colored my whole view of him, I may have thought his interests would stay "perseverative." I saw the link that his interest had to the typical right-brained creative outlet of the electronics passion. That was where his true nature was meant to lead him.

The right-brained label helped me give value to my builder son's passion for building and see the extraordinary spatial competence he developed because of it. I had to step back and see my child as a whole person: introverted, highly sensitive and perceptive, a builder-type, and a person with delayed language acquisition. My builder son's lack of interest in friends is a result of *all* of these attributes. Being introverted, highly sensitive and perceptive, and a builder-type are all associated with being right-brained. Only the delayed language is primarily autism-related. If I zeroed in on the autism aspect alone to determine his learning needs, he wouldn't achieve optimal balance.

When I observed the overall picture of my child's needs, I knew I needed to focus on the core autism need (advancing language), understand the needs of the developmental stages (before age 11 requires honoring one's social style—introversion in this case), and observe his overall competency (developing interests—being a builder-type), and happiness level in his current stage (developing emotional intelligence—highly sensitive and perceptive). The big picture view of each child needs to help us create the learning environment suited to each individual's unique development. Children with autism are just as apt to benefit from strengths-based learning as any other person. If strengths come first, weaknesses are minimized by waiting for the appropriate developmental time frame best suited to be most successful.

References and Notes

[1] Images were created by my electronics son from the software program: Chief Architect. *Better Homes and Gardens® Home Designer® Suite.* ©2008 Chief Architect, Inc.

[2] My son's favorite site at the time was located at http://www. lampsplus.com/.

[3] Beyoncé Knowles' album, *I Am...Sasha Fierce,* was recorded and released in 2008. Her song from the album, "Halo," released as a single in 2009.

[4] This is one of my forever son's senior pictures. The photo is taken by grown homeschooler and professional photographer, Jennifer Pinkerton. You can find her website at http://jennimarie.com/.

[5] Freed, Jeffrey and Laurie Parsons. *Right-Brained Children in a Left-Brained World: Unlocking the Potential of your ADD Child.* New York: Fireside, 1998.

[6] Ibid.

Chapter Twenty-Two

Shift Begins with Us

Shift Begins with Me

I presented at a homeschooling conference in 2005 where the majority of presenters were educational, medical, or research professionals. Only a few homeschooling parents gave workshops, and most conference goers attended workshops of those with more formal expertise. After a few moments into my final workshop, with more attendees than my previous one, a woman entered the room as a participant. She became an active member of the discussion, asking poignant questions throughout. I felt drawn to connect with her after the session. She began our discussion by stating, "I didn't know what session to take and yours looked good, but I thought, 'She's just a parent; what could she know?' but I decided to go and check it out anyway. Well, it was the best session of the entire conference for me!"

Earlier, I listened to a conference panel with some of the most esteemed professionals in attendance: Dr. Thomas Armstrong, Dr. Richard Falzone, Dr. Robert Kay, and Dr. Ken Jacobson. Each had a perspective on the learning-disabled child (i.e., the right-brained, creative learner) that promoted the idea that they aren't broken. Some of these professionals offer lots of ideas in their books and practices to support that, so my question to the panel was, "Why is it that since you are professionals, and you've been advocating for a change to occur to better support these learners, that it hasn't happened?" They looked at each other and simply and sadly replied, "I don't know." I sat back over the next few months and pondered their answer.

It got me thinking about a life-shaping experience where both professionals and parents personally impacted my life. In the spring of 1996, my fourth child was diagnosed with autism and my world turned upside down. As I threw myself into researching the most effective way to help him reach his potential, the work of several professionals gave me hope for helping my child learn. To make an informed choice of which intervention would work for my child, and to learn how to best implement that information, I discovered the best resource was the knowledge and experience of parents. As parents, we have a pure motive—help our children. Others can become clouded in self-importance, personal research goals, administrative requirements, specialization, or other elements that potentially interfere with a professional staying focused on the important goal of helping children.

A quote by Robert Desmarais Sullivan encapsulates the parental perspective in this arena well: "Not being an expert on anything, I rush in where experts fear to tread." I wasn't afraid to try new things if they meant helping my child. I wasn't afraid to learn different ideas if they made my child's life more fulfilling. I wasn't afraid to be humble and look in diverse places if the search unlocked better information that brought joy to my child's life. The common initial reaction to the choice of who to value more, a parent or a professional, often coincides with what the conference attendee in the above story felt—a professional gets more initial respect than "just a parent." Historically, though, empowered parents have the ability to move mountains, especially when you're talking about their children.

Shift Begins with Us—Empowered Parents

Looking at the personal experience I had with autism and noticing the national fights for changes for the autism community, I see that global changes all began with parents—empowered parents! For instance, parents of children with autism clambered for the Centers for Disease Control and Prevention (CDC) to consider that the preservative Thimerasol used in childhood immunizations was a potential cause of autism (first, the child having a predisposition towards a chemical sensitivity). The government performed some studies and concluded there was no evidence to support the claim. Parents disagreed wholeheartedly and sought others to look over the results, but the CDC would not budge. Empowered parents took out full-page ads in major newspapers, warning other parents not to immunize their babies due to the potential risk of autism developing as a result of the preservative. Due to pressure, and the number of immunizations declining, the government decided to remove Thimerasol from the immunizations "as a precautionary measure."[1]

This type of pressure from empowered parents of children with autism also occurred in disseminating information about a particular style of therapy intervention called applied behavioral analysis (ABA). Originally, the professionals wouldn't publicly release program ideas and explanations for fear that parents would "misuse it." Bah humbug! The parents whose children benefited from the program wanted the information available that it might benefit even one more child. A few stalwart parents felt a duty to others as they witnessed their children flourish with this program. They

decided to offer the programs they bought and paid for to others on the Internet or in book form. The professionals quickly followed.

Using ABA principles, my forever son learned his first words at 3.5 years old—colors.

Grassroots changes effected by many movements often began with empowered parents, or the common folk. Think about the civil rights movement, the women's rights movement, the movement to provide education for the handicapped, and the homeschooling movement. Empowered parents and others can move mountains where dedicated professionals can't!

It's up to all of us to say "enough is enough" with regard to the right-brained labeling epidemic and the mismatched right-brained learning scope and sequence in schools. It's time to stop the inequalities that exist in our schools toward our right-brained, creative children. It's time to upgrade to the 21st century and utilize all of the information we have available on how children learn. It's time for a change!

Shift Begins with Us—At Home

Change starts with learning about the new and better information regarding the best environment in which a right-brained, creative learner will thrive. I hope this book serves as a great resource toward that end. I've included some of the best information available from professionals who have had an interest in this topic or have dedicated their careers to supporting right-brained learners *in the left-brained schooling practices.* Now it's time to give mindful value to the way our right-brained children learn, grow, and flourish *in their own learning process.* For me, it started with learning how to be a careful observer.

The Power of Observation

Reading the works of John Holt taught me the power of observation. His most famous work, *How Children Fail,* records his observations of school children's actions, reactions, and emotional responses to a teacher's attempts at typical instructional practices in school. Holt was a student teacher who was supposed to be observing the teaching techniques of the instructor, but his observations of the children ended up much more informative to how learning does or doesn't occur. [2] I encourage you to observe your children as well. As you read through this book and discover a new idea here and another perspective there, take the time to sit and watch your child(ren) in action. Do you notice in your child what I noticed in mine? The best "evidence" is seeing the right-brained traits play out in your own home with your own children.

When you observe right-brained traits in your child(ren), I encourage you to adopt a wait and see mentality. Observe with the intent to discover what unfolds—a day down the road, or a week, or a month. When I observed my child doing something that either made me uncomfortable (which was usually because I was conditioned to view certain actions as wrong, cheating, or lazy) or seemed counter-productive (which was usually because I was conditioned to view certain activities as useless, ineffective, or extra-curricular), I didn't allow myself to react toward my child in that moment. I made myself sit and continue to observe the task at hand over the day, the week, or the month, to see where it led. Inevitably, *I* was the one who learned, as I eventually saw the value of the activity. Sometimes, to help myself grant the time needed, I might journal what I observed, my reactions, or insights about it. As an investigator of the situation, I tried to look beyond my own understanding to allow myself to be taught. In other words, I tried to stay open-minded and teachable. To see your own right-brained learner blossom in his natural time frame or resource on his own is more persuasive than my words and experiences alone.

Bring Them Home

The observations of my children provided evidence that schools are *not* set up to support the way or the time frame in which my children learned. More importantly, these observations proved my children loved to learn and engage in diverse, meaningful topics. The choice to homeschool was an obvious one for our family. Homeschooling is the fastest growing alternative schooling option today. Statistics vary starting at a low end estimate of a 2% to 8% increase annually, and move as high as 15% to 25% per year growth in the homeschooling ranks.[3]

My builder son said to me at age 18, "If you hadn't homeschooled me, I wouldn't be where I am now in all realms." (Image[4])

After writing *How Children Fail,* John Holt initially advocated for positive changes within the school system. When those attempts seemed to fall on deaf ears, he supported the homeschooling community as the best action to affect change in the way children are allowed to learn. Today's educators also recommend choosing homeschooling to families when school isn't working for their

451

children. Lisa Nielson wrote a blog post entitled, "12 Most Compelling Reasons to Homeschool Your Children," in which she introduces her background and explains her reasons for recommending homeschool: "I've been a public school educator and administrator for more than a decade, so you may be surprised that when parents ask for my advice about education, I often suggest they allow their children to leave school. Education reform is happening today, but it's slow and often ineffective. Parents need to do what is in the best interest of their children, right now."[5]

Holt never imagined homeschooling would reach even 1% of the childhood population, but it surpassed that at an estimated 2.9% in 2007. In a survey, more parents chose homeschooling because schools are failing to meet the educational needs of their children and are a negative learning environment (38%) than because they wanted to homeschool for religious reasons (36%).[6] Where's the tipping point when the successes of homeschooling will impact positive changes in school? As empowered homeschooling parents, we can share what we learn from our children, like I'm doing with this book, with as many others (parents, educators, researchers, and professionals) who are interested in advocating for change in schools.

Shift Begins with Us—At School

I have confidence that if we pool together, parents *and* educators, we can create changes in the school system. In my research I discovered a few attributes of education that I validated through the process of organically educating my children. To benefit *all* children, including honoring the right-brained scope and sequence, a good education should:

- ✓ Respect and support alternative time frames for formal learning
- ✓ Support the early natural process of gift discovery and development with a strengths-based focus

✓ Offer several teaching methods to meet the learning style needs of every student

✓ Utilize individual assessments instead of high stakes generalized testing

✓ Encourage the natural process of developing higher level gifts through goal setting starting in the middle school years

✓ Allow diversification through different options for publicly-funded schools

Alternative Time Frames

A good education should respect and support alternative time frames for formal learning. Long-standing research as outlined in the book, *Better Late than Early,* by Raymond and Dorothy Moore, and global successes as described in Chapter Four, support changing the compulsory attendance law to age 7 for all children. In *Raising Cain*, researchers suggest the option of delaying the entry age of boys (who receive 60 to 80 percent of all learning labels) by two years in relation to their typically advanced girl peers.[7] (Exceptions could always be made on both sides for a boy who's ready earlier or a girl who needs to wait longer.) If changes are made to align formal education start times with brain development for all children, there would be less problems for right-brained children who, as a group, specifically need the later school entry.

SOLUTION: Delayed compulsory attendance laws to age 7.

An Early Strengths-Based Focus

A good education should support the early natural process of gift discovery and development with a strengths-based focus. A combination of a Montessori-infused learning environment of self-exploration and discovery, a Waldorf-inspired learning environment of creative outlet opportunities and picture-based exposure, and a preschool-style environment of diverse learning centers and play are ideal for the 5 to 7 year range. The children in this age range should experience ongoing opportunities for physical activity, play, and creative outlet development.

The negative consequences to a nation and generations of children deprived of these important childhood developmental activities are childhood obesity, screens-as-babysitters social model, and loss of creativity. For at-risk children, the cost is even greater. An extensive study showed those in an instructional early learning environment needed more special education services later, had a higher arrest record, and were more likely to be suspended from work.[8] On the flip side, Germany hosted a study that showed a play-based early learning environment reaped higher math and reading skills later, a better adjusted social and emotional outlook, a stronger work ethic, and a higher level of speaking ability, to name a few.[9] A strengths-based, child-centered approach for the 5 to 7 year time frame would reap enormous benefits to later learning.

SOLUTION: Create an open-ended, learning center-based, interactive environment for 5 to 7 year old children.

Diverse Teaching Methods

A good education should offer several teaching methods to meet the learning style needs of every student. Right-brained children need a different scope and sequence, as outlined in Chapter Seven, which introduces and develops subjects at times better suited to their needs. If the 5 to 7 year time frame is supported in the manner described above, and if the compulsory attendance laws are changed to make age 7 the first reporting year, then we could begin formal academics as research indicates is optimal at age 8.

Diverse teaching methods meet the needs of various learning styles, such as using hands-on experimentation and technology for creating stop-motion movies.

The 8 to 10 year time frame needs the most teaching and resource adjustments to best support the learning style of right-brained children. Encouraging the use of more "living books," as described in Montessori education, would enrich the learning experience for all children. Offering several teaching methods and resources to meet the learning style needs of every student could bridge the discrepancy between the needs of both brain processing preferences. Encouraging project-based learning opportunities so that a wide variety of student-directed options are available to prove competence could also bridge the discrepancy between the needs of both brain processing preferences. Encouraging questions and child-initiated discoveries in the elementary level learning environments will increase creativity and curiosity, two ingredients that have seriously decreased in the past decade, especially in this age range,[10] and is sorely needed in our fast-paced, technology-driven society.

SOLUTION: Use at least two to three methods or resources to teach subjects (such as phonics, sight word, and kinesthetic versions of reading study), and encourage alternative, process-based projects for those who don't prefer simplified checkbox tests.

Individualized Assessments

A good education should focus on individual assessments instead of high stakes generalized testing. To provide the unpressured learning environment required when honoring

455

diverse learning time frames, standardized testing shouldn't be allowed until middle school, if not done away with completely. (Waldorf education allows no testing during the elementary years.) In my state, homeschooling laws require yearly standardized tests. Admittedly, I find them sorely lacking in relevance. First of all, they test only two subjects—grammar and arithmetic. Sure, comprehension is in there, but it's a stilted representation. Language is *way* bigger than grammar: writing (poetry, fantasy, scripts, short story, journals), oral expression (plays, storytelling, puppets, conversation, debate), books (atlases, magazines, manga, interactive, adventure), vocabulary (technical, social sciences, cultural, linguistics, interest-based). Math is greater than arithmetic: patterns, problem-solving, comparative, spatial, application. Even if science is included on such tests, it's vocabulary-based instead of exploring, analyzing, questioning, investigating, discovering—experiencing the true nature of our world and how it works. Standardized tests address a mere drop in the bucket of what my children learn. They certainly don't include "testing" any passion or gift. What are we thinking?

Is the sheer simplicity of easily sorting and categorizing based on a multiple choice test better than celebrating the complexity of the human potential? Individualized assessments, written narratives, and portfolios that showcase strengths and gifts as well as overall progress would unleash the creative and innovative traits of both teacher and student in a world that begs for these attributes. If we replace the weeks and months of "test preparation" with nurturing and developing individual aptitudes, love of learning and student self-initiative will grow. Lisa Nielsen invites parents to join in her mission to opt out of standardized testing for your child(ren) as she offers a forum to gather from every state.[11]

SOLUTION: Trade in high stakes standardized testing measures for portfolios, individualized assessments, and written narratives that recognize and encourage personal progress.

456

SEMESTER ONE

In addition to those listed as daily subjects, the following topics were covered each day this first semester, unless otherwise noted:

Title

Science		
	Sky and Earth	Dog Eyewitness Video
	Animal Friends	Cat Eyewitness Video
	Lightning	Skeleton Eyewitness Video
	Wild Animals	Dinosaur Eyewitness Video
	The Magic School Bus Series	How Things Work
	Inside the Earth	Insect World
	Inside a Beehive	The World We Live In
	Inside a Hurricane	Dog Eyewitness Video
	& the Electric Field Trip	Cat Eyewitness Video
	in the Time of Dinosaur	Skeleton Eyewitness Video
	101 Fun Science Experiments	Dinosaur Eyewitness Video
	101 Great Science Experiments	Fish Eyewitness Video
		Bird Eyewitness Video

History		
	Dear America series	The American Girl Series
	Across the Wide and	Molly
	Lonesome Prairie	Kirsten
	The Winter of Red Snow	Addie
	Atlas - Exploration	Samantha
	George Washington: A Picture	Felicity
	Book Biography	Josephina

Two different children, two different focuses, and two different types of resources within the same subject areas. A portfolio captures the difference as well as the richness each offers.

SEMESTER ONE

In addition to those listed as daily subjects, the following topics were covered each day this first semester, unless otherwise noted:

Title

Science		
	The Earth Atlas	Space and Planets
	Galaxies	The Visual Dictionary
	Lightning	of Chemistry
	Black Holes	101 Great Science Experiment.
	New Way Things Work	101 Fun Science Experiments
	The Brain	

History		
	From Colony to Country	Time Traveller Books
	George Washington: A	The Encyclopedia of Native
	Picture Book Biography	America
	Will Rogers	

Gift Development through Goal Setting

A good education should encourage the natural process of higher gift development through goal setting starting in the middle school years. In her book, *Your Child's Strengths,* Jenifer Fox, M.Ed., calls for all parents to join her in what she's calling "the strength's movement." She has a comprehensive plan for the high school years in her own school where she's an administrator.[12] I feel Fox's high school plan could actually start during the middle school years, a time during which I found achieving self-discipline through formal learning goal-setting is best developed. I want to take this idea beyond her vision, though, to include the strengths-based movement in the early years especially, where most of the labeling and broken child mentality begins. The strengths-based movement looks different in elementary school than middle and high school. We need to demand a better matched educational environment for our children to support our gift-centered, specialized culture.

SOLUTION: Teachers become coaches in middle school and mentor each student to meet class goals by collaborating with the student to choose appropriate resources, methods, and reporting systems that work for that student.

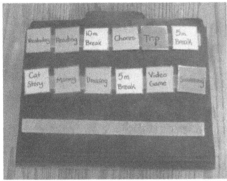

Goal setting work and creating individual reporting systems was developed between 11 and 13 years old in our homeschool.

Additional School Options

One of the best additions to our public school system that has come along is charter schools. The online *Mirriam-Webster* dictionary defines a charter school as "a tax-supported school established by a charter between a granting body (as a school board) and an outside group (as of teachers and parents) which operates the school without most local and state educational regulations so as to achieve set goals."[13] From what I understand, charters were created to provide a different focus or philosophy of learning, diversifying options to traditional school. Yet, attendance is free, as it is for the local public school. I know Montessori education has gained positive notoriety through the use of charter schools. I've noticed that Montessori schools are often a good fit for the right-brained child. If public schools can't change enough to integrate right-brained methods into each classroom, charter schools are a great option to fight for and establish in local communities.

SOLUTION: If schools aren't willing to change, create and support charter schools set up to honor the right-brained time frame and resources.

Shift Begins with Us—In Research

When enough parents start requiring change at the local level, change at the research level will begin. If we as parents no longer accept the idea of all the different labels used to explain why our right-brained children aren't following the school's left-brained scope and sequence, researchers and innovative educators will need to come up with new ways to support our right-brained children in their learning lives. New right-brained resources will be created. New right-brained scopes and sequences will emerge. New right-brained textbooks will be published. Good things can happen for our right-brained children.

Research is driven by current theories. If the new theory is that brain processing preferences creates a different way of learning that affects physical attributes as well as *how* a person learns, then we'll see new research to prove it. I would *love* to see research regarding the connection between three-dimensionality for right-brained learners and the eye-brain connection. I would *love* to see research regarding waiting until children are 8 to 10 years old before introducing reading to identified right-brained learners to see if the percentage of dyslexia is greatly reduced or eliminated. I would *love* to see research regarding long-term memory versus short-term memory based on one's brain processing preference. What exciting research and educational methods will develop as the right-brained/left-brained paradigm is accepted and applied in our educational systems.

Shift Begins with Us—
In the Right-Brained Movement

When I moved to North Carolina in the year 2000, a parent of a child with autism created a new charter school to provide him with an appropriate learning environment. There would be small class sizes of 12 students, with one teacher and one aide. Each class would include one child with autism, and the aide would be specifically trained to especially support that student. A well-qualified behavioral specialist would be on staff to teach all staff with regard to systems, procedures, and supports to best help that child with autism succeed in a regular classroom. The charter school was to open that fall, would start with the children with autism in the kindergarten level, and a new group of children with autism would be added each year after that. It seemed perfect, and I felt fortunate that my son was chosen in the lottery for one of four spaces open to children with autism in the kindergarten classes.

Little did I initially suspect that the parent who created the charter school wasn't being as forthcoming with the school staff about the purpose of the charter as we had been informed. No staff knew about the autism component of the

460

school, no one had yet been specifically trained to support the autism component, and it soon became clear that the parent who created the charter seemed to want to proceed with the (crucial) autism aspect of the charter kept under the radar. Later I discovered that she created the school to keep her third grade son's diagnosis of autism secret, as no one on staff realized he had a diagnosis. Her goal was to have a *normal* child by controlling his environment. Unfortunately for the kindergarten staff, the school year got off to an extremely rocky start because of lack of knowledge and training. Within three weeks, I pulled my son out. Two of the other three pulled out their children with autism within the next couple of months. We wouldn't allow our precious children to be guinea pigs.

My forever son on the outside not looking in at his charter school.

There's a decision we all must make. Do we leave our precious right-brained, creative children in a learning environment that doesn't support them or help them flourish? One of the four children's families decided to stick it out and make it work. The mother was constantly involved to continually demand the purpose of the charter be fulfilled. This mother provided information, ideas, and even personal involvement as the transition continued throughout the year. It did consistently improve. We need parents like this mother to dive into the school system and help it move along in the right direction for our right-brained children. We need parents like the three who wouldn't put up with their children's miseducation. We need all of us in all realms to make a difference!

> ➤ Some of us will advocate within our public schools for change.
> ➤ Some of us will try to start a private school or a charter school option.
> ➤ Some of us will pull our children out and homeschool.
> ➤ Some of us will combine approaches that work just for our child and family.

Within these choices,

> ➤ Some of us will be the leaders and creators.
> ➤ Some of us will be the followers and gather more followers.
> ➤ Some of us will be a right-hand man.
> ➤ Some of us will be organizational support.
> ➤ Some of us will be online voices.
> ➤ Some of us will become politically active.
> ➤ Some of us will advocate locally.

As a result of these choices,

> ➤ An opinion will change.
> ➤ A classroom will change.
> ➤ A school will change.
> ➤ A district will change.
> ➤ A state will change.
> ➤ A nation will change.

Shift Begins with Us—
Empowered Parents in Action

When we realize we've inadvertently placed our right-brained, creative learners in a disadvantaged position, we have to act on the knowledge we've gained. It begins with each of us finding our place in the right-brained movement. The common goal of each empowered and involved parent or teacher will be to get this better information out there about how right-brained children learn, and how they grow and flourish with the right educational environment.

Collectively

Together, we can make huge changes over time, such as changing the compulsory attendance laws or creating a left- and right-brained classroom for every grade level. We may need to create new laws, or we could take advantage of existing laws. For instance, recently in California, a group of empowered parents have banned together to activate a controversial law called the Parent Trigger Law. This law allows parents unhappy with a school's performance to gather a pre-set number of signatures to force the school to close, make significant changes in school staff, or turn it into a charter school. A few other states also have passed this law, and more are considering adopting it. Doreen Diaz, a parent of a child attending the California school in question, and quoted in a CBS News report, speaks for all of us: "Somewhere along the line we lost our right, or they thought we lost our right, to speak for our children. Well no, we're taking back that right to speak for our children." [14] Empowered parents are a force to be reckoned with. Empowered and emboldened parents have proven their ability to make global, lasting changes.

Individually

Individually, we may provide a singular example that inspires bigger changes because the individualized action plan proved effective. Inspired by my right-brained information as outlined in this book, a mother whose child attends public school in England shared a successful, significant classroom modification on behalf of her gifted, right-brained son, who learns on a traditional right-brained time frame.

I don't have the choice to home-school because I'm a single mum, the sole provider for my kids, and work full time at home. But by the time my son was six, I couldn't bear his unhappiness at school anymore. When I asked him what the problem was, he always gave me the same answer: "It's the teaching." I had discovered his strong visual side by then and had found this group,[15] which gave me the confidence to continue making demands on the school. At the same time, I explained to my son that he was a right-brained thinker and for that reason, he wouldn't be able to read until he was much older, so not to worry about it (he was very relieved to hear this).

I demanded a series of changes during the two years he spent at that school, including allowing him to skip their religious assembly and not take reading lessons; I refused speech therapy and obtained agreement that he could get up, leave the classroom, and bounce around when needed. He was also allowed to skip homework because he felt it intruded on his "personal time." In return for these "privileges," my son agreed to obey by the school rules (which he hadn't been doing before). It took a lot of convincing the school and it was with great reluctance that they agreed to stop teaching him (i.e., let him play with LEGO® or draw in the corner).

Getting the first school to accept my demands was the hardest part. I spent two hours in a room with the headmistress and an aging educational psychologist (whom I took an almost instant dislike to) arguing my case. I am very strong-willed and I was determined not to leave that room until they agreed to stop teaching him. This was the only angle I could come from because it was the one thing my son kept repeating was making him sad. I was getting nowhere in the discussions until I threatened to take him out of school and educate him at home. (Looking back I realize that I was close to a meltdown at that point—I was on the verge of tears and livid at the injustice of it all, I probably looked a bit scary!) They told me that home-education was illegal and thankfully I knew this to be a lie and told them so. It was only then that the headmistress finally, and very reluctantly, agreed, but they both went on to warn me that by treating him differently from the other kids in such an obvious way, I was setting my son up for failure and it was highly likely he would abuse his freedom and see himself as beyond reproach.

The next two weeks were pretty grim because my son did indeed flaunt his freedom and caused havoc in the classroom, and the headmistress gave me an "I told you so" lecture in the corridor one morning. It was then that I told my son that I needed him to keep his side of the bargain, to keep to the school rules, otherwise I would lose my power to change things for him. True to his word (as he always has been), he kept to the rules after that and things settled down. His teacher's attitude towards me softened after one afternoon when she had been getting all the kids to write a three-lined riddle. My son had spent the afternoon drawing in his corner and taking no part. At the end of the school day she asked him if he was going to write a riddle for her, too, and he blew her away by reciting back the one he had made up in his head, and then continuing on and reciting the other 30 or so riddles the rest of the kids had made up.

The head did insist on providing reading lessons with a Special Education Needs teacher, but when I asked my son how these were going he said, "No offense, but no effect." By this time, his intelligence was becoming apparent to them, and his obvious happiness and improved behavior were all contributing to a much easier ride for me. So, when I passed on this nugget to the headmistress, she smiled and agreed to my request to stop the reading lessons.

As far as religious assembly is concerned, I was told by the head that the school didn't have the right to force religious teaching on any child, so this one was easy. Allowing him a creative outlet in the classroom wasn't so straightforward. LEGO® was finally banned because he made too much noise raking around the box looking for the bits he needed, but he contented himself with other quiet activities, drawing mainly. He was also provided with a visual time-table and given ten minute warnings when class activities were about to change—this was the head's idea because she had realized he was having trouble transitioning from one activity to the next.

Eighteen months ago, I moved my family to a small village—the school was very sympathetic to his needs and gave him all the privileges he had at his previous school. After a year at his school, he himself requested reading lessons. A few months later, he suddenly got up and dragged his desk over to join the other kids. He also chose to start attending religious teaching with the rest of the class and despite his self-proclaimed atheism (at age 5), absolutely loves hearing the parables of Jesus and enjoys reading them to his sister. He complained to me about not being able to make friends, and with the support of a teacher he was able to stand up in front of his class

466

and explain his problem and that he felt lonely. I wasn't there to witness this but heard afterwards that the other kids were very sympathetic and they all "brainstormed" ways they could help.

I have regular meetings with the school to address any concerns and the last week when I asked my son if there was anything troubling him, he said proudly, "I have no issues at school that I can't deal with myself, thank you." I felt so very proud of him because I know that it has all been one long struggle for him. My point is though that he's coping, and coping extremely well! He's currently reading *The Lord of the Rings*, is excelling in math, and has recently made a good friend.

His current teacher tells me he's a delight to have in the classroom. Two of his past teachers have stopped me in the playground and told me that they have learned a lot from my son and I feel that in a very, very small way, I have contributed to improving knowledge in schools about right-brained kids. Okay, it's only one head and a couple of teachers, but they all saw the complete turnaround in my son when they responded to his needs, and they all finally realized that his intelligence was far beyond what they had imagined. I hope I have expanded their view on "different." My son has definitely expanded my view!

I'm very resistant to taking him down the diagnosis route because the word "diagnosis" means you have something wrong with you. Since when did "not being that social" mean you have something wrong with you? I understand he has hypersensitivity issues, but I don't see that as having something wrong with you either. It's just something you have to understand and deal with. I don't believe my son needs therapy, but instead he needs his school to understand and be sympathetic to his needs, *and* allow him to show off his strength areas. He does need help with social issues, but I do provide this as a parent and he loves our little chats about "how most people work." He tries out my advice and reports back to me with his successes. I do tell him he's different from most folks but emphasize that he has a funky and cool brain and that he isn't the only one out there like him.

I too am hanging my hat on the right-brained label because it has zero negative connotations, and, more importantly, verbally points to the child's strengths! Many of my friends and family have listened in fascination to my explanation of my son's quirkiness as being due to the fact that he's predominantly working with the right side of his brain. I know I would just have got a sympathetic look if I had told them he had Asperger's Syndrome.

My son started me on this journey. He's now coming up for age 9 and is a happy, caring child and is doing well in mainstream school.

With courage and tenacity, this mother established a delayed time frame for acquiring the subjects that require later development for right-brained children within her son's school. He was allowed to learn in a way that worked for him, to develop and use creative outlets that were catalysts to listen to those topics that interested him. He was allowed to stop the teaching that didn't work for him, and join in when the timing was right. He was able to address his sensory and social needs through collaboration with the attentive educators involved. In the end, instead of resulting in a labeled *or mislabeled* (as I think Asperger's would have been) child who hated learning, we have a confident young man who loves to learn and does so competently. This is an example of just *one* parent and *one* child whose successful modification may open doors for others within these schools and with the educators involved down the road. A seed has been sown.

When we realize we've inadvertently placed our right-brained, creative learners in a disadvantaged position, we have to act on the knowledge we've gained.

We need to give our creative, innovative, right-brained children a better start in our schools than what they have historically received up until now. Especially in the elementary ages, right-brained children have been labeled, misunderstood, and undervalued for their way of learning. Right-brained children deserve a scope and sequence that favors their universal gifts. It's time to reclaim our creative children and their rightful place in the educational realm by understanding and honoring the natural learning path for right-brained children. Let's celebrate the right side of normal!

References and Notes

[1] *Centers for Disease Control and Prevention.* "Vaccine Safety: Thimerasol." http://www.cdc.gov/vaccinesafety/concerns/thimerosal/ (Last Updated February 8, 2011).

[2] Holt, John. *How Children Fail.* Da Capo Press, 1995.

[3] Lines, Patricia M. "How Many Children are Homeschooled?" *ERIC Clearinghouse on Educational Management.* Eugene, 2001. ERIC Identifier ED457539. http://www.ericdigests.org/2002-2/homeschooling.htm. Another resource is: Bunday, Karl M. "Homeschooling Is Growing Worldwide," *Learning in Freedom.* 1995. http:// learninfreedom.org/homeschool_growth.html.

[4] This is one of my builder son's senior pictures. The photo is taken by grown homeschooler and professional photographer, Jennifer Pinkerton. You can find her website at http://jennimarie.com/.

[5] Nielsen, Lisa. "12 Most Compelling Reasons to Homeschool Your Children," *12 Most.* February 7, 2012. http://12most.com/2012/02/07/ compelling-reasons-to-homeschool-children/.

[6] National Center for Education Statistics. U.S. Department of Education. *Fast Facts.* http://nces.ed.gov/fastfacts/display.asp?id= 91 (accessed June, 2012).

[7] Kindlon, Dan and Michael Thompson. *Raising Cain: Protecting the Emotional Life of Boys.* New York: Random House Inc., 2000.

[8] Almon, Joan and Edward Miller, "The Crisis in Early Educaton: A Research-Based Case for More Play and Less Pressure," *Alliance for Childhood.* November, 2011. http://www.allianceforchildhood.org/. (The study was called the HighScope Preschool Curriculum Comparison Study (PCCS).)

[9] Ibid.

[10] Ibid.

[11] Opt Out of State Standardized Tests can be found at http://opt outofstandardizedtests.wikispaces.com/.

[12] Fox, Jenifer. *Your Child's Strengths: Discover Them, Develop Them, Use Them.* New York: Viking Penguin, 2008.

[13] *Merriam-Webster.* "Charter school." http://www.merriam-webster.com/ dictionary/charter%20school.

[14] Tracy, Ben. "SoCal parents may succeed in school takeover," *CBS Evening News.* February 20, 2012. http://www.cbsnews.com/ 8301-18563_162-57381430/ socal-parents-may-succeed-in-school-takeover/.

[15] My *Homeschooling Creatively* e-mail list advocating for the right-brained learning environment can be found at http://groups.yahoo.com/group/ homeschoolingcreatively/.

Index